D0521720

LIVING SMART, SPENDING LESS

LIVING SMART, SPENDING LESS

Creative Ways to Stretch Your Income... and Have Fun Doing It

Stephen and Amanda Sorenson

MOODY PRESS

CHICAGO

© 1993 by
STEPHEN SORENSON
AND AMANDA SORENSON

ISBN: 0-8024-4930-1

1 3 5 7 9 10 8 6 4 2

Printed in the United States of America

Contents

Acknowledgments

To try to thank all the people who have passed along money-saving tips to us through the years would be impossible, just as it would be impossible to thank all those who have assisted us in various projects in and around our home and vehicles. So we'll mention only a few of those who have helped along the way.

Our parents taught us by example how to work hard, save money, spend with restraint, and do without sometimes in order to accomplish a larger goal. They also instilled in us a love for God and other people that has motivated and directed many of our choices and actions.

Friends and neighbors have also bestowed much practical wisdom and help upon us: Bob, who has saved the day many times in our country adventure; Rick, who knows more about more practical things than anyone we know born after 1950; Susan and Ed, whose prayers and friendship have meant a great deal during tough times.

And a warm thank you to others who passed along encouraging words as we pulled this book together. Many people have given us much in order that we may now share with others what we have learned.

Note to Reader

This book is designed to be a general guide; its purpose is to entertain and educate. The tips and guidelines are supported by research and/or the authors' experience. Not every tip or guideline will apply to everyone. Readers should use their own judgment and common sense when deciding which tips they choose to implement.

Although much effort has been expended to ensure that the information herein is as accurate and as complete as possible, this book is sold with the understanding that the authors and publisher assume no responsibility for errors, inconsistencies, or inaccuracies.

Remarks from the Authors

Countless books have been written on ways to invest, how to get rich quickly, and how to start your own business and be your own boss. Such books meet needs—or at least the need for hope—and millions of them are bought every year. But few books offer proven, simple tips on how to stretch dollars and enjoy life at the same time. This one does. If you use the tips here, you will save money. In fact, you'll easily pay for the price of this book many times over.

The tips included here come from our experience and reliable research. No matter how old you are, how much or how little money you make, or what your family situation may be, this book will help you save money and have fun doing it.

We know that your situation is unique. You may rent an apartment or own a home. You may be retired or work sixty hours a week. You may love to do fix-it projects, or you may not even own a hammer. You may live in a warm climate or in an area where it's cold much of the year.

That's why we have organized this book so that you can pick and choose which tips apply to you and your particular situation. If you don't own a car, for instance, you may skip the section on car maintenance. Some of the tips are simple, based on common sense, and require no tools or further research. Other tips are more detailed and will require you to spend some time in order to implement them. Still others require you to seek the advice of professionals.

Living smart and spending less is an adventure. It requires that we get out of our ruts, see things from new perspectives, and do some things differently. For some people, getting out of a rut is bothersome or scary. We understand that. But we know that changing one's lifestyle in order to save money is worth the risk and can be a great stepping stone toward meeting financial goals in an uncertain economy.

So keep this book handy where you can refer to it frequently. Have fun with it and its ideas. Experiment and enjoy discovering how much money you can save. You may be surprised by how much fun you and your family or friends can have as you embark on the adventure of saving money.

Best of all, practicing the tips in this book will help you discover something about yourself—what you can do, how you can take charge of some areas of your life, how you can channel resources to more productive areas and enhance your family's overall lifestyle, and how you can assist others.

These tips certainly have made a meaningful difference in our lives. Our discussions with friends on saving money have lasted hours, and now we look forward to sharing this book with others we won't have the privilege of meeting personally.

Our credentials? At various points in our lives we have struggled to make ends meet and have learned many things the hard way. We've been seeking saving-money tips for more than forty combined years.

- During his "starving writer days," Stephen only earned $452 in one year. He began learning much about obtaining items for free and sharing with others during that time.

- Amanda commuted by train to a job in Chicago and didn't receive a high wage. By the time she paid rent and utilities and bought food and train passes, she had little left. She, too, learned how to stretch her dollars.

- When Stephen's Toyota's engine burned a valve, he had about eighty dollars for emergencies—which didn't nearly cover a valve job. So he and a friend bought an instruction book and pulled off the top of the engine, step by step, in the parking lot of his apartment. (Amazingly, the engine ran when they put it back together.)

- When we bought our current home, the roof was leaking by the bucketful, the electric bill was sky high, paint was peeling off the outside walls, the kitchen sink was leaking, the little room in which the pressure tank sat was full of water, and the chimney didn't work. Today our utility bills average thirty dollars a month less than they were before we purchased our home, despite the fact that we have doubled the capacity of our electric water heater and have added electric-resistance heat to a three-hundred-square-foot addition.

Because we've never made a great deal of money, we've had to build up our assets slowly and learn new ways to stretch our dollars.

The bottom line? We enjoy saving money and love to share what we've learned with others. Writing this book has been fun because it has given us the chance to combine thousands of tips in one place.

We hope that you'll try some of these ideas and add your own so that you, too, can improve your lifestyle by living smart and spending less.

FOUNDATIONAL CONCEPTS
FOR LIVING SMART

1

Build a Solid Foundation for Smart Living

The cool, spring breeze rustled the curtains of our apartment as the three of us sat in the living room. Barbara, a legal secretary who was visiting from California, shook her head. "I don't see how you do it on what you make. I mean, I'm making nearly twice what you are, yet I don't have anything to show for it." She paused. "Could you tell me what you do? My parents never taught me how to save money. In fact," she added wistfully, "they only taught me how to spend it."

Barbara isn't alone. Many people feel helpless and frustrated as they watch their hard-earned money slip away.

"I don't know how we're going to make it."

"We're working hard but not getting ahead."

"We'd like to contribute more, but we can't."

"My money just doesn't stretch far enough."

"I can't put money away for the future!"

We've heard such comments often—in our living room, at friends' apartments, during church retreats. You've probably heard them, too. Perhaps you've said them yourself.

These words don't just come from people who are fighting off bill collectors. They come from people who are working hard to make ends meet, who are trying to be responsible with what they have and yet can't

---

Certain societal factors tend to put the squeeze on our finances:

Extended families often don't live in the same town or city anymore, which means that the family support network is less effective. Instead of a family member helping out with baby-sitting, one must pay a baby-sitter. Instead of calling a brother or father to lend a hand with a project, one has to call a contractor or repair shop.

Many people, schooled in the philosophy that they must buy material possessions *now*, go into debt and severely limit their financial options.

People fall victim to serious health problems or circumstances beyond their control and have to learn new ways of "getting by."

The economy is volatile. If people use credit to spend money they don't have, economists say the economy is picking up but bemoan the fact that people aren't saving much money. If people cut their spending and save money for fear that things won't get better, economists talk about recession and attribute the lack of consumer confidence to a host of economic ills.

---

seem to stretch their dollars far enough. They come from people who earn good incomes and want to be better stewards of what they earn.

Many people today are concerned about finances, and rightly so. Times have changed. Corporations that were once loyal to long-time employees now lay them off and hire younger replacements whose salaries are lower. Senior citizens watch the buying power of their fixed incomes erode. Salaries are frozen or cut. Families are saddled with debt. Young people fear that they won't be able to count on Social Security when they retire, and rightly so. Middle-aged baby boomers suddenly realize that their kids will need help with college tuition and that their parents may need help with living arrangements. Families that once enjoyed the benefits of two incomes suddenly are forced to live on one. Sometimes they can't make the adjustment and lose their homes through foreclosures.

Learn to Make Wise Spending Choices

There's no doubt that we all face challenging financial pressures. And there is little doubt that an increasing number of cracks in our financial flooring appear to swallow up our earnings. Yet the situation is not hopeless. All of us can learn to make wiser choices in how we use the money we earn.

We can take control of our finances rather than allowing ourselves to become victims of our finances.

In fact, our greatest personal and financial problems are rarely due to outside economic influences. Most occur because we give little thought to the future as we form our spending habits. Like Barbara, few of us have had the opportunity to learn from good role models or easy-to-understand classes on saving money. No one has showed us how to link up financial preparedness and opportunity. Yet everyone has the potential to learn how to be better stewards of his or her resources. We can take control of our finances rather than allowing ourselves to become victims of our finances.

You may be saying, "But you don't understand my situation. I don't make enough money to have financial choices." If that's how you tend to think, consider the following illustrations.

A person who earns an average of $500 a month will earn $240,000 between the ages of twenty-five and sixty-five.

An individual whose average earnings are $1,050 a month will earn more than half a million dollars during the same time period.

And many people earn far more than those figures. Certainly a quarter of a million dollars or more provides some financial options. The challenge lies in living smart and learning how to keep resources from vanishing. Perhaps you are pretty good at saving money. Great! But there's always more to learn, isn't there?

Not long ago we went to see Rick and Janice, friends who are always figuring out new ways to enhance their quality of life and save money at the same time. One short visit gave us a glimpse of how they do it.

Rick was in the garage, puttering, when we arrived. "How're you doing?" Stephen asked.

"Fine."

"Your pile of scrap wood is growing."

"Yes. Our neighbor still gives it to us. It's left over from his woodworking shop. It should heat the stove through the winter."

"What're you doing over there?" Stephen pointed.

"Getting ready to build a fence."

"You sure have lots of pickets."

"I got them at that lumber yard off Fillmore Street. The regular ones cost a dollar nineteen each. So I asked if they had any others, and they showed me their 'seconds' stack where the tops of the pickets weren't cut quite perfectly. I got these for seventy-nine cents apiece and saved one hundred ninety dollars."

And on it went. In the course of normal conversation, we exchanged simple instructions on ways to save money.

Through the years, we've talked with many people like Rick and Janice about their philosophies of saving money and the ways in which they have saved or spent it. Based on those discussions and our experience, we believe that several key assumptions affect the way we each view the adventure and challenge of saving money.

As we considered why some people save money and make it go far and some people can't or won't, we realized that more than individual personality is involved. Each of us makes decisions based on a complex grid of underlying beliefs, habits, and attitudes. These may have developed when we were young or older. We may have picked up correct, partially correct, or incorrect teaching on our own without anybody's guidance. Or we may have learned about finances from a parent, friend, grandparent, business associate, or books. Sometimes we "inherit" views of money without realizing it and have had years of experience in living out those views—sometimes with mixed results.

Every individual was reared differently—that's no secret. Perhaps, like Barbara, your parents never taught you basic financial principles; then suddenly you realized one day that making your dollars stretch was important. Maybe you're a single parent who must be an expert on saving money in order to survive, yet you have to learn how to do it on the run. Maybe you have a family but no job, and your teenage children will soon enter college but the money for their education just isn't there. Perhaps you and your spouse have good jobs but don't seem to have enough money to cover the growing bills. Maybe you just got married and find it easier to use credit cards than to pay cash.

Regardless of our backgrounds, experiences, or situations, we all must accept four underlying principles before we can start living smart and spending less.

1. The way we spend our money is a choice, whether we make that choice consciously or unconsciously.

2. Consumer debt limits our choices more than any other single factor. Therefore, if we desire to expand our choices, we must manage, reduce, and preferably eliminate consumer debt.

3. The amount of money we earn isn't nearly as important as how we use what we earn.

4. The benefits of living smart truly make life more enjoyable.

In light of these foundational principles, we invite you to consider the following thoughts about money, values, and other subjects with us. Some may seem so simple that you smile and wonder why we bothered to include them. Others may be new to you and will require careful thought and evaluation. Some points may challenge you in ways you don't like, but we hope you'll keep reading anyway. If you become uneasy, try to figure out why. As you think about each point, honestly consider whether you agree or disagree, and why or why not. In doing so, you will prepare yourself for the rest of this book—and the life-changing decisions you may make.

Above all, remember that this is a no-guilt book. Everyone approaches saving and spending money differently. We offer no "right" or "wrong" formulas. We merely suggest new possibilities to consider as you progress on your own journey of smart living. We will be the first to admit that we're "not there yet." So if you think we left out a major point, let us know—perhaps we'll include it in the next volume.

Make Your Own Decisions About How to Spend Your Money

Advertisers spend billions of dollars every year to convince you and millions of others to buy or lease items you don't need so that you will achieve a certain quality of life, prestige, or other benefit. Stores use the most modern techniques to entice you and create a buying atmosphere.

Evaluate every purchase, no matter how small. And then make choices with gusto.

But as an intelligent consumer, you can take practical steps to control your money no matter how effective the advertising techniques may be. As you do, you will experience the pleasure of watching your money grow and of gaining financial options. By making careful decisions about your money—conserving it, preserving it, and spending it wisely—you can achieve financial goals that will bring you satisfaction. You can carefully sculpt your lifestyle, reduce your need for cash, and more fully enjoy all aspects of life.

Saving money can be fun when viewed from this perspective because the ways in which you choose to save money reflect who you are. Your choices reflect your personality, your values, and your goals. You'll certainly have the opportunity to enjoy life more if you are able and willing to choose whether or not to buy a particular item. *Evaluate every purchase, no matter how small.* And then make choices with gusto.

If you don't really need something, don't buy it. And consider the money you didn't spend to be a *gift to yourself*—a gift you can use to purchase something you do need. A gift you can share with someone you love. A gift you can freely give to someone in need. Or a gift you can joyously contribute to further God's work.

Many people spend money to feel good about themselves, to gain the affection or loyalty of other people, to fit in with others, to gain control over others, and so on. And the advertising industry encourages that line of thinking. Yet making money choices for those reasons is a form of bondage that limits people's ability to exercise financial control and experience financial freedom. In and of itself, money never satisfies anyone's unmet needs for peace, purpose, and meaning in life. Only God can do that.

You are the only one who can choose whether or not you will take a different path. So it's up to you to think about how and why you spend your money the way you do. Each of us is responsible to bring our financial decisions into the realm of conscious thought where we can evaluate our options and make the decisions *we* choose to make.

For years, friends and friends of friends have come up to us and said, "Gee, I wish I could work at home and write and edit books like you do. I've done a little writing, but I don't know where to start."

"Great," we respond. "We'd like to see what you've done. Perhaps we can help you along. Call us. Let's get together."

Only a few would-be writers or editors have called us. Those who have are taking steps toward realizing their dreams; those who haven't are, for the most part, living with daydreams. Learning to make conscious financial choices is part of realizing your financial dreams.

We all can take small steps that lead us closer to (or farther away from) our dreams. For years, we longed to be self-employed, free from the constraints of nine-to-five jobs. (We also had an inkling of how demanding self-employment is.) After years of working for others, we reached our goal. It's the right place for us now, but it hasn't been easy. We've had to do lots of doing without. We've had to take risks, wondering if we really could complete particular projects on time. We've had to wade through inner doubts, face empty bank accounts, and listen to people who couldn't understand our willingness to sacrifice to allow our dreams to become realities. Some experienced writers and editors even told us that what we had in mind couldn't be done. But by making many small choices along the way, we have seen a dream become a reality.

If you were to list your dreams, what would they be? Buying a boat? Taking a trip around the world? Participating in short-term missions? Helping a son or daughter go to college or buy a first home? Working in a mission hospital? Caring for an elderly parent? Volunteering at an inner-city clinic? It's your life, and *your choices do matter.*

What steps could you take to make your dreams a reality? How can saving money fit into those steps? In a sense, we each have to choose the obstacles we are willing to overcome in order for our daydreams to become dreams and then realities. The fact that you are reading this book indicates that you'd like to make some changes in your life and progress toward your financial dreams. You also may be concerned about the state of the economy and your financial condition.

Whatever is going to happen to you in relation to your dreams will happen gradually, as a result of choices you make and actions you take. There is no middle ground because every decision either carries you closer to your dreams or farther away from them. It is our hope that as you learn how to save money, you may come closer to your dreams and develop the inner parts of yourself that make living much more joyous.

Consumer Debt Must Be Managed, Reduced, and Eventually Eliminated

Consumer debt is one of the most insidious, destructive forces facing individuals and families today. It is also an alarmingly easy trap to fall into. In contrast to reducing needs to minimal but satisfying levels, consumer debt feeds a never-ending hunger for more. It can play a large part in destroying families and robbing people of self-esteem. It erodes choices. It deprives people of the joy of sharing with others in need. It mortgages the future and weakens a person's ability to ride out tough economic times. It's a psychological burden because it reduces future freedoms, and it can cause the loss of nearly everything people own.

A fundamental principle of saving money is not to allow it to be siphoned off by consumer debt. It's hard enough to get ahead when taxes, insurance, food, clothing, transportation, housing, tuition, and other essential items and expenses already take such big bites out of our incomes. So when people have to earn more money just to cover the interest on their consumer debt, the scenario worsens in a hurry. And if a key income is lost, unforeseen expenses arise, or wages are frozen, the economic house built on the sand of consumer debt can tumble down in a hurry.

Some debt may be unavoidable in order to meet certain goals. Few of us can afford to pay cash for a home, for example. But often people use debt to buy items that don't provide lasting benefits. They charge vacations on their cards and pay for them for years afterward. They take equity from their homes to buy boats and cars at high annual percentage rates. In many respects, they mortgage their futures, just as Uncle Sam mortgages our future by his ever-increasing debt.[1]

"We pay eight hundred dollars a month on our two car loans," a woman told me. "You bet we work hard." How much less strain would she and her husband face if they had purchased cars differently or purchased different cars?

The most recent statistic we've heard on consumer debt is that 75 percent of Americans who use credit cards carry a monthly balance on those cards. Even if that statistic is too high or low, figuring the high interest that credit cards typically charge is between 12.5 and 19 percent, that adds up to billions of owed money.

How can you know if your debt is a problem? Consider these points of alarm. If they are true for you, seek financial counseling.

- You use credit cards because you don't have—or can't muster up—cash.

- You can't pay more than the minimum balances every month, and what you owe keeps increasing.

- You are thinking about taking out a consolidation loan to cover the debts you've incurred.

- You consistently pay late-payment charges.

- You won't be able to pay off your nonmortgage debt in a year's time, and you are buying on credit now based on what you expect to earn next year.

- You or your family aren't protected against emergency situations.

- You keep using new credit cards because the other ones are "filled up."

- You have never laid out all your bills to determine how much you owe, and to whom.

- Creditors call or write you.

- You buy things you don't want or need.

- Your debt is more than 29 percent of your after-tax income, after you subtract your rent or mortgage payment.

- Your fears about your financial situation are increasing.

- You get cash from one credit card to pay off another one.

- You "juggle" which card to use for each purchase so you don't go over your limits.
- You've given up trying to pay everything off.
- You keep asking for higher limits on your cards.
- If you weren't doing side jobs, you'd go under.
- You borrow money from people.
- You bounce checks.
- You don't want to talk to anybody about the above—or think about it.

There are many way to get a handle on debt. Entire books have been written on this subject, among them Larry Burkett's book, *Debt-Free Living.*[2] If consumer debt is limiting your financial choices, consider the following points.

DEAL WITH THE PROBLEM BEFORE YOUR CREDITORS DO

If your debt is out of control, face that fact and take drastic action immediately. You have a great advantage if you deal with your credit problems before your creditors deal with you. Seek a wise, numbers-oriented person who can help you get your debt (and your spending) under control. Be prepared to hear things you don't want to hear. As a wise man once wrote, "He who rebukes a man will in the end gain more favor than he who has a flattering tongue. . . . He who trusts in himself is a fool, but he who walks in wisdom is kept safe."[3] The person you talk to will most likely encourage you to take the following steps.

1. Set up a realistic spending plan or start living within the spending plan you already have. (See chapter 13 on setting up a spending plan.)
2. Carefully determine all outstanding debts and keep up-to-date on obligations. Know what each bill costs you in interest charges and the late penalties. Pay off the bills that cost you the most first if you can do so without incurring severe penalties from other creditors.
3. Cut up your credit cards, and start paying cash for what you buy. Studies have shown that people who pay cash spend less than those who buy on credit.

4. Don't take on any more debt. Be willing to "live without" for as long as it takes to get your situation straightened out. Don't spend money you don't have to spend. Put off getting new furniture, a new car, a home, or a new kitchen addition until you strengthen your financial position.

5. Be willing to sell assets in order to pay off your debts. Check with a professional, such as an accountant or attorney, before you do this.

WHEN YOU CAN'T MEET MINIMUM OBLIGATIONS TO YOUR CREDITORS

Meet with your creditors, if need be, as soon as you realize you can't pay them. Approach them first! Show them your spending plan. If they know you are attempting to solve your credit problems, they may allow you to make lower payments for a while. Whatever you do, don't put your credit rating at risk. It's like your reputation: it takes a long time to build up and can come crashing down quickly.

If debt collectors are already hounding you, learn your rights under the Fair Debt Collection Practices Act. Write for a copy of *Fair Debt Collection* provided by the Federal Trade Commission.[4] Or contact your regional Federal Trade Commission Office.

If things have gone too far and you don't know how to straighten them out, get help. One option is to locate the nearest low-cost, non-profit, consumer credit counseling service and set up an appointment. The service can help you develop a financial plan to get out of debt or arrange repayment schedules with creditors. When you have turned your situation around, ask to see your credit report from the local credit bureau and correct any mistakes. That is your right under the Fair Credit Reporting Act.

Other books have dealt with bankruptcy and its consequences, so we'll just say here that bankruptcy should be your last resort.

Living smart and spending less has little to do with how much money we make.

Once you get through this time of debt reduction or debt elimination, promise yourself that you'll never get into it again. Realize that marketing departments spend billions to create "needs" in people's lives and that you and you alone can determine your own needs. Don't buy into materialistic, consumer mentalities. A car is transportation, not a way to gain prestige. Choose to buy the car that meets your transportation needs. A home is a place to live, not a showpiece of status to impress your friends. Live in a home that suits your lifestyle and spending plan. Your child doesn't need the latest video game or brand of cereal. Learn to make better choices so you can pass that gift of wisdom on to your children. Show by example that the way you use money is more significant than how much you earn.

How Much You Spend
Is More Important Than How Much You Earn

Have you noticed how much attention our society focuses on earning power? We encourage higher education because it's the ticket to better-pay-ing jobs. We raise the minimum wage for all workers. When masses of workers are laid off, we cry out not just for jobs but for better jobs, meaning jobs that pay more. We work hard to get promotions, not just because we want the challenge but because we want the pay raises. It's easy to fall into the trap of thinking that our financial condition will improve dramatically if we just get that next raise—or if we just make a few thousand more.

The harsh reality is that living smart and spending less has little to do with how much money we make. Instead, it has everything to do with how we spend what we make. Consider this example. Two single people each earn $25,300 a year. One of them shares a house with two roommates, uses public transportation, saves most of his or her earned income, and in a year's time places a sizable down payment on a house. The other person buys a new car, joins a fancy health club, eats out often, travels nearly every weekend, and ends up spending everything he or she earns. Both started out with the same financial resources, but they ended up with vastly different results. How one spends money is more important than how much one earns. This is true whether one earns $12,000 or $120,000 a year.

When we were first married, we just managed to get by. Amanda's father, knowing how little we were earning, encouraged us to put twenty-five dollars a month—fifty dollars when we had it—into a long-term mutual fund and to set additional money aside in a savings account for immediate use. As a result, we established a habit of saving and investing that continues to make a big difference in our lifestyle. It was not how much we earned that made the difference; it was how we used what we did make. And before interest rates went up, we used some of the money we'd saved for a down payment on our first house. When we purchased our second home years later, we also used a portion of the money we had originally invested.

GIVE YOURSELF A RAISE

Even though we all may realize that wise spending has more impact on our long-term financial condition than how much we earn, it's still nice to get a raise. It's nice to have more money than we thought we would. But there's more than one way to increase our income.

One way many people try to give themselves a raise is by playing the lottery. They hope to win big, to suddenly have a large, guaranteed income every year. Unfortunately, few players win. Everybody else still must continue to live on their regular income, which is actually decreased by the choice to spend money for lottery tickets.

Another way people seek raises is by trying to convince others to give them raises. Believing that they are what they do and that how much they earn reveals their worth as individuals, they push to achieve recognition in the workplace and earn higher salaries. They work late, miss breakfast, miss their children's school events, and buy the latest technological magic in order to increase productivity. Often they "succeed" at their careers, but often at the expense of their relationships.

Yet there's another way to give yourself a "raise." Figure out how to spend less money and do it. When you choose to spend less money, you earn the same amount, but you're able to pay bills and enjoy a more balanced lifestyle.

THE BENEFITS OF SAVING MONEY
AREN'T ALWAYS DOLLARS AND CENTS

Let's say that you choose to save money in a certain way, such as gardening. You spend hours preparing the soil, planting the seeds, and watering the soil. In a few weeks, the seeds begin to germinate. Soon plants are popping up everywhere. You weed, water, fertilize, and care for those plants.

At the end of the summer, you may have $275 worth of vegetables to show for your labors. If you had taken a part-time job, could you have made more money? Probably. If you had not planted the garden, would you have done something else "productive" with your time? Possibly. Would you have enjoyed the benefits of gardening? No.

In the end, saving money is a bit like gardening; its value can't be judged in dollars-and-cents terms alone. Its value must also be judged in light of the joy of trying new things, learning, doing things with family and friends, experimenting with lifestyle changes, discovering what it means to conserve and preserve and not get stuck in a lifestyle rut, working hard to do something worthwhile to you and to society as a whole, and in living out deep spiritual values. When you save money, that's often the icing on the cake.

Here's an example: you need another dining room table because the old one is falling apart. So you buy one at a furniture store on credit for six hundred dollars, and pay off the loan in fourteen months. The table costs you the six hundred dollars plus the interest you paid and the additional pretax money you had to earn to pay for it.

The way each of us views money has a profound impact on how we save and spend it.

Now let's go back in time. You spot a great dining room table at a flea market. It's constructed of solid wood and has a beautiful finish. You bargain the seller down about thirty dollars, pay two hundred dollars cash, and take the table home with you.

Clearly you come out ahead in the second scenario. You saved four hundred dollars on the purchase price, didn't pay interest charges, plus you needed fewer after-tax dollars to buy the table. And if you invested the four hundred dollars you didn't spend, you'd be earning interest or dividends, which would continue to increase as time passes.

By paying cash for a good deal, you have extra money that you wouldn't otherwise have. You have, in effect, given yourself a raise.

Enjoy the Benefits of Smart Living

When you save money by practicing the tips in this book, you will have extra money—perhaps for the first time in your life. Your challenge will be to use that money in wise ways that reflect your spiritual values.

Your challenge will be to enjoy the full range of options smart living can provide.

The way each of us views money has a profound impact on how we save and spend it. If you have gone through difficult financial times and view money as a way to ensure security, it may be difficult for you to use your resources to help others who are less fortunate. If you have used money and the pleasure it can buy as a substitute for happiness, it may be difficult for you to view money as a tool to be used in furthering your goals. If you tend to be impatient and want big results immediately, it may be difficult to wait for the results of smart living to pay off. Such attitudes can make you susceptible to the temptation of get-rich-quick schemes. But greed is not the answer.

Get-rich schemes have caused many a heartache. The next time one such scheme comes your way, keep your financial and life priorities clearly in mind. Ask yourself, *How much money will I have to risk? Who stands to benefit if I become involved? Why am I drawn to this? Could I use my money in a better way? What would a financially astute friend think about this?*

Obviously a few people have made lots of money by getting in on the right deal at the right time. But most haven't. If you can be content to plug along and practice what you read in this book, you'll not only have more money to use and share with others; you will also have more lifestyle options and opportunities to invest your money.

Living Smart Is Better
When You Share It with Others

For years, we tried to save money on our own with varied degrees of success. We read books and tried to implement what we'd learned. Sometimes we asked friends how they did it and learned from them. But we weren't good at asking for help. Usually we'd just push harder, get less sleep, and accomplish what we could.

Today we've learned that friends will help us, and we are willing to help them in return. You see, *saving money isn't a solitary adventure.* It often requires interaction with others. The term *community* was a buzzword in the 1960s. Today community is even more important. When we stand together, caring for one another and helping one another get ahead, exciting things happen.

For instance, last summer a hail storm tore up the roof of our house. Since part of it has a low pitch, we had to act quickly. Often it rains late in the afternoon, and repairs had to be weatherproof (though not necessarily completed) by around 3:00 each afternoon.

A week later, a young man rear-ended Amanda's car at a high rate of speed. Stiff and sore, she couldn't work on the roof. So Stephen called some friends, and on the following Saturday morning five of them pitched in for most of the day.

Saving money is an adventure that people you know have been experiencing for years. Maybe you're a pro at saving money; maybe you're just starting out. Either way, you can benefit from others' help and from helping them in return. That's what community is all about.

This decade is being called the "decade of frugality." People in all walks of life are looking for ways to save money, enhance the quality of their lifestyles, gain more financial options, and prepare for tough economic times ahead.

When you come across a good idea that works, don't hoard it. Share it with others who can benefit. (Send it to us c/o Moody Press, 820 North LaSalle, Chicago, IL 60610, for possible inclusion in our next book.) Discover the joy that sharing can bring.

Maybe you're the only one in your neighborhood or family who is interested in reading this book. Maybe nobody else "computes" the idea of spending less. That's OK. Experiment. Find out what works for you and your family or friends, and sensitively share it with others. Perhaps your example will encourage others to also begin enjoying the benefits of saving money.

2

Make Money-
Saving Choices
and Changes
That Make
a Difference

Remember the story about the turtle that won the race against the quick but lazy hare? Saving money is a bit like that story. If you race until you're dead tired, trying to fix everything at once, taking advantage of great deals all at once, and trying to save a lifetime's worth of earnings in a few months, you'll be tempted to collapse under a tree and fall asleep. But if you act carefully, safely, and wisely, you'll win the race, even when no one else is watching.

This book is about *turtle power*. Turtle power means taking small but significant steps in the right direction—making choices that save you money—so you win the race ahead of you. Let's look at some of the life-changing choices you can make to set your feet firmly on the path to smart living.

Pay Yourself Regularly

Regardless of how little you earn or how much debt you have, you can begin to save money regularly. It may be a very small amount at first, or it may be quite a bit. You may be able to put the money you save immediately into long-term investments. Or you may need to direct it into debt reduction before you tackle long-term goals. No matter where you start, you can do it. Saving just ten dollars a week can add up in a hurry, particularly if you shop around for the best ways to invest it. Ten dollars a week invested at a 10 percent return will be worth more than $2,500 in four years, and more than $8,700 in ten years.

Paying yourself for the future is important. If you have saved money, you are better prepared to meet unexpected expenses and ongoing bills without having to borrow money and pay high credit charges. You can protect your assets by riding out a layoff or other tough times. Best of all, you can begin to take steps to meet your long-term financial goals.

We know an elderly woman who lives in a house that's paid for and manages to save money even though her only income is Social Security. A single friend in his mid-twenties earns little more than minimum wage, yet has paid off his debts and purchased a used truck that he uses in his wood-cutting business. A single mom who attends our church has been able to set money aside because she and her daughter enjoy activities that cost little or no money.

What do those people have in common? They have learned that a part of what they earn is theirs to keep. And they realize that even little purchases or expenses—such as paying for each use of the automatic teller machine—make a difference.

Some people find it easy to set money aside. For others, it is more difficult. They need specific objectives and time frames in order to stay motivated. Yet if you look at your expenses and start at a basic level, you'll see ways to cut costs and save money.

You can't live on less than you earn without financial discipline.

Perhaps your company has a viable pension plan and you can have a sum of money deducted regularly from your paycheck. Perhaps you can stop buying soft drinks and toss the quarters you save into a jar. Perhaps you can pay off a loan and save the money you used to pay on it each month. When you practice money-saving habits on a regular basis, you are making choices that will make a vast difference in your life and in the lives of others.

If your situation is particularly difficult—you've been laid off, for example, and have little money saved—you'll certainly need to meet your basic needs before you think about long-term finances. But you can set small financial goals and achieve them. In time you will be able to make choices that will yield greater dividends.

Live on Less Than You Earn

Living on less than you earn is perhaps the most fundamental principle of living smart and spending less. If you consistently spend as much or more than you earn, you cannot save money. Spending more than you earn is a decision that eliminates most, if not all, other options. Consider a few of the options you may lose if you spend more than you earn:

You can't spend time with your family and friends because you have to work all the time just to keep up with the bills.

When good, money-saving deals come along, you can't take advantage of them because you're "cash poor."

It is difficult to recognize ways to save money because you are not aware of how much you spend on wants rather than needs and have not developed the discipline of practicing wise stewardship.

You save money in one area by practicing the money-saving ideas in this book but don't use the money you save wisely, so you may still end up living on more than you earn.

FINANCIAL DISCIPLINE CAN BE LEARNED

Obviously you can't live on less than you earn without financial discipline. And financial discipline doesn't come easily for many people. As we speak with people about learning to make financial choices, some say, "I wasn't raised like that," or, "I don't know how to begin saving money," or, "Nobody in my family saved money." If making wise financial decisions is new or difficult for you but you are willing to get out of that rut, turn left or right and start doing it. This is one area of life in which you must take charge.

If you can't balance a checkbook, ask a friend to help you. If you're deeply in debt, get help. If you spend too much money, ask a friend to help you sort things out and hold you accountable to a spending plan.

If you don't know how to start saving, take a look at the small areas of spending. If you are serious about saving money, watch those coins. And get ready to experience the satisfaction of learning how to use money as the resource it is meant to be rather than as a fishing line that yanks you more often than you do the yanking.

We buy gas at generic stations that charge us a few cents less per gallon if they're convenient. (But it isn't worth a ten-minute drive to save two cents a gallon.) We buy our milk at a wholesale warehouse and save about fifty cents a gallon. We put a nickel in the parking meter rather than a dime when we'll only be parked there a few minutes. In time, pennies, nickels, and quarters add up to dollars.

GOOD THINGS COME TO THOSE WHO WAIT

Patience is key to saving money. It's a necessary ingredient in locating the best insurance company, finding the best shopping deal, and waiting for your choices to yield fruit. Needing things *now* is a by-product of our age of instant information, and the result of our expectations of immediate gratification that can create dissatisfaction. *Instant* almost defines our culture—instant dinners, instant pudding, instant communication. But it takes time and determination to save money.

Understanding the difference between needs and wants is key to saving money.

In 1973, Stephen had the opportunity to work in Afghanistan with a Christian ministry. He flew from Chicago to New York to London to Rome to Istanbul to Kabul for about four hundred dollars round trip. When he returned at the end of the summer, a friend asked him how his trip was.

"Great!"

"I wish I could do something like that," the woman said.

"You could. Just save up and do it. Or choose someplace closer that doesn't cost as much in air fare."

The woman shook her head and left. She wasn't willing to make the choices that would give her the opportunities she desired.

With patience and consistent pursuit of the right choices, it is possible to make the dreams of your heart happen. For example, we want to take a trip overseas as a family someday. We don't know yet how it will work out, but we're planning on it and working hard toward that goal. If we continue to have the patience to tinker with our old Scout when something goes wrong with it instead of buying another vehicle (that we'll still have to tinker with), if we continue to do our own home maintenance, if we continue to eat low-cost foods, we expect to reach that goal eventually.

Do you want to know a secret? Sometimes we get tired of waiting too. Sometimes we feel as if we're doing too much living for the future. So we treat ourselves to a nice meal at a moderately priced restaurant. At the end of the evening, we know we can face the tired Scout one more year. We can deal with one more plumbing problem. We can be thankful for what we do have and for our hope in the future. (And dinner out is cheaper than buying another car!)

Don't Mix up Your Needs and Wants

Allow us to tell you more about our dear old Scout. It's sixteen years old and runs great (except on the occasional days when it doesn't run at all). It has its share of rust spots. The door locks sometimes come out in your hand when you pull the key out of the lock. If you don't find just the right spot in "park," the ignition lock won't release and it won't start. We could list more of its unique features, but let's just say it would be nice—some days *very* nice—to have a new four-wheel-drive vehicle.

No matter how much we would like to replace our aging Scout, however, we realize that at this point our desire is merely a want. We need a four-wheel-drive vehicle, and what we presently have meets that need. The day will come when the Scout sputters for the last time and our desire for a replacement vehicle will then become a need. But until that time, we dare not think we *need* something that is merely a *want*.

Understanding the difference between needs and wants is key to saving money. Although marketing people (and many government officials concerned about words such as *recession*) want us to believe that what we want is what we need, they are not the same. You can enhance your quality of life in many ways without necessarily fulfilling all your wants. (Let other consumers expand the economy by consuming more and more goods and services.)

"JUST SAY NO" TO THE NEED/WANT TRAP

How many families today are fearful of financial ruin because they confused wants and needs and ended up with beautiful homes, great furniture, huge mortgages, and nearly unbearable credit-card debts? Ironically, many people wish they were making choices to satisfy their own needs and wants instead of pursuing the wants and needs that others have persuaded them to seek. In our state, an appliance company commercial reminds viewers to ask our neighbor about them, implying that because other people shop there, we should too. Those of us who want to take charge of our finances must learn to say no to the "wants" others place before us as needs.

A computer executive friend recently explored positions with several Fortune 500 companies. After his interviews, he said to us:

> I saw all those salesmen running around to gain sales, and I saw something I hadn't seen before. I saw how much their companies encouraged them to satisfy their wants. I saw how overextended they were financially and how they *had* to sell merchandise or go under. I don't want to live like that, being motivated by fear.

Of course, needs vary, depending on people's unique situations. As we've explained, we need a four-wheel-drive to negotiate our country driveway during the winter. Another family may not even need a car. But needs have a way of creating other needs, causing a multiplication effect. The Scout needs trips to the repair shop, rust removal, ongoing insurance coverage, and tires.

Wants can become needs out of habit, too. If the television dies, is replacing it a need or a want? Is redecorating a need or a want? Is it necessary to keep the house at seventy-two degrees during the winter? As you begin to say no to wants, you may also begin to ask more questions about your purchases. You may begin to discover more accurately what your needs are, what other people are saying your needs are, and the differences between the two. And as the cart gets rolling, you may find yourself gaining an increased ability to determine which motivations underlie and influence your perceived needs. When you say no to the wants that can wait and look at alternative ways to meet your needs, you may discover that those needs are quite different than you first thought they were.

One of the rewards of concentrating on needs first and taking small steps to save money is that you'll be free to indulge in more wants of your own choosing. Perhaps some of these wants will include caring for others in need and supporting special ministries. Generosity can be a life-changing by-product of saving money.

IT ISN'T EASY TO GO "BACKWARD"

No matter who you are, it isn't easy to downscale. Once you fulfill a desire or need and become used to fulfilling it, it's hard not to have it anymore. Take garage-door openers, for example. While we were growing up, our families never had garage-door openers. The regular garage doors were heavy and inconvenient, especially during a snowstorm. But for the most part we didn't miss something we had never had. Now we have a garage-door opener, and we're used to it. If we sold our house next week, would we want our next house to have a garage-door opener? You bet! It has become something we think we need.

If you are serious about saving money, you need to be careful about how you view the opportunities around you. If you prime your pump for the latest and greatest, you are creating your own internal dissatisfaction that most likely will cost you money. For instance, perhaps you love a certain chair. It's comfortable for reading and it reclines so you can take a nap. But when you visit a store and sit in a new model, you suddenly realize that your old one doesn't look quite as nice and the armrest isn't quite as comfortable as the new one. Instead of your glass being half-full, it's suddenly half-empty.

We're not saying that you shouldn't compare various items. But creating dissatisfaction when you don't have the means of resolving it can be a strong motivation to spend impulsively, purchase the wrong item, or pay too much for an item.

In order to achieve your important goals, you will, in most instances, have to choose whether to accept an easy solution that will mask your dissatisfaction but cost more money in the long run, or take that temporary step "backward." How you respond to those challenges will make the difference between fulfilling long-term goals and short-term desires.

Making Your Own Choices Isn't Always Comfortable

Years ago, Stephen went skiing on the slopes of Breckenridge. He wore layered clothing, including a patched down jacket and baggy, wool army pants. As he rounded a bend, he noticed a skier who was dressed in a similar style.

Aha! Stephen thought. *At last there's somebody like me. No matching outfit. Just simple clothing that works.*

When he met with friends after the lift closed, he mentioned that he finally had seen someone like him and described the man.

"Oh," the friend said. "That was Bo-Bo. He's a mountain man who lives in the national forest. He just comes into town for groceries and a shower."

The point is simple. If you are committed to saving money in a balanced way (doing what you can without going overboard and becoming angry, weird, or miserly), you'll stand out in the crowd. You won't stand out as if you're wearing purple hair in a mall or baggy, unmatched clothing on a ski slope. Rather, people will notice something different about you, your lifestyle, and the way you think.

When others pull into the parking lot, your car may be a little older than theirs. When they visit your home, they may see it furnished with shelves you built yourself. In your garage they may see a fine set of used tools that you purchased at garage sales, auctions, and flea markets instead of at well-known stores. Your utility bill may be half what they pay each month, or less, and you may order two smaller hamburgers at a fast-food restaurant instead of the larger one that costs three or four times as much. And you might be better dressed than they are—for pennies on the dollar.

NONCONFORMITY CREATES DISCOMFORT

Be prepared for flack. Nonconformists always have an uphill battle. People have an inherent desire to be like each other and want other people to be like them because it's safer; deep down everyone wants to be loved and accepted, not criticized. Unfortunately, those who lead the pack usually have ulterior motives.

Have you ever noticed how often people tempt you to do what they do? After all, no one likes to feel as if he or she is going where nobody else is going (unless we're really trying to get away from it all). A child who gets excited about a particular game will run toward it and try to get his or her friends to follow. But if none of them follows, usually the child returns to the group.

When people want you to do certain things that require more money than you'd prefer to spend, pay attention to what they say to convince you. Usually they reveal their philosophy of spending, with which you may choose to agree or disagree. Worse, they may have a philosophy altogether different from the one they mention and seek to take advantage of you.

A neighbor has purchased three vehicles this past year. He buys one, keeps it for a few months, and then gets another one. When Stephen stopped by to say hello one afternoon, the neighbor looked at our Scout and said, "You still driving that thing? Why don't you get one that looks better?"

Stephen didn't say much. Driving a pretty vehicle means little to us. What matters is whether it will do what it needs to do. Other priorities are more important than buying a car that people will admire.

Nonconformists shake up the system by not playing by the usual rules. But the status-oriented boss who drives a fancy car with four-hundred-dol-lar-a month payments may not like to be reminded that the attractive but older car in the parking lot was paid for long ago on a salary less than half what he or she makes. A good rule to follow here is to be socially conscious; choose the areas in which you will compromise. Eat your peanut butter and jelly sandwich and fruit for lunch, but join your co-workers for an occasional lunch out, too. If you invite guests to your home during the winter, don't have the thermostat down so low that they freeze. If you must dress well for work, do so, but look for deals on clothing at a consignment shop. Also, don't talk about your savings adventures unless someone asks. You'll drive people away who don't yet understand what saving money is all about. (You could give them a copy of this book to get them started, however.)

If you start taking the path of nonconformity and begin to practice the tips in this book, you may feel some initial discomfort. Your values may change, and that isn't always comfortable. Habits are hard to unlearn. Seeing potential in what others throw away—and stopping to pick up what they discard—isn't always easy. Learning to do new things carries some risk. And when the money isn't going out of your pocket as fast, you'll be faced with the decision of what you'll do with it. Will you help others in God's name? Or will you simply use the money to satisfy another want?

Jesus challenged people's values. Pompous religious leaders of His day looked down on normal "sinful" folks. But Jesus invited Himself to the homes of those folks for meals.[1] When people ostracized lepers, Jesus felt compassion and touched them.[2] When rich people made a show of giving money to charity, Jesus praised the widow who gave two small coins—all she had.[3] We, too, can challenge unfair values by changing our lifestyles.

Choosing Between Bigger and Smaller

Whenever one faces a decision between bigger and smaller, certain factors win out. It's important to think about why we choose bigger or smaller. After all, marketing people at large corporations spend much of their time trying to figure out why we make decisions the way we do.

If you drive up Ute Pass in Colorado, you'll pass a unique home. Nestled near the mountains, it has a variety of rooms, seemingly distinct, yet pleasantly tied together in loose architectural form. The home is not large, but it is inviting. We suspect that the owner built the home in stages as he or she had the need and resources.

Not far away is another distinctive home. Carefully packaged and obviously built all at one time, its size and unique design also stand out.

Which home is better? Both are nice. In the end, one isn't really better than the other as long as each owner is happy with the outcome. There is plenty of room in this world for both *bigger* and *smaller*. What's important is that we understand why we choose one over the other, and are willing to make decisions that may vary widely from the status quo.

NOT EVERYONE CAN SAVE MONEY THE SAME WAYS

Some people are great at fixing things. No matter how intricate the tasks, they can take things apart and fix them. Some people are skilled at sewing or bookkeeping, some at marketing or teaching. If you're like most people, you are good at some things and not so good at others. For instance, a friend of ours is skilled at stretching dollars through creative cooking. She can cook amazing meals for five people for a surprisingly small amount of money. But when it comes to changing the oil in her car, forget it!

Stephen is great at physical activities, such as logging, building a road, and fixing things that aren't too detailed. But let him take apart a lawn mower engine and watch out. When he is "done," a leftover piece always seems to be sitting on the table or workbench.

Because you don't have the aptitude to save money one way doesn't mean you can't save money in another area. Thousands of ways to save money await you.

Look for Alternative Solutions

Stores make it possible for us to meet our needs with easy solutions. "You need it; we have it!" they say. But a key to saving money is to think through your problems thoroughly enough to come up with your own, cheaper alternatives that may work even better than store-bought ones.

During a cold trip to Illinois, for example, Stephen stopped at a budget motel. The next morning, he checked the oil and was horrified to discover that the oil cap was gone. Oil had begun to spray everywhere.

One way to save money is to be willing to improvise, to find new ways to do things, to look at situations differently.

He checked the local phone book. No car dealership. So he put a plastic bag over the hole, tied it down as well as he could, and drove slowly to an auto parts store a mile away.

"No, we don't have a cap for your car," the man said, looking in his book of parts numbers.

"Well, think with me for a minute. A hole has to be filled. You have more parts in here than exist in many Third World cities. What else will work?"

The man thought. "We do have other caps that might go over the top." And the wheels began to roll.

Half an hour later, Stephen and his new acquaintance had fixed the car. An oil cap, albeit not the right size, covered the hole, and sheet-metal screws on the cap were attached to short bungee cords that were hooked to nearby engine points. The funny-looking solution took Stephen 1,300 miles until he bought a cap that fit at his local dealership. Finding alternative solutions can be an intellectual challenge as well as a means to keep within your spending plan.

Make an Item Yourself

Sometimes it doesn't pay to make something yourself. Maybe special expertise is required, the cost of individual parts is more than a new item will cost, or you don't have the time. But when circumstances are favorable, you can save a great deal of money by making items yourself.

We have built bookshelves, garage shelves, an outdoor swing, bird houses, and a large playhouse for our daughter, not to mention the house addition that gave us an office and garage. We've had fun as a family, saved money, and ended up with higher-quality items than we could otherwise have afforded.

IMPROVISE

One way to save money is to be willing to improvise, to find new ways to do things, to look at situations differently, and to pursue a course even when others don't understand what you are doing.

Creating your own solutions instead of depending on those that people are ready to sell you can be a game, and the better you get at it the more you'll save. Perhaps that old riding lawn mower chassis could be a good start on a go-cart, those old boards would make a great playhouse, and that old stereo cabinet could be modified and used for something else.

Stephen uses a twenty-foot pole saw he made from a piece of conduit pipe a contractor gave him. Instead of paying several hundred dollars for a pole saw that long, he mounted a Swedish steel blade on top of the pipe. Is it as convenient to store as a telescoping saw? No. Does it look as nice as the commercial saw? No. Does it cut hard-to-reach branches just as well? You bet!

NOT SPENDING MONEY
CAN BECOME EASIER THAN SPENDING IT

If you're like most people, you like to spend money. When we make a purchase we've anticipated for a while, we enjoy spending money too. But when you get in the habit of saving money, get ready for a surprise.

Believe it or not, when you become skilled at not spending money, it's easier to come up with your own creative solutions than it is to spend money on other people's solutions and ready-made products. Maybe you'll fix the item yourself. Maybe you'll borrow something from a neighbor. Maybe you'll wait until what you need shows up at an auction. Maybe you'll trade for it. Maybe you'll junk the whole idea and start over. Your resourcefulness, sense of accomplishment, and learning will often make spending money the least desirable choice.

Learn New Skills, Make New Choices

As you embark on the adventure of living smart and spending less, you'll begin to observe things you didn't see before. You (and your friends or family) will become interested in new activities. You'll be drawn to learn new skills that apply to virtually every aspect of life.

EVALUATE WHAT YOU THROW AWAY

Have you ever gone to a city dump or landfill? The dust, the noise of diesel equipment pushing and flattening, and the lines of cars and trucks are memorable. But what you may remember most is what people throw away.

We don't spend much time picking through landfills. However, we have been known to take loads of brush and other junk to landfills in our pickup truck and return with such items as bicycles, a reinforcing bar used in construction, tire chains, tarps, wood, and so on.

That brings us back to our central point. Look at items creatively before you throw them away; could they have another use? Maybe the cracked bucket could cover the rose bushes during the winter. Maybe you could use that piece of wood to make a birdhouse. Maybe that old towel could become a great car-washing rag or should be reserved to dry off the dog when he comes in dripping wet. And the shower curtain might make a dandy drop cloth when you paint.

If you can't easily put an item to good use, consider who else could. Give it to a needy family if it is in good shape. Donate it to a charitable organization. Use the trash can or landfill as a last resort.

PRACTICE REGULAR MAINTENANCE TO PRESERVE WHAT YOU HAVE

Routine maintenance is seldom fun. It may mean getting oily or greasy or taking apart an appliance for the first time. It may mean hunting for misplaced manuals or calling knowledgeable friends and asking questions about subjects you don't fully understand. It may mean buying a tool that's required to do the job correctly.

Maintenance requires time and the awareness of what needs to be done even when the baby is crying, the boss is demanding, the priority list is already too long, and/or your spouse wants to take an unexpected vacation. (Right now, the lights on our old camping trailer are out, the barn roof needs to be replaced, and the lawn mower needs oil in the spark plug hole before we store it for the winter.) But if you don't do necessary maintenance or ask someone else to do it, you'll likely end up having to fix items under financial or time pressure and paying much more money in the long run.

By caring for what you own properly, you'll save on repair bills, time, and the cost of buying new items to replace the ones that didn't last as long as they would have otherwise.

ASK THE RIGHT PEOPLE FOR HELP

There is an army of people available for you to consult about virtually anything you need to learn. Most people enjoy talking about what they know best—themselves and what they've learned. And asking before you get into trouble is a lot easier than asking afterward.

One time Stephen was trying to put some grease into a fitting on our old pickup truck. He kept trying to push a certain part down, but it wouldn't move. Just as he was getting angry, he decided to call the service manager at the dealership.

"Oh," he said, "that part unscrews."

We have asked people about generators, engines, painting, trees, gardens, grass, weeds, clothes, tools, and more. And we're constantly surprised by the number of gifted people who freely offer their good advice.

There's a saying, "Don't make the same mistake twice; make a new one." Often it's possible to avoid making the first costly error by asking an expert for advice. Stephen once bought a 1962 Jeep for $1,200 without asking anyone's advice. (He liked the winch on the front bumper.) The vehicle ended up costing us lots of money, conked out various times in isolated areas, and was a terrible time waster. We wish we had a dollar for every time we thought, *Why did we get this thing?*

There's another benefit to asking the right people for advice: it gives them an opportunity to feel good about what they know and to share the benefits of their creativity and expertise. For instance, when we had to do major excavating work on our long driveway (it was a mudhole in the spring when the snow melted), we hired a "payloader" to move the dirt and then a road grader to do the final grading. When the driver of the road grader pulled up, he called out, "What kind of grade do you want?"

Stephen's answer surprised him. "Well, my wife drives this road all the time during the winter. We want the water to drain off the sides, and we need it to last for a while. You do this all the time. Can you fix it for us?"

The driver smiled. "I know exactly what you want." And in less than an hour, he had done a superb job and had even done a little extra work that we couldn't pay him for. Why did he do such a good job? It wasn't because Stephen was watching him as he worked or because Stephen gave exact grading percentages—he didn't. What mattered was that Stephen acknowledged the man's expertise and allowed him the freedom to use it.

The same thing has happened with electricians, plumbers, contractors, and so on. We sketch out what we think we need and then say, "You do this all the time. What do you suggest? Is there a better way?" Quite often, we end up with a better job at a cheaper price, and the people doing the work are happy because their opinions matter. Plus, they give us advice along the way that allows us to do more ourselves the next time around. Granted, sometimes you do need to provide close instruction. But it is worth it to find people who have both skill and initiative so we don't have to be experts in areas beyond our knowledge.

SHARE AND TRADE WITH BUDDIES

Every household seems to accumulate things. That might be called the "Law of the Household." Material goods expand to fit the space available—which leads to crowded closets, garages, and storerooms. But there's a plus: other people may be able to lend or give you what you need so you don't have to rent or buy it and vice versa.

Recently a friend asked to borrow the thirty-two-foot extension ladder that we purchased four years ago so we could shingle the steep roof on our addition. In return, he will adjust the clutch on our truck—not to repay us or because we expect it. He will do it because he wants to help us save money, too.

Sharing tools and knowledge can be a way to get to know people and avoid having to buy or rent duplicate items. For example, we let the neighbor use our lawn mower whenever he needs it, and he lets us use his tractor. When we rent a wood splitter, we lend it to a neighbor, who also lets us use his rototiller to cultivate our garden.

Several rules apply to sharing. First, realize that things sometimes break during normal use, so don't get mad if your friend or neighbor has a problem with one of your hoozy whip tootles. Second, communicate expectations ahead of time. If you want your fertilizer spreader to be washed out as soon as it's used so it won't corrode, mention that. Third, return anything you borrow in at least as good a shape as it was when you borrowed it. Stephen used a neighbor's saw enough to dull the blade, so he had it sharpened professionally before returning it. Finally, consider buying items you use regularly or use hard, and borrow and lend specialized items or those you don't often use. There's no point in spending money unnecessarily.

YOU CAN DO AND LEARN
MORE THAN YOU THINK YOU CAN

When Stephen traveled overseas as a journalist, he'd sometimes be gone for weeks at a time. Upon returning from India one spring, he was delighted to discover that Amanda had completely redone the bathroom: new countertop made with leftover tile from a friend, new sink, new fixtures, new vanity (from a custom cabinetmaker who was selling his overstock), new wallpaper, and new carpeting. She had also replaced some plumbing in the process.

How did she do it? She believed she could. She'd never done anything like that before, but she realized that she had enough ability to succeed. She knew her limits, so water didn't end up everywhere. She asked questions and used the right tools. She refused to believe that only a plumber or contractor could do the job, so she jumped in and did it at a substantial savings.

You can tackle new projects, even if your picture of yourself is as far from a "save-money-by-doing" person as anyone could get. The key lies in believing that you (and your family or friends) can do it and being willing to learn what you don't know or seek help from a knowledgeable friend or expert.

Read owner's manuals. Ask people for advice. Take basic courses at a local college. Stephen once took a house-framing course at a junior college, and what he learned came in handy when we built our addition. And when you're not sure whether you can do something, try it anyway, as long as there is little risk of permanent damage or injury. You may be pleasantly surprised.

During his travels, Stephen has seen people make houses out of grass, shape boats out of logs, tie nets out of hand-woven rope, and butcher their own animals. They have learned to accomplish those tasks because such knowledge is valued, because they had virtually no money for anything but necessities, and because they needed to accomplish certain tasks in order to survive.

Procrastination is the enemy of saving money.

Without thinking about other possibilities, many people hire professionals to do routine tasks. Sometimes it is appropriate to use experts. But think about what you could do this week or this year that would save you money and bring you satisfaction. Throughout this book, you'll read about ways in which you can save money. Some of them are relatively easy. Others will require more effort. How much you do is up to you. But if you are willing to develop new skills—by reading, experimenting, watching friends and skilled professionals do certain tasks, and asking questions—you will learn skills that will help you save money, that may become hobbies, or that may provide additional income.

There Is No Better Time to Start Saving Than Today!

It's easy to put off tasks that require effort, especially considering the pressures we all face today. There's no denying that living smart and spending less requires effort. Money seldom comes to us on its own. If we want to build up our financial resources, we must use existing resources wisely, *today*. Procrastination is the enemy of saving money.

Many people have never met with a financial planner to map out their financial future. If they did, they'd realize how much money they should be investing every month in order to achieve their minimal financial goals, such as being able to maintain the standard of living they enjoy today when they retire. And when other financial goals are factored in, such as paying off a mortgage, having the resources to visit grandchildren, or paying for a college education, the amount needed increases.

Is that a cause for alarm or fear? No. Should you do something about it now? By all means. The longer you wait, the more difficult it will be to save and invest enough money to meet your financial goals. No matter how small or great an amount you can put away for the future, the best time to start is *now*. Delaying is far more costly than you might imagine. Consider these examples.

If your goal is to put away fifty dollars per month and you do that every month for thirty years and receive a modest return of 12 percent, you will have $154,050 in thirty years. But if you delay your plan by just one year and put away the same amount per month at the same rate of return, you will have only $136,950 after twenty-nine years. A delay of one year can cost you $17,100, or $46.85 per day—nearly as much per day as you planned to invest per month!

If you were able to put away as much as three hundred dollars per month (which is 10 percent of a $36,000 per year salary), you would have $924,300 at the end of thirty years (figuring a 12 percent rate of return). But if you were to delay only one year, you would have $821,700 at the end of twenty-nine years. Once again, the cost of delay is expensive—in this case, $281.10 per day.

Today is a good day to start your adventure of living smart and spending less.

3

Shop
Smart

A simple formula is at work in our country: People earn money, and other people want it. To get it, businesses try all sorts of methods. They conduct expensive tests to see which jingle is most memorable, experiment with package designs, and create different versions of direct-mail letters. They pay "personalities" to hawk their products, banking on your belief that you will be as popular, desirable, or powerful as those personalities if you use the same products. Or they use "neighbors" to induce you to think, *Hey, people just like me use that. I should use it too.* They use the implied authority of doctors' recommendations to sell health products and images of patriotism, motherhood, pets, and sex to play on your emotions.

The bottom line? Whenever you shop, marketing pressures can influence you to spend your money on things you don't need. So it is important that you learn to shop smart and buy according to your needs, your research, your choices, and your spending plan.

Protect Yourself from Bad Decisions

It's easy to let external influences, personal wishes, and impatience overrule common sense when it comes to shopping. In spite of our best efforts to save money, we all make bad shopping decisions occasionally. But there are ways to protect yourself from expensive mistakes.

GUARD AGAINST IMPULSE SPENDING

Buying on impulse is a hazardous spending habit. Impulse buying costs people money because:

- They haven't compared prices.
- They rarely need the items anyway.
- The items may not be well made.
- The items may have little value a year (or even a few days) after the purchase.
- A little impulse buying can easily grow into an out-of-control habit.

Take a close look the next time you're in a store. See those toys at kid level? See the cookies on a shelf near the counter, the candy by the checkout register? Notice how you have to pass rows of nonessential items to get to the other necessities? See the items on the aisle display when you first walk into the store? The magazines? The cosmetic counters in the department stores? All of those are examples of retailers' attempts to entice us to buy on impulse.

Whenever you shop for anything other than a low-cost item, it's time to comparison shop.

Many people can't resist the impulse. If you want to spend less, learn to resist spending temptations. Here are some suggestions:

- Don't be afraid to say no.
- Don't allow high-pressure tactics to wear down your resistance.

- Go into a store armed with a list, and buy only what is on it.

- Think carefully about both major and minor purchases. Don't rush into them.

DO YOUR HOMEWORK BEFORE YOU BUY

Saving money often requires advance planning. Whenever you shop for anything other than a low-cost item, it's time to comparison shop. Look at various products. Talk with other people. Check prices and quality. And don't allow anyone to pressure you. You'll save money and learn much in the process that will help you to make other effective product decisions.

Research and compare. We know a man in the East who literally spends a year researching which car or wood stove he should buy. That may be a bit extreme, but he does have the right idea. Here's how you can begin your comparison shopping homework.

- Look up big-ticket items in *Consumer Reports* and similar publications. Compare the test results.

- Evaluate the quality and price of similar merchandise in several stores before buying an item.

- Compare the cost of the same or similar items in several stores, by telephone if possible. Some items you just have to see; others, such as car oil, are standardized.

- Consider the possibility of buying used or rebuilt items that are backed by warranties. Compare the cost of these products with the costs and guarantees of new ones.

Evaluate features and costs carefully. Do you really need the top-of-the-line model? Perhaps the more basic (often less expensive) model will work as well, or even better, for your needs. Most people never use more than the basic features anyway.

A former neighbor of ours repaired electrical appliances. When we decided to buy a microwave, we asked him what kind to buy. "Many good ones are out now," he replied. "Stick with one that has a simple timer and not all the touch-button computerized control panels. The timer will work just as well, and if it goes out it's much cheaper to repair. I can replace a manual timer for less than twenty dollars. A computer control panel can cost more than one hundred dollars, just for parts."

We followed his advice and have had trouble-free service from that microwave for ten years.

When we bought our fax machine, we researched various consumer magazines to learn about features. Some of the machines were so complicated, with options such as polling and multiple number recall, that we knew we'd get lost in the manuals. So we bought a basic model, and it has worked faithfully for several years. We can only put in five sheets of paper at a time, but we saved more than sixty dollars by being willing to feed the pages in the few times we send more than five sheets.

Salespeople often want to sell you the "latest and the greatest." But when you know (or research so you know) what you need and what you can pay, you have the upper hand. Plus, you have to live with the product—and the price; the salespeople don't.

The other day the temperature dropped, and we knew that winter would soon arrive. So Stephen called a few tire shops to get a price on a specific snow tire we've used for years.

"Yes, we've got that in stock. Four of them, with the mounting and balancing, will be $307.00."

"Yes, we have that tire in stock," the second man said. "Four of them mounted and balanced—that'll come to $366.24."

"No, we won't carry tires like that," the third man at the discount warehouse said. "We have others, but not that one."

"We can get those tires for you," the fourth guy said. "They'll be $333.75, and we'll have them tomorrow."

We bought the tires at the first shop—and one of the men helped Stephen fix a gas-line leak on the Scout in the parking lot. So, for fifteen minutes on the telephone, including discussions about other tires that might work equally well, we saved a minimum of $26.75 and a maximum of $59.24.

We also evaluated watering cans not long ago, and to our surprise found one that was much better designed than the others, and it cost just a dollar more. But we didn't spend a lot of time comparing cans, which brings us to the next point.

Consider your time and energy when you shop. If a store offers a product you use quite often at fifty cents off, that may be a great price. But if you have to drive half an hour out of your way to save fifty cents, you will come out ahead if you pay the higher price at a store close to home. The same principle applies to how much research you choose to do. If an item such as a sponge is cheap, you may determine whether you can buy a package of six for the price of two. But it would be silly to go from store to store hunting for a cheaper sponge. In contrast, items that cost hundreds or thousands of dollars that you plan to use for five, ten, or twenty years or longer, are worth the time and energy spent in research.

Compare and understand
warranties, guarantees, and service contracts

Warranties and guarantees vary. By comparing them closely, you can buy makes and models that will cost you less money if something goes wrong. For example, if the item you buy develops a problem covered by a warranty, will it be fixed locally or shipped somewhere else, forcing you to wait weeks for repairs to be made?

Service contracts can be costly, so make sure you evaluate your needs before you buy them. Ask yourself a few basic questions:

Will this really save me money?

What if I just saved this money on my own and used it to pay for the repairs?

What kinds of problems am I likely to have with this product?

We talk with service technicians about specific models before making our choices. If you buy quality products, you'll often come out ahead even if you don't purchase the service contracts.

Evaluate some purchases on an ongoing basis. It may be important to evaluate certain purchases, such as major appliances, again and again. By planning ahead, you can save money because you won't have to replace a broken item blindly. An appliance can break unexpectedly, but even if the worst scenario occurs, you will know where to shop for the best deals on a replacement.

For example, Amanda noticed that our twenty-eight-year-old refrigerator was beginning to run more frequently and cool less effectively. She knew that it wouldn't be worth repairing again, so she started looking for a replacement. She knew exactly what she wanted and checked the classified ads for eight weeks without finding one. She then began checking ads for new appliances. In several weeks, she found exactly what she wanted—for more than 30 percent off the regular price. We bought it gladly.

You will also benefit by regularly comparing prices on food, homeowner and car insurance, and other goods and services. Sometimes you may need to shift policies or change your customary shopping places in order to spend less.

Homework builds on itself. As you learn about one subject, others become more understandable. Gradually you'll gain a thorough understanding of some subjects. So watch out—smart folks will then start coming to you. Allow time in your schedule for sharing what you learn.

Never sign anything you haven't read. Sounds logical, right? But many people sign contracts without being aware of the consequences. No matter what kind of contract you are dealing with, read the fine print on every side. If you don't, you will probably lose. If you don't understand something, find out what it means. Never allow yourself to be pressured or embarrassed into signing something you don't understand. Using that simple principle can protect your wallet to the tune of thousands of dollars and save you big headaches.

Buy Quality at the Right Price

CHEAPER ISN'T ALWAYS BETTER

Remember the time when you bought that thingamijig for twelve dollars, smiled all the way home, and then a week later it broke? Stores today are full of poorly made and poorly designed products. As a result, consumers should be wary. For example, years ago Stephen purchased a short pole saw for cutting tree branches. At the top was a curved saw blade built of Swedish steel. That blade worked well without a sharpening until he accidentally snapped the blade off. When he went to buy another blade, the replacement blades were made of cheaper steel, which didn't cut nearly as well.

You could probably provide your own examples of poor-quality goods that you bought because you thought you were getting a good buy: the clothes that didn't hold up well, the appliance you wish you could get rid of, the discount power tool that started to smoke just after the limited warranty expired.

The key principle here is this: When you can, buy quality and take care of what you buy. Don't buy one doodad that will break down each year when a more expensive one could provide years of hassle-free service. Always consider *value*.

Remember, there are exceptions, however. Quality often is less important than price if you plan to use something once. But weigh quality, price, and value carefully. All merchandise is not created equal. Check out such factors as product warranties, operational costs, whether or not the product has been rated by a recognized testing organization, whether the product has the features you really need, and where you'll need to have servicing done if you can't service it yourself.

BE WILLING TO HAGGLE ON THE PRICE

Just because the television has a price tag on it doesn't mean the dealer won't reduce the price (particularly at the end of the month). Obviously many items, such as those in a grocery store, are seldom open to negotiation. (One friend did manage to buy forty pounds of bananas for a dollar.) But larger-ticket items often are negotiable, although that fact may not be publicized.

Remember, selling is a game of sorts. Sellers have goods and services they hope you or someone else will be willing to buy. But if people don't rush to buy the item or service, what happens? It sits in a showroom or warehouse, costing the seller money. Plus, retailers have to pay interest on goods and equipment, storage, and utilities. Perhaps they can't order a newer model until the older one is sold. That is just the time to strike a bargain.

It's easier to bargain if you buy more than one item at once. Three of our friends were in the market for new skis. They looked in several ski shops and all decided on the same kind of skis and bindings. The next day, one of them went back to the stores and asked to speak with the sales managers. She explained that she wanted three pairs of skis and bindings and asked how much of a price break each store would give her on three pairs. One manager took her challenge and sold the skis at a substantial deduction—seventy dollars per pair!

Another way to buy what you want for less is to inquire about slightly damaged or display models. Often you can purchase those items for a reduced price and get the same warranty.

Creative bargaining can seem a bit difficult at first because no one wants to appear "cheap," but once you get the basics down, it's not hard unless the retailer refuses to consider a price reduction. In that case, you can always shop in another store.

Sellers have almost come to expect buyers to bargain. It's part of the game. We've bargained for everything from tools to clothing to professional services. To do it, you must:

- Know what items are worth to you (and have a good idea of what they are worth to others).
- Be willing to search to find exactly the right object.
- Be friendly. (Nobody wants to deal with a sourpuss.)
- Pay cash.
- Be willing to take a risk. ("Hey, will you take ten bucks for this instead of thirteen?")

TAKE THE TIME TO HAND SELECT CERTAIN ITEMS

If you are buying certain products, such as paneling or wood for that addition or special shelf you are going to make, we recommend that you hand select them. Why? Stores are busy. If you need something, an employee may grab the nearest item that fits your description. Sometimes that's OK, but if the boards for your project must be very straight, you may be better off selecting them yourself.

That holds true for other items as well. Glassware and china may be chipped. Books may have shopworn covers. Fabric items may have flaws. If you select items yourself, you can guard against getting stuck with inferior merchandise.

EXPECT QUALITY PRODUCTS FROM SUPPLIERS

You are paying the bill, so ask for quality products. No matter how busy they are, people generally respect courteous customers who know what they want and won't settle for less. If you pay more attention to quality, you'll usually get it. For example, when we first ordered materials for our home addition, we received warped two-by-fours. But since the supplier had a generous return policy, we sent the warped ones back for credit and asked for straighter ones. The next boards were much straighter, and that trend continued until the project ended. The men loading the trucks in the warehouse knew what we wanted and gave it to us. And when we had occasion to enter the warehouse, we thanked them personally.

RETURN DEFECTIVE OR UNUSED MERCHANDISE

Remember that little gadget you bought for three bucks and never used because it wasn't the right size? Did you take it back for a full refund or exchange it for store credit? What about that item that seemed perfect in the store but when you tried it out at home didn't work well? Not long ago we bought our daughter a new fishing rod and reel. It seemed great and passed all the mental tests, price comparisons, and simple evaluations. But whether it was us or the reel, we couldn't cast worth a hoot with it. Since we had kept the box the reel came in and the receipts, we took it back for a full refund. The rod and reel cost less than fifteen dollars, but we were able to use that money to buy a better rod and reel that work well together.

Unless you have to drive many miles and stand in line for hours, make it a practice to return unused items, new gifts that can be exchanged, and defective merchandise.

If you're buying anything of consequence, read the store's return policy before you buy. You may not be able to return the item, no matter what the reason. (This is one place where using a credit card can be helpful, since this gives you certain product rights.) Or you may have to pay a "restocking" fee or accept a credit refund. If the policy is not what you want, shop at another store.

Always return defective merchandise. First, you deserve to get your money back, or at least receive a store credit. Second, you need to let the store buyers know that you won't accept shoddy merchandise. It's all part of shopping smart so you can spend less.

Timing Makes a Difference

Have you ever spent Christmas Eve running around to find a special gift, only to discover that stores have been sold out of what you wanted to buy for days? Ever run out of eggs you needed for a recipe that had to go into the oven in ten minutes? It's not much fun to scramble to cover your bases. But by stocking up on sale items and buying ahead for special occasions, you can save money, time, and transportation costs. Sometimes spending money now can save you money later.

When you find a perfect gift for
a loved one, buy it now and save it
for the next gift-giving occasion.

For instance, if you have a freezer or a pantry, you can take advantage of special sales on food items you use regularly. By keeping an eye on your inventory, you can anticipate when you're running low and replenish supplies at your convenience when items are on sale.

You can accomplish similar savings by making seasonal and gift purchases at the right times.

SHOP AT THE RIGHT TIME

Various items go on sale at different times of the year. Businesses don't want "dead" inventory to sit on their shelves. So when summer things such as fishing tackle don't sell well, the sporting goods store discounts them to make room for other items. For the same reason, Christmas wrapping paper is much cheaper right after Christmas than it is before Christmas. Fans go on sale in the fall. Skates and ski wear are cleared out in the spring. And so on. If your family enjoys outdoor activities, buy next year's bathing suits, fishing line, ski clothing, or camping equipment at the end of the season when this year's items go on sale.

When you find a perfect gift for a loved one, buy it now and save it for the next gift-giving occasion. You not only save money by shopping that way, but you may be able to spread your gift expenses out over the whole year rather than concentrating them in a few weeks' time.

WAIT FOR SALES

.   Even though everyone knows that stores have periodic sales, people are often not willing to wait or don't plan ahead to determine what their needs will be. Try to anticipate what you'll need ahead of time. If it goes on sale, buy it now. If you plan to replace an item, try to make it last until the sales start.

When evaluating sale items, consider:

- Is it really a sale item? (Perhaps it's always priced lower at competing stores.)
- Is the item comparable in quality to a similar item in another store?
- Can you buy the same item cheaper through another source?
- Is the store having a "final closeout" sale really closing its doors or simply trying to get rid of unwanted merchandise?
- Have items been made especially to be sold at the "sale"?
- Have the good items been distributed to other stores in the chain, leaving only the dregs?
- If you only buy three items instead of four, will you get the same deal? For example, "Four packages for a dollar" may mean, "Each one costs twenty-five cents."
- Has other merchandise been substituted for the advertised merchandise? Ask to see the advertised merchandise. If they don't have it, leave.
- Are a few items sale priced to get you into the store, whereas the rest of the items are regularly priced?
- What guarantees, return policy, or warranty will you receive on a given item? You may buy it cheaper one place, but if "all sales are final" you may be out of luck if you need to return it.
- Are goods priced at just below the next dollar jump ($18.97 instead of $19.00, for example)? People like lower numbers, even if the savings is minuscule. Smart shoppers make it a point to know exactly what they are buying and whether it is worth the price.

Don't let the gimmicks fool you.

RAIN CHECKS ARE WORTH THE WAIT

If the merchant is allowed to give a rain check on a low-priced, out-of-stock item (not all states, we understand, allow this), by all means ask for one and wait until the product comes in. Note the rain check to see when it expires, how many items you can buy, and where you must purchase them.

Take Up the Challenge

Are you ready to put these tips into practice? Start today. Protecting yourself from bad buying decisions, buying quality at the right prices, and timing your shopping so that you can pay the lowest prices will help you spend less—and give you other benefits too.

SAVING MONEY ON WHERE YOU LIVE

4

Choosing a Place to Live

When we first started out, we had no choice about whether we'd rent a place to live or buy one. We had several hundred dollars to our name, school debts, and Stephen was making a rather modest salary as a publishing-house editor. Perhaps your situation is similar to ours at that time. You may be renting until you can buy a home. Or you may be renting because the financial commitment and responsibility of home ownership would interfere with your personal goals or priorities. Perhaps you are in the position of having saved or inherited enough money to choose whether you will buy or rent a place to live.

Regardless of your present situation or future goals, housing costs probably consume the largest chunk of your income. It is no secret that housing costs will continue to rise. But by asking the right questions and following basic guidelines, you can save quite a bit of money on housing costs while enhancing your lifestyle too.

Determine Your Housing Requirements Carefully

If you want an enjoyable living situation and want to spend the least amount of money possible for it, determine ahead of time what you need. That principle applies whether you rent or buy. So list your housing requirements—what you would like but don't need and the things that annoy you about where you're living now. This basic step will help you avoid making an unfortunate decision that may prove to be expensive and that you may later regret. Consider the following requirements.

INTERIOR REQUIREMENTS

- The number of bedrooms and their locations. Will an elderly relative be moving in with you? Will you need a first-floor bedroom? Do you want secondary bedrooms to be close to or separated from the master bedroom?
- The size, layout, and condition of the kitchen.
- Number of bathrooms in specific locations.
- A den or family room.
- A formal dining room.
- The convenience and overall feel of the layout.
- The square footage.
- A garage for projects, safe storage, and to ensure the car will start on cold mornings.

EXTERIOR REQUIREMENTS

- Condition of the lawn and/or landscaping.
- Size and security of the yard or play area for children.

LOCATION REQUIREMENTS

- The proximity to busy roads and traffic noise or to neighbors.
- Quality of the school district.
- Environment—semirural, country club, city, urban, planned community, rural, suburban.
- Distance from schools, work, and recreational opportunities. (You can save money on transportation costs by living close to places you tend to frequent.)

- Convenience of public transportation.
- Quality of fire and police protection.
- Neighborhood character. Is it well kept or in decline? Do you want to live in a new or old neighborhood? Do you want to be near young families? Do you want to live within walking distance of stores and services you use regularly?
- Is it important to live near an airport for business travel?
- What kind of a view will you be content with?

UTILITY AND MAINTENANCE REQUIREMENTS

- Utility bill history. If money will be tight, high utility bills caused by poor construction and/or a lack of insulation may tip you over the edge financially. If you are renting your living space, find out exactly which utilities you will be required to pay.
- Type of heat (hot-water baseboard, forced-air, electric, gas, propane, solar?) and air conditioning (central or certain rooms only?).
- Number of repairs needed to meet your requirements. Is the landlord or manager eager to make those repairs? If you are buying, how much repair work can you or family and friends do? How much will you have to pay professionals to do?

The question of whether you should buy or rent your living space depends on many personal factors.

REQUIREMENTS OF SPECIAL CONCERN TO POTENTIAL BUYERS

- Is the property prone to flooding or severe erosion? We nearly purchased a beautiful home on seven acres, but after a hard rain, we visited the property and saw that the water had cut a six-foot-deep channel in the hillside next to the home.
- Is there enough land to suit your needs and future goals?
- Do you need to generate income with the property? If so, consider buying a duplex and renting out one unit.

- Taxes. Some areas have much higher taxes than others or will have tax increases as new facilities and services are added. Call the county assessor's office to check on special assessments.
- Insurance. (Is the home in an area with higher insurance rates or in a higher-priced fire-protection district?)
- The property's ability to accommodate your unique needs, such as RV parking, an oversized garage, a guesthouse, space for a garden, and so on.

To Rent or Buy: That Is the Question

The question of whether you should buy or rent your living space depends on many personal factors. You and/or your spouse or family can save a great deal of money by asking basic questions about your lifestyle and goals that will help clarify which option suits you best.

WHAT ARE YOUR LIFESTYLE NEEDS?

☐ Might I/we be moving soon? Do I/we value mobility?

☐ Do I/we anticipate a major lifestyle change that will affect this decision, i.e., having a child, going back to school full time, changing careers, or retiring?

☐ What kind of housing is best suited for my/our lifestyle? (For instance, if you travel frequently on business, who will watch your home while you're gone? A condominium or townhome community may provide better security while you are away than a home in the country.)

☐ Do I/we enjoy "puttering" around fixing and improving things? (If so, consider buying an older home. If not, consider buying a newer home or plan to pay someone to do necessary repairs.)

☐ Do I/we have special requirements that a landlord/manager might not want to accommodate? Can I/we live with the restrictions most landlords/ managers place on tenants?

☐ Do I/we really want the security that home ownership can provide? Do I/we want to assume the responsibilities as well?

WHAT IS YOUR FINANCIAL CONDITION?

☐ What kind of down payment could I/we make on a home? What kind of house could I/we afford? What are mortgage rates doing? (Contact mortgage lenders to find out.)

☐ Can I/we afford mortgage payments, taxes, house insurance, and maintenance? Or would I/we be better off paying rent and tenant's insurance and saving as much as possible for a while?

☐ Is my/our credit rating good enough? Have I/we had credit problems or changed career fields within the past three years?

☐ Do I/we need rental income from our home?

☐ What is my/our income projected to be during the coming years? Will it be steady or erratic? If it will be erratic, have I/we demonstrated the ability to put money aside regularly, which indicates that I/we could make house payments regularly?

What Are Your Goals?

How important is gaining home equity? "Don't buy a home just for an investment," a realtor told us. "View it primarily as a place to live."

IS NOW A GOOD TIME FOR YOU TO BUY?

☐ What is the housing market doing in my/our area? Are housing prices going up, holding steady, or going down? (The odds are that the value of the home you buy will appreciate at a rate similar to the rate of inflation. But no one can predict whether the value of a particular home will go up or down while you own it.)

☐ If I/we wait a while, might we get a better deal in a few months? In a year? (Price and interest rates determine the cost of buying a home. Obviously no one knows for sure what real estate prices or rates will be in twelve months.)

A best-selling realtor gave us these guidelines: "If prices are declining, you might buy if you can get a great deal and plan to stay in the house long term. If prices are going up rapidly and you plan to live in the home at least a year, buy it now."

Renting a Place to Live

If you have reviewed the list of housing requirements in this chapter and have chosen to rent your living space, you may take advantage of a number of money-saving strategies. Most of them will apply to other kinds of residences as well.

CONSIDER CREATIVE OPTIONS

Although most renters live in apartments or single-family homes, there are special options that may be worth considering.

- Pay little or nothing by doing specific work around the home or property. Recently a friend of ours found a rancher in the country who needed someone to live in the ranch house and do a few maintenance jobs. Sometimes camps or other recreational facilities offer similar opportunities in the off season. Sometimes such arrangements can accommodate families, too.

- Rent a portion of a large house.

- Join with several friends to rent a house or large apartment.

- Rent a manufactured (mobile) home instead of a small apartment.

- If you are caught without a place to live and need to rent for a short time, such as a month or less, store your belongings and borrow a camper or recreational trailer to live in. If local laws permit, you may be able to live that way in a friend's backyard. Or you may find a nearby campground where you can stay for five to ten dollars a day. This option isn't for everyone, but it can be fun if the weather isn't extreme.

- Try long-term housesitting. Some people leave their homes for two to six months at a time. If they do that regularly, they may like to have a reliable person stay in their home while they're gone. Some of them even pay their housesitters! We know people who have moved from one housesitting job to another—never paying rent—for several years now. If you don't mind being mobile, this can be a great way to save money. However, this kind of opportunity is generally only extended to responsible, childless adults who don't own pets.

RENT THE HOUSE OR APARTMENT THAT'S RIGHT FOR YOU

If you've decided that a traditional renting arrangement is more your style, then make every effort to find the living space that's best for you. Review the list on page 60 for evaluating the inside of a home. In addition, consider the following points. (But be aware that in a tight rental market, you may have to take whatever you can find. If that's your situation, try to arrange a short-term lease so you are free to make a change when rental conditions improve.)

- Does the apartment or house feel right to you? Is the layout comfortable? Are the rooms big enough?
- Are the front entrance and hallways well lighted?
- How is entrance to the building controlled? An intercom? Automatic locks?
- Is there a resident landlord or manager?
- Does the apartment door have a strong deadbolt lock on it?
- Are the rooms clean? Are the walls, carpet, and appliances clean?
- What external sounds can you hear?
- Do the kitchen and bathroom(s) look well maintained? Do all the appliances work? Do the plumbing fixtures work?
- Do the heaters and air conditioners work?
- Are there adequate electrical outlets? Adequate telephone jacks? If these are inadequate, will the landlord/manager improve them?
- Do you see bugs or evidence of bugs?
- What are the other tenants or neighbors like? (We never lived above a drummer, but our walls vibrated from neighbors' stereos quite often.)
- Is there adequate storage in the apartment, a separate storage area, or a garage?
- What about the neighborhood? Is it safe? Convenient? Well maintained? Quiet?
- Is there adequate parking?
- Are there adequate stores (the type you typically use) nearby?

✔ What do other tenants or neighbors say about the complex or area? What is the landlord/manager like? Why is the unit vacant? Ask other tenants or neighbors so you can find out if something is wrong with it.

✔ If you are renting a house, particularly note its condition. Does it need painting? Is there evidence of water damage? Does everything work well? Make sure you understand which repairs or maintenance will be your responsibility and which will be the owner's.

UNDERSTAND YOUR LEASE

Read the entire lease carefully before you sign it. If you don't understand it completely, don't sign it until your questions are answered satisfactorily. Find someone who can explain the lease to you or pay a lawyer to read it. Perhaps a local housing official can advise you.

Make sure your lease addresses the following points. If it doesn't, you may be required to pay more money than you originally planned.

Terms of occupancy.

✔ The rental unit's location.

✔ Dates of your occupancy.

✔ How large of a security or cleaning deposit will you have to provide? What are the terms for getting it back? Find out how long the landlord/manager can legally keep it after you move out.

Rental payment terms.

✔ How much will you pay each month for rent?

✔ When is the rent due? What are the related terms? Is there a few days' grace period? What are the late charges?

✔ Can your rent increase? If so, by how much and how often? (If there is no lease, the landlord/manager may be able to raise your rent arbitrarily.)

✔ How long will the lease last? Can you renew the lease? If so, at what rent? (Try to get the option of renewing the lease at the same terms or of staying on a month-to-month basis after the lease expires unless another lease goes into effect.)

Utilities. Which utilities will be included in the lease payments? Will you share the average utility cost with others or be on your own meter? (If there is only one meter, you may end up paying the bills of a neighbor who wastes a lot of energy.)

Your restrictions and obligations.

✔ What are your restrictions and obligations? Is it OK if a child or another person comes to live with you? What if you want to work out of your apartment, cook on a balcony, store items by the back door, or put up a television antenna? What are the rules and regulations for the complex pool, laundry equipment, storage space, and so on? Who enforces them? Does the landlord/manager want you to agree in advance to rules he or she may develop in the future?

✔ Can you have pets? If so, what kind(s)?

✔ Can you sublet to someone else if you have to move before the lease is up?

✔ How many people can live in the apartment?

Maintenance.

✔ Which services, such as snow removal and lawn care, will the landlord/manager provide, and which will you pay extra for?

✔ What about any problems that you noticed when you toured the apartment? Will the landlord/manager agree in writing to fix them? (Or do you have to accept the unit "as is"?)

✔ Which items does the landlord/manager agree to furnish? (If you are renting a furnished apartment, take photographs of the apartment's furnishings and carpeting before you move in. This will give you a record of the items that were in the rooms and help you document their condition.)

✔ Does the landlord/manager accept the obligation to make future repairs?

✔ Who will be responsible for painting, cleaning, and general upkeep and repair?

✔ Who will fix things that break under normal use? How does the landlord/manager define "adequate maintenance"?

Miscellaneous.

✔ Will the landlord/manager give you advance warning before entering your rental unit?

✔ Who is the owner of the building?

✔ Can you have your own washing machine?

✔ What parking facilities are provided? Are they adequate?

---

*Buying a house is both an emotional
and a rational decision. . . .
Give appropriate weight to both aspects.*

FINAL CHECKS BEFORE YOU SIGN THE LEASE

✔ If you can't live with a specific clause, and the landlord/manager is willing to delete it, cross it off. Initial and date the deletion and have the landlord/manager initial and date it, too.

✔ Make a dated list of all the problems with the apartment before you rent it and have the landlord/manager sign the list. If he or she won't sign, and you still want to rent the unit, take photos to document the list and send a certified copy to the landlord/manager. Also learn what your rights as a tenant are under state law if the landlord/manager doesn't make necessary repairs. When you move out, take more photos of the apartment.

✔ Be sure the lease contains no blank spaces and that all blanks are filled in correctly. If changes are made on the contract, both you and the landlord/manager must initial and date them. If the changes won't all fit on the contract, make an addendum to the contract that lists other points and write on the main contract that all parties agree to the attached and signed addendum.

So You're Going to Buy

For most people, buying a home is the investment of a lifetime. Making the right choice is critical because you have to live with what you buy, and buying the wrong house can cost you lots of money.

Buying a house is both an emotional and a rational decision. In order to make the right choice, you must give appropriate weight to both aspects. For example, it is unwise to buy a house that you know is a bad financial risk, no matter how much you like it. Conversely, it doesn't make sense to buy a house you absolutely hate, no matter how good a deal it may be. Go into it with your eyes open, and make as knowledge-able a choice as you can.

Although people's needs and tastes in houses vary widely, the following basic tips can save you big bucks.

CONSIDER YOUR OPTIONS

When you're ready to take the big step of buying a home, it is wise to consider the options available to you.

For instance, if you are renting a home you like and you don't want to change neighborhoods, find out whether your landlord will sell it to you. If you already own a home, decide whether or not your current home could be renovated to meet your needs for less than you'd spend to buy another one. Be sure any changes or improvements you make will actually add to your home's value when you sell. Remodeling certain areas such as the kitchen and bathroom(s) usually pays off at least fifty cents on the dollar. Other remodeling projects may not add to the value of your home, but may make your home more saleable.

Are you handy with tools? Perhaps you could renovate a wreck. Some foreclosed homes are in such bad shape that they scare away many buyers; yet they are "redeemable" if you have the skills, patience, money, and "long-suffering" to do so. As we write this, new neighbors who bought a house a few weeks ago are pulling out cat-tainted carpeting, carting away trash, and scraping dirt off kitchen cabinets with razor blades. As a result of their willingness to work hard, they will have a fine, much larger home than they could otherwise have afforded.

If you can't afford the home you desire in your present location, perhaps you can find one in an area that is farther from work. If you have the flexibility, determine what your options are in other states. Perhaps you can find the kind of house you want and can afford in the kind of community you prefer and find good employment opportunities too. (Contact a local realtor for a "housing comparison guide" that will help you compare housing costs in various areas of the country.)

A few months ago, we met a couple from New York who are looking for a place to "retire" and begin second careers. Both of them will receive pensions, so they are "state" shopping. They started out in Arizona and worked their way to Colorado, looking at housing, taxes, food prices, and other details. You can be certain that they'll know where to move when the time comes.

Review your list of home requirements and consider the many types of housing you might purchase. Options include: condominium, town-home, co-op, manufactured (mobile) home, multifamily dwelling, or a single-fam-ily dwelling. Each option has pros and cons. Also consider the various housing styles that are available. A single-family home, for example, may be a split level, raised ranch, colonial, cape cod, log home, traditional, southwestern, contemporary, and so on.

FIGURE OUT HOW MUCH YOU CAN AFFORD TO PAY

A lender or knowledgeable real estate broker should be able to tell you quickly how large a loan you will qualify for. Finding that out first may seem to be common sense, but the significance of that figure is often overlooked. Before you buy, you need to determine how much you can really afford to pay for housing each month. You'll need to figure your after-tax monthly income and your monthly expenses and subtract the one from the other. If you aren't already using a spending plan or aren't sure what you can afford, we recommend that you meet with a knowledgeable accountant who can help you evaluate your financial situation. It is imperative that you decide whether or not you really can afford to repay a loan of the maximum qualifying amount.

Know your personal financial needs and habits . . . to determine if specific loan and repayment amounts will actually work.

For example, do you really want to take a week's take-home pay (or even more) out of your budget for a mortgage? Are you dependent on two incomes to get into the house and keep it, yet thinking about having children? How might your income(s) change within the next few years? Do you plan to change careers? Are you content to live without extras for a while? All of these factors affect your willingness and ability to pay your mortgage.

Conversely, some people who are thinking about buying a home believe they can afford less than they really can. We were the same way. We didn't think we could qualify for our first home, yet we did. In fact, the first lender we approached told us we qualified for only two-thirds of what we eventually qualified for. It's important to know your personal financial needs and habits in order to determine if specific loan and repayment amounts will actually work for you.

Generally, a lender will allow your monthly mortgage payment and other housing expenses (insurance, taxes, interest) to total no more than 29 percent of your monthly gross income.[1] The lender will also add up all your debt obligations to see if the total is more than 41 percent of your gross income. If your obligations exceed the lender's allowable amounts, you will not qualify for the loan. If you have assets you could sell quickly to cover mortgage payments and have low consumer debt, a lender might give you a few percentage points of grace on the usual allowable limits.

Can you put more money down to reduce the amount you'll need to borrow? Doing so will reduce your monthly payments, lower your closing costs, and perhaps give you a lower rate of interest. But if you can earn more money with your money than the interest rate of the loan, you might choose to keep the down payment small. Be aware, however, that a small down payment may mean that you'll have to come up with additional cash in order to sell your home if its value has not appreciated enough to cover the costs and commissions for the sale of your property.

If you're ready to buy but don't have quite enough money to buy what you need, consider additional options and sources for funding. If this will be your first home, for instance, are you eligible for a first-time housing deal in your area? Can you borrow additional funds for a down payment from your company's profit-sharing plan? Can you lease with an option to buy (which often requires no down payment)? Can you liquidate any stocks, mutual funds, or other investments? Can you assume an existing low-rate mortgage?

Start Shopping

FIND A COMPETENT REALTOR

A realtor can be a tremendous help in finding the home you want and in walking you through the process of purchasing it. The right realtor will make home buying relaxed by helping you sift through options and legalities. However, you must understand your agent's position and loyalties in order to gain the greatest benefit from his or her expertise.

Although it may seem strange, the real estate agent you choose may be representing the seller because the seller pays the agent's commission. In a number of states, real estate agents can have several different types of working relationships with buyers. The exact nature of the relationship—whether the agent is a seller's, buyer's, or dual agent—can significantly affect your level of satisfaction.

Seller's agent. This kind of agent works on the seller's behalf and maintains undivided loyalty and confidentiality to the seller. A seller's agent must mention any material defects of the seller's real estate property to the potential buyer. However, if you work with a seller's agent, any information you reveal, such as how much money you are able to offer, will be relayed to the seller.

Buyer's agent. This, in our opinion, is the best type of agent to have. He or she will work solely on your behalf and can be counted on to keep your confidences and be loyal to you. The buyer's agent must deal fairly with the seller and cannot falsely represent the buyer's financial condition. To get this kind of arrangement, you and the agent should draw up a written, buyer agency contract. Otherwise, your agent may be legally presumed to be an agent of the seller.

Dual agent. A dual agent serves as an agent for both buyer and seller. An example would be when a realtor shows a buyer a property that is listed with his or her real estate company or when a realtor knows both the buyer and the seller.

We've used three agents to purchase two houses. Two were very helpful, but the third made us so angry by some things he said and did that only his absence at the time we drew up the final contract made the purchase of our second home a reality. He used a number of ways to try to force us to pay more money. But part of it was our fault. We did not realize the difference between a buyer's and seller's agent. We didn't realize that he was a seller's agent and that our best interest was not his primary concern.

ASK QUESTIONS

Fortunately, many good agents are available to assist you as buyer agents. Since you will be spending quite a bit of time with your agent and since he or she can make a significant difference in the property you find and in how much money you spend to purchase it, it is important to find a good agent. Criteria to evaluate include:

- Is the agent licensed in your state? Is he or she a realtor, a member in good standing with the local board of realtors?

- Has the agent helped one of your friends or family members?

- Has the agent been in the area long enough to be familiar with it? Does he or she know which areas are appreciating, which neighborhoods show signs of decline, the current home prices in specific areas, financing options, and so on? Having worked in the same area for a number of years can make a significant difference.

- Is the agent's company well established and well respected?

- Is the realtor friendly and pleasant to be with? (Why spend hours with a morose person?)

- Does the agent understand what you're looking for and show you properties that fit your requirements?

- Is the agent working in real estate full time? If not, does he or she have a good knowledge of the area?

- Is the agent willing to show you government "repos" that may suit your needs but not necessarily provide a big commission? Will he or she handle all the paperwork?

- Will the agent enthusiastically take your "low" offers to sellers, even if the offers may be lower than he or she would like? (By law the agent may be required to present all offers, but attitude can be important.) When we bought our first home in 1978, it was listed for $45,500. We offered $40,500 and made no plans to respond to a counteroffer because we couldn't afford anything more expensive. Our realtor balked a little, but submitted our offer. And the seller took it—within two hours.

- Are you relaxed or uptight when you come home from seeing houses? (Perhaps you are being subjected to unnecessary pressure from your agent without realizing it. Or perhaps you've seen some great houses and are uptight simply because you can't make up your mind.)

- Does your agent really add insight to your observations about a house? Or does he or she overlook obvious drawbacks and hope you do, too? A good realtor will act as a sounding board for you, distilling information and helping you make decisions.

- Has anyone filed formal complaints against the agent or agent's company with the Better Business Bureau, board of realtors, or state real estate commission?

SHOP FOR A MORTGAGE LOAN

Interest rates are fickle. They rise like helium balloons and tumble like barn swallows chasing mosquitoes. But whether they are high or low, paying a mortgage every month takes a chunk out of the spending plan. So it is wise to shop around to see what you can do to reduce that bite. Here are some suggestions:

Shop around for the best interest rates. Even a fraction of a percentage point could save you thousands of dollars over the life of your loan. For example, let's say Eddie and Susan go shopping for rates. They want to borrow $100,000 using a fixed-rate, thirty-year loan. One lender offers them 9 percent, another offers 9¼ percent. If they simply make the required payments, the difference between those two percentages is $28,859 over the thirty years.

Mortgage deals can vary widely, so compare what is offered by mortgage banks, savings and loan associations, credit unions, and commercial banks. A good real estate agent (or broker) should know which lenders in your area offer the cheapest mortgages of the type you prefer.

Select your lender carefully

There's much more to a lender than interest rates, however. How long has your potential lender been in business in your area? What is the lender's reputation? Is the staff competent? Cooperative? As one realtor said to us, "The last thing you want to have happen is for the lender to make last-minute requirements just before closing or to back out just before closing." An experienced real estate agent usually works with several lenders and has some "pull" to ensure that you'll be treated fairly.

Evaluate the kinds of available loans. Determine which loan will best suit your needs. A good real estate agent, accountant, or real estate lawyer can provide valuable assistance here. Common mortgage options include: conventional fixed-rate, adjustable-rate, graduated-payment, and balloon. This area is complicated, so be cautious. Ask the Federal Trade Commission to send you the sixteen-page booklet titled, *The Mortgage Money Guide* and the Federal Reserve Board to send you the twenty-four-page *Consumer Handbook on Adjustable Rate Mortgages.*[2]

An adjustable-rate loan, for instance, may be good if, in order to qualify, you need a lower starting interest rate. It may also be good if you plan to make extra principal payments to reduce your interest payments or if you don't plan to stay in the home very long. But carefully evaluate which factors (U.S. Treasury Bill rate, Federal Home Loan Bank Board's national average mortgage rate, and so on) determine the index to which the variable interest rate, the amount you pay, or the term of the loan is connected. Generally the more sensitive the index is to changes, the more frequently the interest rate will increase or decrease. Also, verify how often and how much the rates may change. What are the annual and lifetime ceiling limits for interest-rate changes? Can you convert your adjustable-rate mortgage to a fixed-rate mortgage after a certain period of time? Can you make sure your interest rate is calculated correctly?

A fixed-rate loan with an interest rate and monthly payments that remain constant during the life of the loan may be preferable if (1) the mortgage rate seems low, (2) you do not anticipate an increase in income so you want to lock in the payment level, (3) you want to avoid rising mortgage payments, or (4) you may be unable to afford higher payments. Inflation and tax deductions also may make a fixed-rate mortgage a good financing method.

Consider all aspects of the loan. When you shop for a loan, you should consider such things as: the amount you'll be financing, the length of the loan, the size of your payments, the stability of payments or rates (whether they can change and, if so, how much), and if you can refinance the loan when it matures. Also consider your tax situation.

- Will the lender charge you "points," each point representing 1 percent of the loan amount at closing? If your loan will be large, will the lender require fewer points? What other closing costs—such as mortgage insurance, appraisals, taxes, advance payments, and filing fees—will you be required to pay?

- Consider the length of the loan (fifteen, twenty, or thirty years). Choosing a shorter-term loan will increase your monthly payments while allowing you to build equity faster and dramatically reduce the amount of interest you will be required to pay. Long-term loans will lower your monthly payments but cost you much more in interest over the length of the loan.

- How much of a down payment is required for the loan you desire? What will your monthly payments be? If you're late with a payment, what will be the penalty?

- Can you pay off the mortgage in advance without penalty? If not, keep shopping. If interest rates go down significantly (two percentage points or more), you may want to refinance—take out a new loan and pay off the old one. (If you have to pay an early payoff penalty, your potential savings through refinancing may decrease significantly.)

- By making extra, separate principal payments each year, you can save thousands of dollars in interest and gain equity. Let's assume that Eddie and Susan have a monthly mortgage payment of $804.62 on a thirty-year loan at 9 percent interest. If they make one extra payment every year and designate it for principal, they can pay off the loan in twenty-one years and nine months and save $62,233 dollars in interest.

- Can you make your own property tax and insurance-premium payments rather than having those funds held in escrow? You'll save money if you pay these yourself because you can gain interest on the money you set aside to cover these costs.

- Does the lender want to include a "call" that allows the firm to force you to repay or refinance a loan at any time? If so, find another lender.

- Does the lender pressure you to buy life or disability insurance? If you need to have that insurance, you can buy it from a regular insurance agent—usu-ally for far less than you would pay a lender.

- How much is the fee if you "lock in" your rate of interest so that the rate won't increase before you close on the home? Will a "lock in" fee be credited toward the mortgage origination fee? When will a "lock in" expire (thirty, sixty, or ninety days)?

- Can you assume a lower, existing loan rate without the interest rate increasing?

Besides finding out the facts, ask yourself the following:

- If the loan requires a balloon payment, will you have the money to pay the balloon or might you have to refinance, perhaps at a higher rate of interest?

- Will the monthly payments leave you badly strapped for cash?
- Are you comfortable with the possible changes in interest rates and monthly payments that your loan may require?

If you can obtain a biweekly mortgage in which you pay what you'd normally pay each month in two biweekly installments, you'll save thousands of dollars in interest. Remember Eddie and Susan? Let's say they hear about biweekly mortgages. Since they want to borrow $100,000 for thirty years at the fixed rate of 9 percent, they discover that if they pay $402.31 every two weeks instead of $804.62 a month, they will save $70,317 dollars over the course of the loan.

SHOP FOR THE HOME YOU WANT

Evaluate the neighborhood of each home you like. The adage says, "Three things are most important when buying a home: location, location, and location." That is true not only from an investment perspective but from a personal viewpoint as well. Will the home you're considering be a suitable and pleasant place for you and/or your family to live?

- Are the neighbors friendly?
- What are the other homes in the area like? Are they of similar value? (An expensive home sandwiched among modest homes will be worth less than it would be if it were located among other expensive homes.)
- Is the home in a secluded location? Consider the risks. Some people want to be in sight of neighbors and close to conveniences and friends.
- What do real estate appraisers say about the area?
- If the area is new, is the developer on solid financial footing?
- Are there many "for sale" signs in the neighborhood? If so, why? What are the resale values like?

✔ How many area homes are rentals?

✔ How tight are the zoning laws? Are there covenants that would pre-vent you from using or enjoying your home in the way you intend?

✔ Do the police and fire departments provide quality service to the area?

✔ Who plows the snow (if applicable)?

✔ Is there garbage service?

✔ Is the home in a good school district? Do you like the school(s) your children would attend? (Evaluate age/condition, curriculum, class size, quality of teachers, play areas and equipment, reputation, busing distances, achievement test scores, and so on.)

✔ Is the area depressed or appreciating? Is the crime rate low or high?

✔ Is the home near businesses or public transportation you'll use fre-quently? (Consider supermarkets, hospitals, doctors, shopping cen-ters, churches, airports, restaurants, and so on.)

Evaluate each house you like. From the work you have already done in determining your housing needs, you will know which properties could suit you. Before you buy, however, you would be wise to evaluate the condition of the house. You don't have to be a contractor to notice problems that could cost you lots of money. Paying a reputable home-in-spection service to check out everything and give you a written report before you buy a home is certainly advisable and well worth the money. Mary, a realtor in our city, says "it's the best money you'll ever spend." But before you hire a home-inspection service, you can do a preliminary inspection yourself. Simply evaluate the following areas of every house that seriously interests you and keep accurate notes on what you find.

Look over the house's exterior first.

☐ Is the foundation cracked or uneven? Are the walls straight or do they appear to lean?

☐ Is the roof in good shape? Are the gutters in good working condition?

☐ Is the landscaping well maintained? Are plantings healthy?

☐ Is the stovepipe/chimney installed well?

☐ Are cracks and holes caulked or weather-stripped?

☐ Is siding newly painted and in good condition?

☐ Are porches, decks, patios, sidewalks, and steps in need of maintenance or repair?

☐ Is there any sign of termites or other insect damage?

Look closely at the house's interior.

☐ Is the floor plan efficient and the square footage sufficient for your needs? Or are there awkward room arrangements and traffic patterns that would be hard to live with (and might make resale difficult)?

☐ How does the house smell? (An odor or stains in the carpet, particularly if they are from pets, often mean new carpeting will be needed. A musty smell in the basement may indicate a leak or a chronically damp condition.)

☐ Is there adequate closet and storage space?

☐ Are there water stains anywhere? (If just one ceiling has been freshly painted, it may have been done to disguise a leaky roof.)

☐ Do the doors and windows fit well? Do they have adequate locks?

☐ Is the interior foundation even? Are there major cracks or settling?

☐ Are the floors sagging, creaky, or uneven?

☐ How is the insulation? Get a ladder and go up to the attic. Find out what you can about the insulation in the walls and above an unheated basement or crawl space.

☐ Are the windows and doors energy efficient?

☐ Look for signs of hazardous substances, particularly if it is an older home. Has asbestos been used in the ceiling texturing or as insulation on the furnace equipment? Is any plumbing made of lead pipes? (The home inspector should tell you these things. Make it a point to ask about these potential problems, and have appropriate laboratory testing done if there is any doubt.)

As much as you are able, check out the mechanical condition of the house.

☐ How old is the heating system? When was it last inspected or repaired? Is it the proper size to heat the house? Does it make loud noises? When you turn up the thermostat, how long does it take for the furnace to kick in and raise the temperature?

☐ How is the sewer system? If the house has a septic system, when was it last pumped and/or inspected? How big is it? Are there any odors, holes, or wet areas in the leach field? Septic tanks can develop serious problems that may cost thousands of dollars to fix.

☐ Is the wiring up to code? Are there enough outlets and switches? Will the circuits take the demands of modern appliances? Do lights flicker or dim, or fuses blow, when appliances are turned on? Is the wiring aluminum? (If so, hire an electrician to check it out.)

☐ Is the lighting adequate?

☐ Is the hot water heater large enough for your needs? Are the hot water pipes insulated?

☐ Is there a stove or fireplace? Does it work well?

☐ Is the plumbing in good repair and up to code? If you turn on several taps and flush the toilet, does the water pressure drop significantly?

☐ Does the air conditioner work? Is it efficient?

☐ Are the appliances that will remain in the home in good working order?

Once you've decided that it's time to buy a home, pursue your search vigorously.

Finally, make sure you know the additional expenses of living in the home.

☐ What taxes will you pay? Look at the property tax statement, and check with the local assessor's office how high taxes in the district may be in the future. Find out how old the existing assessment is and when it will be reviewed.

☐ Can you afford the utilities? Ask to see previous electric, gas, oil, propane, water, or sewer bills, preferably those during winter months if you live in a cold climate and during summer months if you live in an area where air conditioning is necessary.

BE READY TO BUY

Once you've decided that it's time to buy a home, pursue your search vigorously. Be willing to shop for a home even when you'd rather not. When it's especially hot or cold outside, or during holiday periods, keep looking. If the market is slow, your offer may be even more attractive to an anxious seller.

When you find the home you want, be willing to make an offer quickly. "In a hot market," one agent told us, "I always tell buyers that I'll show them many houses that meet their requirements. In return, I want them to be prepared to write an offer on the first house they see. If they really like a house, chances are good that other buyers will like it, too. So they need to act quickly or it'll be gone."

When You Find What You Want

In one sense, when you find the house you'd like to buy, your work is just beginning. It is now time for you and your agent to negotiate numerous details with the seller. The more attention you pay to the negotiating process, the more likely you are to save money and end up with a deal you can live with.

You and your real estate agent should draw up a contract carefully. This is one area in which your agent's expertise is extremely important. In most cases, a good agent can handle this aspect of buying a home. (In some states, realtors must use real estate commission-approved contracts, which decreases the likelihood of a poor contract being drawn up.)

Present any and all offers formally, in writing. The seller will have to consider and respond to each offer within the time frame you specify.

COVER ALL THE BASICS IN YOUR OFFER

The following key items should be included in your offer.

1. Make sure the property is described legally.
2. If you want certain items to be left in or near the home—window coverings, air conditioners, appliances that are not built in, light fixtures, storage shed, and so on—put those items into the description. We know a family that listed a huge pool table in the description and ended up getting it. (The reason was that the owners had finished the basement after the pool table was in place, and the only way to take the pool table out of the house was to remove a wall!)

   If the current owner promises to leave the refrigerator/freezer or range that is in the house now, be sure that its model and serial numbers are listed in the offer. Otherwise, a different model could be substituted.

3. State how much earnest money you are willing to put down on the house, and which third party will hold that deposit.

4. State the price you are willing to pay. Be prepared to negotiate over the price and possibly make several offers. As you determine how much money to offer, think about how much you can take off the asking price without losing the house. (Is the owner desperate to move? Has the house been on the market a long time? Is another serious buyer involved?)

   If you know the house needs work, reflect the cost of that work in the price you offer. If you will have to contract for the work, obviously it will cost more than if you do much or all of the work yourself.

   In most instances, your first offer should be lower—possibly much lower—than the asking price. You can always offer more later, unless the market is so hot that someone else immediately offers more. When we made the offer on our second house—the one we live in now—we offered the seller twenty thousand dollars less than the asking price, although the asking price was reasonable. The property needed lots of repair, it had been on the market for more than two years, and we couldn't offer any more. To our delight, the seller accepted.

5. Be sure the conditions that will void your offer without penalizing you are clarified. Typically these include such clauses as: obtaining satisfactory financing, selling an existing home by a certain date and at a certain price, and favorable inspections.

6. In the contract, list everything that the present owner agrees to fix before you buy the house, along with all terms and conditions contained in the original offer. A verbal promise to replace the shingles on the roof is easily forgotten or denied. Cover the bases in case the house is damaged in some way before the closing—when the transfer of ownership takes place.

7. Clarify when you will take possession of the home.

ADD CONTINGENCIES TO THE OFFER WHEN NECESSARY

Don't hesitate to make your offer contingent on verification of the condition of certain aspects of the property. That may include a favorable inspection report, repairs being completed to your satisfaction, and so on. If the seller has nothing to hide, he or she will usually accept an offer with such contingencies. When we bought our present home, for example, we specified that the septic tank had be inspected and serviced accordingly and that the junk car by the front door had to be removed from the property.

If you already own a home and cannot afford to own two homes, make your offer contingent upon the sale of your home. Some sellers will reject such a contingency, but owning two homes at the same time can be a devastating financial burden.

Consult an Attorney If the Deal Is Complicated

If you are working out a complicated arrangement, it is best to consult your own real estate lawyer who can steer you through and around any pitfalls your real estate agent may have missed. You may save money in legal fees if your real estate agent draws up the contract and the lawyer simply reviews it. If you consult an attorney, he or she should also review the sale's financial arrangements and possibly attend the closing.

BE SURE THE SELLER CAN SIGN THE OFFER YOU PRESENT

It is futile to make an offer that the seller cannot sign, such as requiring the seller to bring cash to the table when he or she is strapped for cash. Be cautious about the contingencies you put into the contract. Excessive contingencies may cause a seller to reject an otherwise satisfactory offer. That is especially true if the seller already has an offer with contingencies in it.

BARGAIN ON CLOSING COSTS WHEN APPROPRIATE

The less you pay, the more you save. You may choose to pay the closing costs but offer less money for the house.

CONSIDER A HOME WARRANTY

Whether you pay or the seller pays for it, consider the advantages and disadvantages of home warranty coverage. Basic coverage can cost as little as a few hundred dollars a year, plus a deductible. If a water heater is all that malfunctions, you'll lose money, but if the furnace, central air conditioner, or major appliance quits, you'll be dollars ahead. If you wish, a warranty can also cover expensive items such as a swimming pool, Jacuzzi®, or spa.

MAKE SURE THE FINAL CONTRACT IS WHAT YOU WANT

As with all contracts, read the final copy carefully before you sign it. Whenever possible, go over it with a real estate attorney who can point out anything that could create problems for you. Make sure you understand and agree with all the implications of the contract. People can tell you numerous horror stories about what can happen when contracts aren't specific enough.

5

Saving Money in All Corners— Reducing Home Energy Costs

R egardless of whether you are a tenant or a homeowner, the costs of living in your home are probably your greatest monthly expenses. Mortgage or rent payments usually account for the largest percentage of monthly residential costs, but utility bills aren't far behind. With ever-increasing utility costs, you may come out many dollars ahead if you take steps to reduce your utility usage.

I've done a few things to save energy in my home, you may be thinking, *but I'm so busy. I don't have time to mess around with little things that won't make much difference. And doesn't it cost money to save money?*

We don't have the time or money to do everything we could do either, but what we have done has saved us at least a thousand dollars a year. And that's a thousand dollars of after-tax money. Although your savings may be more or less (there is more room for improvement in an

old, drafty house than in a new, energy-efficient one), you could probably use any amount of extra cash.

Whether you rent or own, you will save money by implementing
the ideas in this chapter that apply to your situation. Perhaps your apartment manager won't let you caulk around the windows, but you can
hang insulated curtains. Perhaps you don't have the money to buy an
energy-efficient water heater, but you can insulate your old one and turn
down the thermostat.

---

*Experiment and see what works for you given
your time, finances, and other constraints.*

Some of these tips require virtually no time or energy, such as turning off unnecessary lights and using the right-sized pan on the range top.
Others, such as changing a furnace filter or installing a flow restrictor in
the shower head, will require ten or fifteen minutes of your time. Other
tips, such as caulking your home or shopping for an energy-efficient appliance, may require hours of commitment.

Don't be afraid to try some of these suggestions, even if you haven't
used tools frequently in the past. It isn't hard to learn to do many basic
repairs and innovative, energy-saving projects. Two of our favorite
"help" and "project" books are the *Reader's Digest Back to Basics* and
Reader's Digest Complete Do-It-Yourself Manual listed in Appendix B.
We've also learned to call experienced tradespeople for advice and to
shop in hardware stores where the personnel know their business.

We suggest that you keep a pencil handy as you read this chapter.
Put a star next to hints you think should be a priority, a check mark next
to ones you'd like to do when you have the time or money, and a question mark by the ones you aren't sure about and may look into later. Every living situation is unique, so you will need to experiment and see
what works for you given your time, finances, and other constraints.

Reduce Your Water Bill

Clean water is a precious resource—one we should conserve even if
its cost isn't a significant expense to us. In many countries, people walk
miles to obtain impure drinking water. Yet most of us simply turn a fau-

cet and take as much water as we want. We even let it run until it reaches the desired temperature!

LANDSCAPING AND OUTDOOR WATER USE

Depending on your climate, you may be using a large amount of clean, drinkable water to keep your lawn, flowers, and trees healthy. The following tips will reduce your water usage and possibly improve the health of your yard and garden, too.

Minimize the need for water.

- Use mulch. Mulch around well-established trees, shrubs, and flowers with shredded or chopped garden matter. We use leaves, pulled weeds (not those that have developed seeds), and grass clippings. The mulch helps the soil retain moisture and retards weed growth.
- Use natural landscaping. Select rocks and natural grasses for landscaping, or plant drought-hardy grasses, plants, and ground coverings.
- Control your children's use of water. Running a sprinkler for two hours uses a lot of water. Why not give them squirt guns, fill up a small wading pool, or help them make water balloons?
- If you own a swimming pool, use a pool cover to slow evaporation and heat loss.
- When you wash the car, use a nozzle that will stop the water flow when you take your finger off the trigger.

Water efficiently.

- Water your garden or lawn early in the morning or in the evening, while it's cool. The water will not evaporate as quickly, so more will reach the roots of the plants.
- Use a soaker hose instead of a regular sprinkler to water your garden. Less water will evaporate.
- Let your grass grow a little taller during hot months. This will protect the roots and increase moisture retention.
- Direct the watering. Adjust sprinklers to water only your lawn and flowers, not the street or driveway. Some people pour gallons of water into nearby sewers every day.

- Watch for leaks in your water system. If your yard is especially green or muddy in one place, check it out.

- Water your lawn and shrubs thoroughly and less frequently rather than watering them a little bit every day. You will save water and promote stronger root growth. Overwatering your lawn will create shallow roots and make the grass more susceptible to burning during a drought.

INDOOR WATER USE

Repair leaky faucets. Fix leaky faucets quickly. Fifty drops a minute can waste many gallons of hot (or cold) water every week. You could be paying as much as fifty dollars a year per leaky faucet. Usually an easy-to-replace washer is the problem. A knowledgeable friend or hardware/lumber store employee can explain how to install a washer, or you can follow directions in a how-to manual.

Use the washing machine efficiently.

- You will save money by washing with cold/cold or warm/cold cycles rather than with hot water cycles. The odds are that the clothes will get just as clean unless they are oily. (And even hot water doesn't take out the oil stains on Stephen's "auto pants.")

  If you decide to wash with only cold water, dissolve the laundry detergent in a small bowl of hot water to make a paste.[1] The detergent should then dissolve more quickly.

- You can also let the clothes agitate longer to get them clean.

- Use the lowest water setting possible. If your washing machine has water-level settings, select the lowest level possible for small loads. Why use a "medium" load of water when a "small" one will do?

- Presoak very dirty items or spray spots with prewash cleaners. Most spots will then come clean during the wash cycle, saving a repeat washing.

- Use the right-sized machine. If you tend to run small loads of special-requirement clothing (gentle cycle, for example), you may be able to use a smaller washing machine that requires less water and electricity. If you wash many large loads, use a machine that's made for the job so you won't have to wash as many loads—thereby saving energy (and money).

- Wash clothing when it is dirty, not just because it has been worn once. Often pants, for instance, can be worn several days before they become dirty.

Flush with Care

Toilets can use a lot of water, and much of it may be unnecessary. Here are some ways to control how much you flush away.

✔ Consider replacing an older toilet with a low-flush toilet that requires less water. Estimate how often the toilet is flushed each day and multiply that by the number of days you or others are in the house each year to figure out how much water the existing toilet uses. Find out how much you must pay for water, and compare the operational cost of your existing toilet to the cost of installing and operating a new toilet.

✔ Don't flush trash down the toilet. Use the wastebasket instead. You'll save water and avoid potential (and expensive) sewer backups.

✔ Evaluate whether you need to flush the toilet after every use.

✔ If your toilet keeps running, take the lid off and see what's wrong. Usually a part is stuck. A broken toilet can waste hundreds of gallons a day.

✔ Reduce the water that's required to flush the toilet. Cut the top off a plastic gallon jug. Place the jug in the toilet tank on the side away from the flushing mechanism and fill it with water. When the toilet is flushed, water will remain in the jug, thus reducing the amount of water that flows out of the toilet. (Some people put bricks in the tank, but after a while the bricks may start to crumble and the grit may wear out rubber seals, fittings, and gaskets, thus causing leaks that will need repair.) If you don't want to use a gallon jug, try using a half-gallon or two-liter jug. You can also reduce the overall level of water in the tank by adjusting the float or carefully bending the float rod.

Run the dishwasher only when necessary. The typical dishwasher uses fourteen gallons of hot water per load.[2] So if you own a dishwasher, you can save dollars every month by following a few simple guidelines:

- Locate it as close to the hot water heater as possible. Less heat will be lost in the pipes.
- Operate it with a full load of dishes. You'll save water and electricity. If you live alone or only have a few dishes (not enough for a full load), it may be most efficient to wash them by hand. You don't have to use a dishwasher just because it's there.
- Load the dishes properly so that the energy used will achieve maximum results.
- Rinse dishes in the sink before you put them into the dishwasher. Particularly if you have an older model, rinsing may enable you to use a shorter wash cycle or at least get the dishes that have cheese, hardened rice, egg, or other food substances on them clean the first time through. But don't rinse by running water over each dish. You'll use as much water and energy as if you had washed the dishes twice.
- Pay attention to the water temperature. Make sure the hot water is hot enough to dissolve the dishwashing detergent. If it isn't, adjust the hot water heater's thermostat or try a different detergent. (Some dishwashers have booster heaters, which raise the hot water temperature in the dishwashers.)
- Use the "rinse hold" cycle cautiously. It uses three to seven gallons of hot water each time you use it.[3]

Use only the water you need in sinks, showers, and tubs.

- Only put as much water into the bathtub as you need. Unless you plan to soak for an hour or so, you probably don't need a lot of water.
- Install an inexpensive flow restrictor in the shower head. Usually installed in a few minutes, it can cut the shower flow rate from a normal four to eight gallons a minute to as few as three gallons a minute without providing a weak spray, thus saving a family of four an average of 1,600 gallons of water every month.[4]
- When you use the shower, turn off the water while you lather up.
- Take brief showers instead of baths.
- If you need to run water until it's hot enough to use, catch the cold water in a jug. One friend has done that for years. "I use it to water the plants," he said.

- Clean the bathtub or shower right after you use it, while the sides are wet. You won't have to run more water to rinse the sides later.
- When you want to cool the temperature of water coming from the tap, turn down the hot water instead of turning up the cold water.
- When you brush your teeth, don't leave the water running.
- If you shave with a razor, try filling the sink with hot water rather than letting the hot water run freely.
- Install a faucet aerator that will reduce the per-minute water flow.
- Wash fruits and vegetables over a bucket or pan instead of letting the tap run. Then put that dirty water on your indoor plants or garden.

---

*Heating water is expensive and
may account for 20 percent or more
of your total utility bill.*

Miscellaneous water-saving tips.

- Use cold water in your coffeepot or teapot unless someone recently used the hot water tap. And by all means use cold water in a mug you'll put into the microwave.
- Follow the example of some restaurants: serve water only when people want it.
- If you live near a beach and need to rinse away the sand and salt when you get home, try making a "solar shower." Amanda's brother painted a barrel black and ran a black hose from the barrel to an enclosed outdoor shower area. He feeds cold water into the solar shower from an outside tap and mixes additional cold water with the solar-heated water as needed. (Yes, on a hot, sunny day the solar-heated water actually gets too hot.) Two or three people can take a comfortably warm shower in the afternoon before the water starts to cool noticeably.
- Take food out of the freezer early enough to allow it to thaw on its own so you don't have to run hot water over it.
- When you use the garbage disposer, run cold water briefly and then turn off the disposer and water. Grease solidifies in cold water and can be washed away.

- Put a pitcher of water in the refrigerator so you don't have to run the tap every time you want a cool drink.

HEATING WATER

In addition to saving water in general, it is especially important to save hot water. Heating water is expensive and may account for 20 percent or more of your total utility bill. Although we have included a few hot water saving tips already, here are additional ways to slash the cost of heating water. There are different kinds of water heaters: demand water heaters that don't store water, heat-pump water heaters, solar water heaters, water heaters that tap into the main heating system, and storage water heaters. Since storage water heaters are the most common, we'll emphasize that kind.

Heat no more water than you need.

- ✔ Make sure your water heater isn't too large for your needs. If it is, energy will be wasted to heat the unused water, and heat will escape from the storage tank.

- ✔ Install a programmable timer on the water heater so it won't heat water when hot water is not needed. Also, you can set the timer to heat water when your electric company may offer reduced rates. Be sure that the timer you buy matches the requirements of your water heater.

- ✔ Gradually turn down the thermostat on the water heater to a temperature level that will meet your needs and comfort level. You don't need to use scalding, 150-degree water (which doesn't kill all the germs in the dishwasher anyway). Try 120 or 125 degrees for starters, unless you own a dishwasher that requires a higher temperature. That will dramatically reduce the money you spend to heat water. For every ten-degree reduction, you will save more than 6 percent in water-heating energy.[5] NOTE: If your water heater has two thermostats, keep both of them adjusted to the same level. Otherwise, the one that is set higher will wear out more quickly.

- ✔ If you are leaving home for longer than a weekend, turn the water heater down or off. (If it has a pilot light, be sure you know how to relight it.)

Heat water efficiently.

↙ Make your own inexpensive solar water heater. We've seen various plans, but we haven't done this ourselves. If you are handy with tools and gadgets, and can spend the money for materials, consider this route.

↙ Raise the temperature of the water that enters the water heater. One way is to add another water tank in which the cold water can warm up before entering the storage water heater. (We hope to do this, since the water coming out of our well is only forty-eight degrees. But at the present time we don't have room for another holding tank.)

↙ Drain the water heater regularly. Remove a few buckets of water from the drain faucet to keep sediment from gathering in the bottom of the water heater and reducing its efficiency.

↙ Consider replacing an inefficient water heater with one that has a high Energy Efficiency Ratio. Even if you end up paying more up-front, a high-efficiency model will save you money year after year. Some utility companies offer rebates when you upgrade to a high-efficiency unit. If you or your family use lots of hot water, consider buying a larger capacity model that won't have to work as hard to keep up.

Minimize heat loss from already heated water.

↙ If you have access to them, insulate the hot water pipes. You'll get hot water sooner with less waste. You can buy various types of "pipe wrap" or insulative sleeves that are slit down one side and fit over the pipes. We've used fiberglass insulation wrapped with a roll of durable plastic made just for that purpose, and it has made a significant difference in our electric bill. (Be careful not to wrap the insulation too tightly; compressed insulation is less effective.) The water in our pipes stays warm, which means we get hot water sooner and therefore don't waste as much water.

↙ Add demand hot water heaters. If you have long runs of piping, consider having a plumber install a hot water heater for each tap that only heats the water when the tap is opened. Demand units are expensive, but they cost less to operate than standard storage heaters.

↙ Add another water heater. If the hot water has to travel a long way to a location that uses lots of hot water or your home has various levels, consider adding a smaller or similar-sized water heater that will serve an individual zone at another part of the house. You may save a great deal of money in the long run because the efficiency will be high.

✔ Consider wrapping the water heater with insulation. In nearly all cases, your water heater will benefit from a wrap of insulation. It can cut your water heating bills up to 9 percent and make the water heater last longer. (Check with a company that carries your model or a similar one first; some models should not be wrapped.)

Insulating the hot water heater is easy, but you must follow certain safety guidelines.[6] First, wrap the outside with a faced, fiberglass insulation so that insulation fibers won't be exposed. (Put the facing on the outside.) Your utility company may provide this insulation for between ten and twenty dollars. Do not use any other type of insulation.

You may be able to reduce your electric or natural gas bills by one-third—or even more.

Tape the insulation seams with duct tape. Be sure not to compress the fiberglass batts; they need to be fluffy. Also, don't cover up the temperature controls or any access panels. And if the heater has a pilot light, leave air space at the bottom so air can enter the burner area.

If you have any questions, talk with a professional or your utility department. We installed a water heater blanket after attending an hour-long class sponsored by an energy-saving group. For ten dollars, we received instructions and the insulation blanket.

Save Electricity (or Natural Gas)

When we bought our present home, we were concerned about the electric bills. The bills the previous occupants had paid were twice as high as our highest bills had ever been, so we started hunting for energy waste as soon as we moved in. We found four high-wattage bulbs in the bathroom that we replaced with three lower-wattage bulbs (we still had plenty of light). We discovered that the twenty-year-old water heater had virtually no insulation, so we replaced it with a high-efficiency model. We replaced the dark-green kitchen carpet with light-colored tile, and painted the mustard-yellow ceilings bright white. And the list went on.

Within a few months, we reduced our electricity usage by about 50 percent.

We've emphasized electricity savings in the next section, but if you use natural gas, the same guidelines apply in most cases. (We will discuss energy use for heating and cooling in later sections of this chapter.) By applying the tips that apply to your situation, you may be able to reduce your electric or natural gas bills by one-third—or even more. (When that happens, don't forget to write. We may include your illustration in the next book.)

THE COST OF NATURAL GAS VERSUS ELECTRICITY

Compare the cost of natural gas to that of electricity in your area. Compare BTUs per kilowatt and gas BTUs per therm. If natural gas service is available, you may want to switch to gas appliances over time. When remodeling your home or updating a heating system, compare the cost of operating electric appliances to that of natural gas appliances, and make your selections accordingly.

Some families still favor electric or gas appliances based on unpleasant experiences they had two generations ago when appliances were often unreliable. Design, quality control, and consumer safeguards make such concerns unwarranted today when dealing with reputable suppliers and installers. When evaluating the value and energy usage of appliances, be aware that gas appliances tend to cost more initially, but at present energy cost levels they have greatly reduced operating costs.

SAVING ENERGY IN THE LAUNDRY ROOM

Ironing.

• Begin with clothes that require the lowest amount of heat and then work on higher-temperature fabrics as the iron heats up.

• If clothes to be ironed must be dried in the dryer first, remove them from the dryer while they're still damp and iron immediately.

• Whenever possible, buy clothing that doesn't require ironing.

Using the dryer.

• Don't use a dryer unless you have to. On sunny days, or if you live in an area with low humidity or prevailing winds, use a clothesline instead. Doing that during summer months could save you about sixty-five dollars a year.[7]

- During winter months, hang laundry on an indoor clothesline or drying rack instead of using a dryer. We've done that for many years now. The humidity the drying clothing adds to the air also reduces our need for the humidifier in our dry climate.

- If you use a clothes dryer, place items of similar thickness in each load. For example, two heavy towels added to a load of lightweight shirts will increase the drying time needed for the whole load.

- If the dryer vent is not straight, air flow may be limited, which will reduce the dryer's effectiveness and cost you money.

- If loads of clothes seem to take forever to dry, perhaps you put too many items in each load.

- Dry clothing in consecutive loads. Once the dryer is warmed up, it requires less energy to dry other loads.

- Keep the lint screen and the outside exhaust vent of your dryer clean, or it will take longer to dry your clothes.

   Using the washing machine.

- Run full loads instead of partial loads.

- Clean the lint filter after each use.

- Placing too many clothes in the washing machine will cause it to run inefficiently, strain the parts, and often leave you with a load that isn't fully clean.

SAVING ENERGY IN THE KITCHEN

   A typical kitchen contains more appliances than any other room in the house or apartment, and some of them are major energy consumers.

   The range.

- Buy a gas oven or range that has an automatic ignition system instead of pilot lights. You will save up to a third of your gas use—53 percent on the top burners and 41 percent in the oven.[8]

- Whenever possible, use small, energy-efficient appliances such as a Crockpot or pressure cooker instead of the range. A crockpot will cook your stew, soup, or roast all day al a low heat, providing substantial savings over conventional cooking methods. A pressure cooker will also reduce your cooking costs because it reduces cooking time by as much as 50 percent while retaining most of the food's nutritional value.

- Turn off the range when food is nearly cooked and let residual heat finish the cooking. (This is less effective on gas ranges than on electric ones.)
- Match the size of the range's heating element or flame to the pan. Putting a small pan on a large burner wastes energy.
- Use the top of the range rather than the oven when you can. The oven requires more energy.
- Copper, cast-iron, and stainless-steel cookware requires a lower heat setting than aluminum to cook food.[9]
- Use pots and pans with flat bottoms and tightly fitting covers that will maintain cooking temperatures. Your food will heat up faster.
- Only boil as much water as you need. Better yet, use a microwave oven to boil water.
- Keep burner reflectors and range-top burners clean. They'll reflect heat more efficiently. (Use appropriate cleaners; certain scouring powders can scratch the metal.)
- Turn on the range when a pan is on the burner, not before.

The oven.

- Turn off the oven a few minutes before the food is cooked. The residual heat will continue to cook the food, particularly if you use ceramic, glass, or heavy-gauge metal cookware.
- Bake in the evenings during the summer. Otherwise, you will heat up your home and need to run fans or air conditioners more often.
- Every time you open an oven door to check on food inside, you let as much as 20 percent of the heat out.[10] So set a timer and minimize your "peeking."
- Don't preheat the broiler longer than necessary.
- Avoid overcooking foods, which reduces the nutritional value and wastes energy. Use a cooking thermometer and timer.
- Warm plates or rolls in the oven after baking is completed.
- Don't preheat the oven for longer than eight or ten minutes. Place food inside the oven quickly.

- When you're cooking in the oven, place several items inside at the same time (potatoes, chicken, a vegetable casserole, and so on). This is also a good way to get ahead on meals that you can use later.
- Use the range top instead of the oven whenever possible.
- Use a portable oven instead of the kitchen range oven when you can.
- Use a microwave oven instead of a conventional oven to cook or re-heat small quantities of food. A microwave uses considerably less energy than other types of ovens and generates little heat, so it will not add to your air conditioning costs.
- Make sure the oven door seals tightly.
- Broiling is more efficient than roasting or baking.
- Use the self-cleaning function sparingly and preferably after the stove has just been used and the temperature is high.
- Bake in continuous loadings to harness the heat generated. Doing so is more efficient than baking one item and baking something else several hours later. (If the house is chilly when the baking is done, turn off the oven, open the oven door, and enjoy the excess heat!)

If your refrigerator is fifteen years old or older, . . . it may benefit you to buy a new, more efficient model.

The freezer. Replacing an old, inefficient freezer with an efficient model can save you a bundle of money. (Our electric bill dropped about ten dollars a month when our old freezer "died" and we replaced it with a newer model.) Consider buying a chest freezer, which keeps most of its cold air inside when you open the lid. An upright model allows cold air to flow toward the floor every time you open it. No matter what kind of freezer you have or how old it is, freezers are expensive, so follow these tips to get the most efficient use out of your model.

- Open the freezer door as seldom as possible.
- Tape foam insulation board several inches thick to the sides of the freezer. (Contact a professional before doing this to make sure this is compatible with your particular model. Some models discharge excess

heat through the sides, and you don't want to prevent it from dissipating.)

- Defrost manual-defrost models before the ice builds up to ¼ of an inch. Frost, an insulator, causes the freezer to consume more power as it maintains temperature.

- Place large quantities of food into the freezer gradually. If you put in too much food at once, the motor will run constantly and could over-heat. Also, the food could spoil if it freezes too slowly.

- If you don't mind the occasional work, buy a high-efficiency, defrost-it-yourself freezer rather than a frost-free one. Frost-free units require as much as 35 percent more energy to operate.

- Keep the freezer as full as possible. The cold mass helps retain cold. If you can't afford to fill up the space with food, fill it with plastic jugs of water that will freeze to provide more cold mass. (Fill gradually, a few at a time.)

- Rather than putting warm foods into the freezer or refrigerator, let them cool down first. That way the freezer or refrigerator won't use as much electricity to cool them. (But remember not to leave the foods out too long.)

- Adjust the freezer thermostat to about zero degrees Fahrenheit. That will keep items cold enough for long-term storage. A colder setting is unnecessary and wastes energy.

- Unplug an unused freezer, making sure it is completely clean and dry first. Lock it shut or remove the door so a child cannot become trapped inside.

- Leaky door seals can cost you money. Stick a dollar bill between the door gasket and frame of the freezer. If it pulls out easily, the door seal needs to be repaired or replaced. Also watch for frost or condensation along the edge of the door, which may indicate a bad seal.

The refrigerator. Refrigerators have become much more efficient in recent years. If your refrigerator is fifteen years old or older, for example, it may benefit you to buy a new, more efficient model that's right for your needs. You may recoup your investment in just a few years, particularly if you live in an area with high electric rates. If you do shop for a new refrigerator, keep this rule of thumb in mind: one that's too large will waste energy, but a big one will be more efficient than two smaller ones.

- Most people have refrigerators/freezers in the kitchen, not far from the oven and sunny windows. If you can, move your unit away from heat sources (stoves, windows) so it will use less energy.

- If your refrigerator has a "power-saver" switch, use it according to the manufacturer's instructions.

- If you leave home for an extended time, clean out your refrigerator, unplug it, and leave the door slightly ajar or remove it if there is any possibility a child could become trapped inside.

- Cover liquids in a frost-free refrigerator. Otherwise, the moisture that evaporates will cause the refrigerator to use more energy.

- When thawing wrapped food in the refrigerator, remove the wrapping, which acts as insulation, but keep the food covered so it will not dry out if you have a frost-free model.

- Don't use an extension cord for a refrigerator or freezer. The farther electricity has to travel, the more electricity will be used.

- Keep track of what you store in the refrigerator (and freezer). Leaving the door(s) open when looking for particular items wastes energy and costs you money.

- Open the refrigerator door as seldom as possible when preparing a meal. That will force your refrigerator to work less. Plus, if the refrigerator/freezer isn't frost free, the frost will build up more slowly.

- Regularly clean underneath and behind the refrigerator/freezer. Dust and dirt can reduce air circulation, reducing the effectiveness of the self-cool-ing motor and coils. To be safe, unplug the unit during your cleaning, and be sure to plug it in again when you are finished.

- Check the seal on the refrigerator door. (Follow the same procedure and recommendations listed in the above section.)

- Consider installing a small fan near the back of the refrigerator (or freezer) to carry away warm air that can accumulate and reduce the unit's efficiency.

- Adjust the refrigerator thermostat so that the inside temperature will be between thirty-four and thirty-eight degrees Fahrenheit. Reducing it further will cost you more money without providing much benefit.

- Whenever possible, don't put your refrigerator in a corner where the air circulation is poor. Also, if your refrigerator has coils in the rear, leave about six inches between the refrigerator and the wall so that the heated air from the coils can dissipate easier.

The microwave. A microwave uses much less energy than a range or standard oven. Covering foods with a glass lid or plastic wrap will cause the food to heat more evenly and faster. (We sometimes turn a microwave-safe plate upside down over another plate.)

You may not need to buy microwave cookware. Most casserole and baking dishes will work. If you are not sure whether a dish is microwave safe, measure one cup of water in a glass cup. Place the cup in the oven on or beside the dish you are testing. Microwave one minute on high. If the water becomes hot, the dish is microwave safe. If the dish heats up, it should not be used for microwave cooking.

The Dishwasher

Use any energy-saving cycles your dishwasher may have.

Open the dishwasher before the drying cycle starts and air-dry the dishes.

You'll save as much as 10 percent of the electricity used. (This also adds heat and humidity to your home during winter months.)

Miscellaneous tip. Use a waste disposer as seldom as possible. Put organic scraps into the garden compost pile, if gardening is an option.

SAVING ENERGY ON OTHER HOUSEHOLD APPLIANCES

- Carefully review energy labels when buying a new appliance (freezer, refrigerator, water heater, and so on). By comparing various models, you can determine whether paying more for a highly efficient model will pay energy-saving dividends over the long haul.

- If you have a heated waterbed—a high-energy using item—you may want to use a timer so it won't heat the water unnecessarily. Or consider replacing the waterbed with a conventional bed.

- Empty vacuum-cleaner bags before they become overloaded.

- Turn off heating pads and other appliances when you are not using them.
- Use portable electric heaters sparingly. Most are not designed for constant use, and they use a lot of electricity. Avoid using extension cords with portable heaters; the cords can heat up and cause a fire.
- If you use a toaster, ascertain whether your model is the right size for you. Heating up unused "slots" wastes energy.
- Don't buy electric gadgets you don't need. Stores are full of deep fryers, popcorn poppers, and sandwich makers. Evaluate carefully which appliances you really need, which ones will use less energy, and which ones the corporate marketers dreamed up in order to "create a need."
- If your television picture is on the screen as soon as you turn on the set, unplug the set when you're not using it. A prewarming unit uses electricity even when the television is turned off.
- Turn off the television and radio when you are not listening or watching.

DON'T BE IN THE DARK ABOUT LIGHTING SAVINGS

Harness natural light. Use natural lighting whenever possible. Open window shades or curtains, for instance, instead of turning on a lamp. Install a skylight or two so you can harness natural light (and perhaps add to the resale value of your home). Arrange your furniture to take advantage of natural light.

Solid-state dimmer switches used with incandescent lights will reduce energy usage. (Rheostat-type dimmers, however, use a large amount of electricity while dimming.)

Turn off unused lights. When you go on vacation, turn off all lights except for security lights attached to timers. Control outdoor electric lights with a photoelectric switch or a timer that turns them off automatically so they don't accidentally burn all day long. Likewise, if you have a decorative gas lamp, turn it off—perhaps for good. A gas lamp uses forty to fifty dollars a year in natural gas. Eight lamps burning year round may use as much natural gas as it takes to heat an average-sized home for a winter heating season.[11]

Make the most of your light.

- Keep lighting fixtures clean, especially the surfaces of light bulbs and fluorescent tubes. Dirt blocks light.

- Use clear light bulbs. They produce more light than frosted ones.

- Replace dark-colored lamp shades that diminish light with light-colored shades.

- Use three-way light bulbs only when you need to vary light intensity. Single-wattage bulbs are more energy efficient.

- Use a few high-wattage bulbs rather than several low-wattage bulbs. High-wattage bulbs give out more lumens (the amount of light produced) per watt than low-wattage bulbs.

- Experiment with low-wattage incandescent bulbs. Often a forty- or sixty-watt bulb will meet your lighting needs as well as a seventy-five or one hundred-watt bulb. But remember that one high-wattage bulb gives more light than two or three low-wattage bulbs that add up to the same total wattage.

- Reflector bulbs provide the same results as high-wattage, standard bulbs and cost less to operate, but they are more expensive to buy. If you need light focused in specific areas, compare the cost of reflector bulbs (that beam light in one direction) to the cost of regular bulbs.

Use area-specific lighting.

- Use lighting in a specific area. If you are reading in a chair late in the evening, turn on the lamp or overhead light and turn off other lights in the room.

- Use a strong reading lamp aimed at what you are reading rather than leaving several lights on.

- Add a solid-state dimmer switch to a lamp so you can choose exactly how much light you want.

- Don't overlight areas of your home. You may only need a sixty- or seventy-five-watt bulb in a hallway instead of a one-hundred-watt bulb, for example.

✔ Whenever possible, use fluorescent lamps instead of incandescent bulbs. Although they are more expensive to buy, fluorescent bulbs provide more lumens per watt and last up to ten times as long. (One forty-watt fluorescent tube provides more light than three sixty-watt incandescent bulbs.) Fluorescent lights work well in areas such as laundry rooms, work rooms, garages, and kitchens. Incandescent bulbs are better in areas where lights are frequently turned on and off.

✔ Take unneeded light bulbs out of multiple-bulb fixtures and replace them with burnt-out ones. Or partially unscrew unneeded bulbs. (Having no bulb in a socket can be dangerous.)

Stick with inexpensive bulbs whenever possible. Buy inexpensive, regular light bulbs rather than expensive, "long-life" bulbs that use more energy. In a fixture that's hard to reach, use a long-life incandescent bulb. Otherwise, use more energy-efficient, regular bulbs.

Care for fluorescent bulbs properly. Replace a flickering fluorescent bulb promptly to save energy and avoid damage to the ballast part of the lighting unit. Leave fluorescent lights turned on if you plan to return to the room shortly. You'll save electricity and cause the lights to last longer.

MONITOR YOUR ELECTRICITY USAGE

Learn how to read your electric meter so you can compute your electricity usage and see how much money your conservation efforts are saving you. Read the meter from left to right and always use the lower number if the arrow is between numbers. Since the number of kilowatt-hours you use is cumulative, you need to subtract your earlier readings from later readings.

---

*The heat flow within your home
is affected by three factors:
conduction, infiltration, and radiation.*

On each electric bill, verify that you are being billed at the correct rate, that the service charge is correct for the residential rate you are on, that you have used as many kilowatt-hours of electricity as you have been charged for, and so on. If what the local utility department is charging you per kilowatt-hour doesn't match your figures, complain to the utility department in person.

- Does your electric utility department offer lower "off-peak" rates? If so, try to use necessary electricity when the rates are lower.

- Become familiar with the residential rate schedules in your area, and be sure the rate you pay is the best one for your situation.

- Find out whether the electric utility department will give you a rebate for purchasing energy-saving appliances such as water heaters, refrigerators, or air conditioners. Our electric company gave us a $150 rebate for upgrading our water heater.

Decorating for Savings

Are you ready to paint the walls? If so, consider the possible energy-use effects of your choices. Light colors dramatically reduce the amount of light needed in a room. White reflects 80 percent of light, beige 66 percent, and peach 53 percent.[12] Remember, too, that light-colored carpeting, draperies, and upholstery also reflect light. (Please note: Saving money on electricity is not a justification for redecorating your home!)

- If you live in an apartment complex and your electric bills are high even when you are not home, see if your neighbor's outlets have been accidentally run through your electric meter.

- Contact your local utility company to find out if they do free energy audits.

- Contact the electric utility department or do research in the library to locate a chart that shows how much money small and large electric appliances cost you to operate. (You may gather some ideas regarding which ones you could operate less or do without altogether.)

- Be sure the utility meter reader can get to your meter. If he or she can't, an estimate may be made that results in a considerably higher bill than you deserve.

GARAGE MOTORS

When you use motor-driven equipment, such as a table saw, let the motor run continuously instead of turning it on and off for each cut. (Most of the electricity is used to get the motor started.) When a motor breaks down, talk with an experienced motor repair person about the possibility of replacing the motor with one that will deliver the required horsepower while using less electricity.

Insulate Yourself Against High Heating and Cooling Bills

THREE INSIDIOUS CULPRITS

The heat flow within your home is affected by three factors: conduction, infiltration, and radiation.

Conduction takes place when heat is transferred through the walls, ceilings, doors, windows, and floors of your home. When your home's interior is colder than the outside air, warm air is conducted into your home and heats the cooler inside air. Conduction in the opposite direction takes place during the winter, when the heat in your home is conducted to the cooler outside air.

For example, if the inside temperature of your home is seventy degrees Fahrenheit and it is zero degrees outside, a single-pane window inside your home will have a temperature of eighteen degrees. A double-glazed window, which has an airspace between the panes to reduce conductivity, will have an inside temperature of thirty-six degrees. A triple-glazed window, which limits conduction even more, will have an inside temperature of fifty-one degrees.[13]

Infiltration allows outside air to penetrate your home through holes and cracks around doors and windows or when someone enters or leaves your home. A strong wind on a cold day will clearly indicate where infiltration is occurring. When we first bought our present home, air infiltration was so great that a strong wind would actually move an *inside* door. It turned out that one room, built in the 1930s, had no insulation.

Even small holes and cracks add up to significant infiltration. A small crack around a large window frame, for example, may be equivalent to having a three- or four-inch hole in your wall! So it isn't surprising that up to half of your annual heating and cooling costs may result from infiltration. Remember, the greater the temperature difference between the inside of your home and the outside air temperature, the greater the air infiltration will be.

Radiation from the sun affects the flow of heat into your home in obvious ways. During the summer, for instance, solar energy enters your home through windows, causing heat to build up rapidly unless you take steps to thwart it. During the winter, solar energy can dramatically reduce your heating bills if you have a way to capture it.

THE BENEFITS OF INSULATION

Simply put, insulation helps keep heat indoors where it belongs during winter months and helps keep outside heat from entering during summer months. Proper levels of insulation will keep the inside temperature of your home from fluctuating a great deal, thus saving money on heating and cooling costs and making the home more comfortable. Appropriate insulation also enables you to operate smaller-capacity cooling and heating systems.

Depending on where you live and how much insulation your home contains, adding insulation can increase temperature-control efficiency in your home by as much as 30 percent, which means you can save money without sacrificing comfort. So adding the right kind and amount of insulation to various parts of your home can be one of your best savings investments.

A number of books contain specific data on determining how much insulation your home may need. But insulation costs money, and you must consider how much you should spend to reduce your heating or cooling bills in light of how long you plan to remain in your home, how great a savings on utility costs you anticipate, how much the work will cost, and other factors. The average family lives in a different house every five years.[14] If you are average, you may not want to put much money into insulation unless high utility bills are threatening to run you out or you think you can recoup some of your investment when you sell your home. If you pay several hundred dollars a month for the privilege of using an air conditioner each summer, and the winter months cause you to mutter under your breath about the heating bills, you probably will benefit a great deal from increased insulation and other methods of reducing heat gain or loss, even if you plan to live in the house for a relatively short time.

Cautions About Insulation Installation

Insulation must be installed properly. If you decide to do your own insulating, first talk with local building code officials, read books on proper insulating techniques, and become familiar with the various types of insulation (loose-fill, batt, rigid-board, and so on), vapor barriers, fire-resistant qualities, and other general rules, precautions, and guidelines. For instance, you should not cover vents, eaves, or electrical sockets in the attic with insulation, and insulation should not be near exhaust flues that become hot. You will want to wear a protective respirator or dust mask and protective clothing, too. When the job is done, wash that clothing separately from other clothing.

HOW MUCH INSULATION DOES YOUR HOME NEED?

If you're not sure where to start, consider having a trained energy auditor pinpoint problem areas and make recommendations. Your local utility department may provide this service free or at a low cost. If you don't have the option of using an energy auditor, you may have to find out on your own if your home has enough insulation.

Climb into the attic and look. You may find a six-inch layer of insulating "batts" neatly placed between each ceiling joist. Or, you may find that the insulation is piled deeply in one place and that other places have no insulation at all. Go into your basement or crawl space to see how well your floors and exterior walls are insulated. Also check the insulation between any heated and unheated areas of your home (such as the wall between an attached garage and heated living space).

The R-value—the resistance of the insulation to heat flow—of the insulation, not necessarily the thickness, is what matters. The higher the R-value, the more effective the insulation is. If you have less than six inches of insulation in the ceiling, for example, you probably need more. Check with a licensed insulation specialist or county regional building official to find out how much more insulation you need.

Other factors to consider are: the climate in which you live, the amount of money you can spend on insulation, which areas of your home need insulation, and what type(s) of insulation your home presently has.

Before adding insulation yourself, find out how much a professional insulation company would charge you to do the job. When we considered various options for insulating our home addition, we discovered that, because companies purchase insulation in bulk, we could hire skilled people to install the insulation for less than it would cost to purchase it ourselves.[15]

CHOOSING PRIORITY SPOTS TO INSULATE

Insulate the top ceiling first, since that is where the bulk of heat loss or gain occurs. Walls are more difficult to insulate, since they are seldom exposed. A professional company usually has to blow the insulation into uninsulated walls. Also, standard two-by-four construction doesn't allow much room for insulation,

An insulation company gave us truckloads of free, loose-fill insulation that had not fully blown into new homes. We took our old pickup truck to the building sites, bagged the loose insulation, brought it home, and spread it in the attic. The price was right, and our heating bill dropped by 40 percent the next winter.

- If your basement is unfinished but heated, consider putting insulative material on the walls. One effective way is to frame two-by-fours against the walls, add insulation, and—when you have the money— put dry wall over it. You could also place foam insulation board around the outside basement walls.

- Insulate the ductwork through which centrally cooled or heated air flows.

- Check the ductwork for air leaks when the fan is operating. Seal any leaks with the kind of tape a heating/cooling contractor in your area recommends. Make sure you insulate and seal leaks properly, and wear protective clothing and a respirator.

- If your home has a crawl space or unheated basement that allows heat to pass through the floor, insulate between the floor joists above the crawl space or basement. But if heating ducts travel through the crawl space or basement, you may want to insulate the entire space rather than just the ducts and floor. Talk with various heating companies or knowledgeable people at "do-it-yourself" stores to determine the best way to proceed.

- Check out the attic access panels. Often they have no insulation on them. You can easily cut batts or foam insulating board to fit.

Keep Air from Infiltrating Your Home

Air is always trying to enter your home through holes, seams, and cracks. Insulation is a good start, but it cannot fully prevent air infiltration. You can dramatically reduce air infiltration by caulking and weather-stripping, which doesn't cost much money or require much training.

PLUG HOLES AND CRACKS

Use caulk to plug holes, seams, and cracks up to a quarter-inch wide. Caulking requires few tools—an inexpensive caulking "gun," caulk, and whatever you need to prepare the spots for caulking—and the payback is great. We caulked our first home for about forty dollars and saved about eighty dollars that first year, and every year afterward. Not a bad return on a half day's work.

Caulk around your home where the walls join the foundation. Air commonly leaks into your home through that space.

Caulk the exterior of your home in any cracks where different building materials meet (such as wood and brick), at corners where siding meets, around exterior openings such as water faucets or vents, around doors and windows, around window air conditioning units, at joints between door and window frames, where wiring and plumbing goes through insulated floors and walls, and so on.

Since caulks are designed for various uses, check with a knowledgeable person about which kind to use. Silicone caulk lasts longest, for instance, but costs more. Acrylic-latex caulk is easy to apply and clean up but doesn't last as long as silicone caulk. Butyl-rubber caulk is good for connections between metal and masonry but is harder to apply. Latex caulk is good for small cracks and is easy to clean up. Be sure to buy caulks that will remain flexible for years and, if the caulking will show, choose the right color.

Make sure that areas you caulk are dry, clean, and free of peeling paint, water, old caulk, grease, and oil. Also note the temperature requirements of the caulk you use. Most caulks should not be applied, for instance, when the temperature is below fifty degrees because they take so long to dry.

Use other methods to plug larger holes, cracks, and seams.

• Cover unused dryer vents and other exhaust vents. Vents can act as chimneys, carrying valuable heated (or cooled) air outside.

- Repair any holes in the ceiling (for example, the stovepipe hole no longer in use) that allow air to enter or leave your home.
- If cold or warm air is entering through electrical outlets located on exterior walls, install a foam gasket behind the cover plate of each outlet and switch plate. Before doing this, be sure to turn off the power to the appropriate electrical circuit.
- Use an expanding foam sealant if your home has holes and cracks that aren't exposed to sunlight and moisture and that caulk won't easily fill.
- If the cracks are wide or deep, use a "crack filler" material. Rope caulk, a thick and flexible material, also works for filling cracks around windows.

WEATHER-STRIP DOORS AND WINDOWS

Poorly designed doors and windows and those that are not insulated or weather-stripped typically account for as much as one-third of a home's total heat loss. If your doors and windows are in bad shape (rotted wood, cracked glass, or poorly fitting seals), you probably need to replace them with energy-efficient ones or ask your landlord to consider doing it. Not long after we purchased our country home, we discovered that the window by the kitchen sink was so rotten that we had to glue and screw it shut—nails wouldn't hold. Needless to say, we replaced it.

People have a love/hate relationship with heat.

Assuming that your windows and doors operate well, weather-stripping is one of the most permanent ways to cut air leakage. It reduces heat loss or heat gain around doors and windows that open and close and can create an airtight seal inside door or window frames. If you've seen a flap of rubber at the bottom of a door that keeps air from moving under the door, you've seen one type of weather-stripping.

If you want to do your own weather-stripping, buy quality materials, preferably those that are premeasured to standard window and door sizes and will hold up well through years of use. Various kinds of weather-stripping are available, each offering advantages and disadvantages. Select those that will best meet your needs.

To determine where weather-stripping is needed, check for air leaks with a hand-held hair dryer. (One person uses the dryer, the other person stands on the opposite side and feels around for heat.) Or, carry a candle around and watch its flame on a cold, windy day to locate air leaks (being very careful, of course). Check underneath and around doors, basement windows, storm windows, and so on.

Replace single-pane windows with thermal-pane windows. If that is too expensive, if you are renting, or if you don't plan to stay in the house long term, buy plastic-film storm window kits or make simple, wooden frames, using plastic sheeting and furring strips. Trim the wooden pieces to the window- or door-frame size, tape the plastic to the frame with masking tape, and nail up the frame. We have built plastic storm windows for several doors and windows that we don't have to open, and we leave them up all year. (NOTE: Try to find plastic that will stand up to some abuse inside your home or lots of abuse outside from wind and rain, heat and cold. We use thick, sun-resistant upholstery plastic on the outside of our home, and it usually lasts four or five seasons.)

If your doors are not in good shape, you have several options: (1) Weather-strip around each door. (2) Consider adding a storm door. (3) Replace one or more doors with new, insulated doors that seal tightly. (4) If you live in a cold or windy climate, consider an "air lock" entry that has double doors with room between them to close the one behind before you open the other.

Keeping Cool for Less Money

No doubt about it, people have a love/hate relationship with heat. They spend much time and money to keep it in their homes during the winter and try their best to keep it out during the summer. They plan vacations around it, traveling many miles to sit on warm sandy beaches, and buy air conditioning systems to avoid it.

People use countless ways to keep cool. Fifty years ago, those who wanted to get cool would run a fan over the top of big blocks of ice placed in tubs. Desert nomads wear loose, light-colored clothing that protects their skin from the sun and allows sweat to evaporate. People in tropical climates typically take a break during the hottest part of the day. Millions of households in the United States have air conditioners that hum away the time (and money). Ceiling fans, attic fans, desk fans, whole-house fans, and hand-held fans push and pull warm air. And on it goes.

How much you spend to keep your home cool depends upon many factors: where you live (temperature, greenery nearby, level of humidity), the type and size of your home, the insulation in your home, local utility rates, how often you use heat-producing appliances, and so on.

The most effective cooling strategy is to use a variety of techniques in combination. As you evaluate the following section, consider which ones you can do easily—perhaps even this week. Note which ones you should do sooner than later, and try to work them in within the next few months. Finally, note the ideas you might like to try someday if you have more money or time.

CONSIDER COMPRESSOR-TYPE AIR CONDITIONING OPTIONS CAREFULLY

Evaluate high-efficiency options. If you currently have an old, central air conditioning unit or are thinking about having one installed, consider a high-efficiency unit that will be quiet and convenient. A unit with a high Seasonal Energy Efficiency Ratio (SEER) can dramatically reduce your cooling costs. Compare the initial cost of the unit, the expected savings compared to your present cooling system, your cash flow, and the length of time you plan to live in your home. Also consider how hot the climate is where you live. (If it's generally cool, you probably don't need a unit with as high an efficiency ratio and may be able to consider less expensive cooling options.) Shop for an energy-efficient air conditioner later in the summer, when the season is nearly over and stores are more willing to lower prices.

Consider using room air conditioning units. Depending on the size and layout of your home and which rooms you use during the summer, you might be able to purchase one or two wall- or window-mounted room air conditioners that have high Energy Efficiency Ratios (EERs), instead of a large, central air conditioning system. Room air conditioners, which cost much less than a central air conditioning unit, can be a good option if nighttime temperatures drop down to manageable levels or if the hot weather doesn't last longer than a few weeks.

Comparison shop. Read independent analyses of various air conditioners before buying one. Evaluate warranties and serviceability as well as dependability.

AIR CONDITIONING TIPS

Buy an air conditioner that is the right size. Buy a correctly sized air conditioner that will take the punishment of the cooling season where you live. If the unit is too small, it will run too often, wear out sooner, and not cool as well. If it's too big, it will only run for short periods of time, use too much electricity, and be inefficient.

If you live in a warm climate and plan to buy central air conditioning, buy a highly efficient unit that will give you the cooling capacity you need—and no more. The proper size is determined by the square footage of the area to be cooled as well as by such factors as the number of stories in your home, shade of trees and shrubbery on the southern and western sides, the amount of humidity in your area, how often you use heat-producing appliances, and whatever conservation measures you have taken or plan to take soon.

Other factors to consider are a switch that will allow you to run only the unit's fan instead of the whole unit and a variable-speed fan if you live in a humid climate. (A lower fan speed removes more humidity from the air.)

Run the air conditioner only on really hot days. When the outside temperature is cooler than the inside temperature, use natural ventilation or window fans unless the outside humidity is high enough to be uncomfortable.

Cut down on humidity. Vent your clothes dryer outside. Use a bathroom exhaust fan to remove humidity after a shower.

Use shade to your advantage. If your air conditioner's compressor unit is outside, shade it with an awning or strategically planted trees or shrubs; that can increase efficiency by up to 10 percent.[16] Placing the unit on the north side, away from direct sunlight, is preferable. Leave enough room around the unit for air to circulate freely. That holds true for window units, too. A window unit operates most efficiently if it is not located in direct sunlight.

Keep the cooled air circulating. Don't block window air conditioning units with shades or draperies that will keep cooler air from circulating.

Position and use the air conditioning thermostat properly. Raise the thermostat five or six degrees during the summer, and you will lower your air conditioning bills by as much as 25 percent.[17] If every household in the United States did that, we would save the equivalent of 190,000 barrels of oil every day.[18] Determine the highest temperature setting you can live with and adjust the thermostat accordingly. Don't keep turning the thermostat up and down.

Place the thermostat away from direct sunlight, the oven, lamps, and so on. Higher temperature readings will cause it to signal the air conditioner to run more than is necessary. Consider installing automatic thermostats that control temperatures during the day and at night, when you're sleeping or not at home. You'll save money and won't have to remember whether or not you adjusted the thermostat correctly.

Cool only areas that need cooling. People commonly cool areas in which they spend little or no time. Close off vents to rooms that don't need to be cooled, but don't close off too many or you may damage your compressor.[19] If you have central-heating ducts and use window air conditioning units, close the heating ducts so the cooler air doesn't flow down to lower areas of your home.

Seal out warm air when you run the air conditioner. Keep warmer air outside by tightly closing exterior doors and windows.

Depending on where you live, a whole-house fan might be a great alternative to more expensive central air conditioning.

When you are not home, turn off window units. Turn off the window air conditioners when you leave home for several hours or longer. You'll save money by cooling the rooms later with the air conditioners, fans, or by opening windows to take in cooler evening air.

Operate the air conditioner during off-rate times. If your electric utility department has off-peak prices, see if you can operate the unit at that time.

Reduce air conditioning maintenance costs. Clean permanent filters regularly according to the manufacturer's instructions. Your equipment will last longer and be more efficient, and you'll reduce operating costs. Replace disposable filters whenever necessary. Check them often. Keep up with all maintenance that you can do, and hire a professional to do specialized annual or biannual maintenance.

Using Fans to Cool Your Home

One or more fans, used correctly, can do a fine job of cooling a room or even your whole home.

Consider using a whole-house fan. You might install a whole-house fan that moves warm household air into the attic and then outside as the fan draws in cooler air from open windows during the evening. The home in which Stephen grew up had a fan like this. It got the air moving, which made the house feel cooler and lowered the actual air temperature inside. One speed cleared the air out in a hurry, the other, slower speed just kept the air circulating.

Depending on where you live, a whole-house fan might be a great alternative to more expensive central air conditioning. Because a whole-house fan has certain requirements (adequate outlet vents in the attic, for example), talk with a cooling professional about your particular situation.

When operating a whole-house fan, you will feel cooler if you only open the windows and doors of the rooms you're using (unless too much air is flowing through them).

Add extra vents or exhaust fans in the attic. If your attic is poorly ventilated and traps heat during the summer, add static roof vents, ridge vents, soffit vents, a turbine-roof fan, or an attic fan to clear out the hot air so your home will cool faster. Even if the attic is well insulated, attic heat gradually works its way down into the living areas. If you use an attic exhaust fan, set it to go on at one hundred degrees Farenheit or higher. If it's set too low, it will run too often and use electricity unnecessarily.

Use exhaust fans to dissipate heat and humidity. Use a kitchen exhaust fan to remove cooking heat during the summer. Turn it off as soon as you can so you don't expel cool air, too. Use a bathroom exhaust fan to remove moisture buildup after a bath or shower. Excess humidity makes the air feel warmer than it really is.

Ceiling fans keep air circulating. Install a variable-speed ceiling fan, with reversible controls, that will keep colder air rising in your rooms instead of settling down at lower levels.

Window fans have certain advantages. Large window fans are cheap to operate. We have two reversible-direction, two-speed fans. We put one fan at one end of the house to push hot air outside and another at the other end to suck in cooler air. Sometimes we run only one fan to bring cooler air into the house.

A large, slow-moving fan that has variable and reversible speeds keeps air circulating and draws in cool, evening air. It may enable you to cut down on a window air conditioner's use—or do without it altogether.

Don't run an attic or window fan when the air conditioner is on. Leave the air conditioner off until the fan has removed the hot air. If your house has a cool cellar or basement, you might put a vent in the floor above it and use a fan to bring cool air into the living area.

USE SHADE TO YOUR ADVANTAGE

Shade can keep the sun's radiant heat from entering windows and from "cooking" the walls and roof of your home. This can save up to 40 percent of your air conditioning energy. There are many ways to shade windows and walls during the summer months to keep the sun out.

Shade southern and western windows.

✔ Install shutters on the outside of your windows to block out the sun. You can close the shutters when the windows receive direct sunlight and open them when the windows are shaded.

✔ Mount insulating shutters on the inside of your windows. These can add about an R-7 insulating value to your existing windows.[20] (Be sure you know how they will operate and what they will look like installed before you buy them.)

✔ Install attractive, insulating window shades. Insulating shades cost much less than shutters and are about half as efficient. They should fit snugly along the inside edges of the windows, open and close easily, be able to be cleaned, be energy efficient, and not create condensation that could rot wood or cause paint to peel. Select thickly woven material that will allow less air to enter and use a colorfast, light-colored liner that will reflect the sun's rays.

✔ Install sunscreens that will allow you to see in or out but will block part of the sun's rays.

✔ Hang light-colored draperies with light-colored linings that will reflect sunlight.

✔ Awnings effectively shade windows, too. Consider how they will affect your home's exterior appearance.

✔ Install adjustable window blinds or shades. We use a white one in our office to cut the flow of heat entering the south-facing window.

✔ Put a film over the window surface. Some transparent window films reduce the light or solar energy that enters the window but still enable you to see out. If you're not sure how to do this without getting bubbles or creases in the film, hire a professional to do the job.

✔ Curtains can be effective and inexpensive. Energy-efficient, light-colored window curtains that fit tightly at the top, bottom, and sides of the windows reflect the sun's heat during the summer (and keep the house warmer during the winter because the heated interior air will not have as much contact with the cold windows).

Additional shading tips.

✔ A shed or garage placed on the eastern, southern, or western wall will help shade the living areas of your home from direct sunlight. (However, placing it on the southern wall will dramatically reduce the solar energy you receive during colder winter months.)

✔ If you can stand dirty windows, don't wash your windows as often during the summer. Dirty windows let in less sunlight, therefore less heat.

✔ Install an operable skylight. Open it to vent heated air and to allow cooler air from lower vents or windows on the northern side of the house to enter.

OTHER OPTIONS TO HELP YOU KEEP COOL

We've covered the major cooling concerns, but various other factors play a key role in keeping your home cool during summer months.

Keep cool air moving in the right directions. Install inexpensive heat deflectors over registers so that cooled air won't simply collect behind floor-length draperies.

Position air conditioning vents to direct the air upward. The cooler air will circulate downward, creating more air flow.

Minimize the impact of indoor heat sources.

- Run the dishwasher in the early morning before the heat builds up or at night before you go to bed, when the outside temperature is cooler.

- Cook dinner and prepare other meals in the evenings, when it's cooler. Depending on where you live, you may be able to open the windows so that cooler outside air will offset the heat your appliances generate.

- When you cook, use low-heat appliances such as a microwave oven to keep heat to a minimum.

- Use heat-producing appliances and incandescent lights sparingly during the day when outside temperatures are warmest.

- Turn off a pilot light when it is not needed. Many furnaces have pilot lights. If yours does, turn it off during the summer, but be sure you know what you are doing. Often local utility companies provide this service for free.

- Try to keep kitchen and bathroom doors closed while cooking and showering. Why let all that heat escape into the rest of the house? Use an exhaust fan to draw out the heat before opening the door.

What you wear in your home can have a great impact on how cool (or warm) you feel. While traveling in India and Burma, Stephen learned that staying cool was an art. Some of the tips he picked up include:

- Wear light-colored, loose clothing that allows air to move across your skin.

- Wear cotton clothing whenever possible, which "breathes" and dissipates body moisture.

- Wear loose shirts and open collars.

- Wear lightweight shoes that allow moisture to evaporate. Avoid shoes made of nonporous materials.

Landscape with cooling in mind. Planting trees in strategic spots can make your home much cooler during the summer and warmer in the winter. Plant deciduous trees on the southern, eastern, and western sides that will provide shade during the summer and still allow the solar energy to enter your windows during the winter.

Trees, shrubbery, and grass around your home cool the ground and the air entering your home. Several large shade trees can cut the summer air conditioning load by 10 to 15 percent.

Paint or stain your home a light color, and select the roofing carefully. Select light-colored exterior house paint or stain and roofing materials that will reflect the sun's heat rather than absorb it. That is particularly effective if you live in an area where winters are mild.

Open the windows. If you live in a breezy area and it's safe to do so, open the windows for cross-ventilation early in the morning and in the evening when the temperature cools down.

Keeping Warm for Less Money

For many people, heating is their largest energy expense, accounting for more than half of their energy costs. Many of us don't have the luxury of living in well-insulated homes with R-19 walls and R-30 ceilings. So we notice if utility companies raise rates on natural gas, heating oil, propane, or electricity.

It is possible to substantially reduce your heating bill if you are willing to put forth some effort and a little expense. How much you'll actually save depends on such factors as where you live, how energy-efficient your home is, how large your home is, its layout, and how efficient your heating system is.

FURNACE-RELATED TIPS

Unless your house is completely heated by solar equipment, wood, or electricity, you probably depend on some kind of oil- or gas-powered furnace or boiler to provide primary heat. Rather than addressing all types of heating in great detail, we'll focus on furnaces and discuss fireplaces as well. If your home has hot-water heat, some of the following tips will also apply.

Install an energy-efficient furnace (or boiler). Why start with this point when a new furnace (or boiler) is expensive? Today's furnaces are much more efficient than those most of us have in our homes. If you plan to remain in your present home, if your furnace is inefficient, worn-out, or the wrong size, and if heating costs are prohibitive, it may be time to buy another furnace with a high Annual Fuel Utilization Efficiency (AFUE) rating.

Contact various heating professionals and evaluate furnaces (and boilers) carefully. Compare warranties, prices, and costs of installation. If you live in a cold climate, the right heating unit could reduce your heating bill by more than 30 percent and pay for its initial cost several times over within a few years. Be sure to consider the advantages of gas versus oil heat.

Investigate energy-saving modifications. Depending on your heating system, one or more modifications may save you a significant amount of money each year. Check with a service technician to see if one of the following modifications—or another one not mentioned—is suitable for your heating system.

- An automatic flue damper installed in the furnace flue will keep warm air from rising when the burner shuts off. The result? More heat will remain in your home.
- Replace or improve inefficient gas or oil burners.
- Adjustable radiator valves and vents may reduce the flow of hot water to unused rooms.
- Electronic ignition can replace a pilot light.

Having your oil furnace serviced at least once a year . . . can save you up to 10 percent in fuel consumption.

Direct heated air where you want it to go.
- Put air deflectors on floor registers so that the furnace's heat will not collect behind long curtains or draperies.
- Move furniture and draperies away from heating ducts, baseboards, and radiators so that heated air can circulate freely.

✔ If your house or apartment has radiators or baseboard convectors, tape heavy-duty aluminum foil to insulation board and slip it between the wall and the radiator/convector. Make sure you do not restrict proper air circulation between the wall and radiator.

✔ Just as a fan can pay great dividends during warm summer months, it can help during the heating season. A variable-speed fan in the ceiling, for example, will circulate warmer air near the ceiling back to lower levels, enabling you to save as much as 25 percent of your heat.

Follow routine maintenance procedures. Furnaces should be inspected and adjusted periodically in order to run more efficiently. Find out if your local utility department offers free inspections. If you use oil heat, ask a serviceperson to make sure the furnace is firing correctly and that the burner is efficient. Having your oil furnace serviced at least once a year, preferably during the summer when service rates are cheaper, can save you up to 10 percent in fuel consumption. [21]

Become familiar with the maintenance requirements of your particular heating system—what you can do and what a heating technician must do. Learn which spots need to be lubricated, cleaned, or routinely replaced. If you have a forced-air system, for example, change or clean the air filters regularly.

Try to spot a problem when it first develops. If a heating-related problem develops, it is important to detect it early. One morning Amanda heard the pump for our propane hot water boiler turn on, but it sounded like a rattling can of bolts instead of the usual hum. So she turned it off and called a repairman. Part of the unit had loosened up and shifted position. "If this had continued to run," the repairman said, "the motor would have burned up inside and might have even caught on fire." Since we had to pay for the standard service call anyway, while he was at our home we asked him questions about the system and the best ways to maintain it.

Use thermostats for greater efficiency. Lower thermostats during winter months. Try setting your thermostats at sixty-eight degrees during the day and sixty degrees at night. Reducing the temperature by just five degrees overnight can save you up to 10 percent on your fuel costs. Be aware that every degree over seventy degrees typically adds an additional 3 percent to your heating bill. [22]

NOTE: Some older people require higher indoor temperatures at all times (above sixty-five degrees) to avoid accidental hypothermia—a possibly fatal drop in body temperature. People with circulatory problems or those taking certain types of drugs may also be vulnerable to lower temperatures.

- ✔ When you leave home for several days or longer, turn down the thermostats, but be sure your pipes won't freeze during your absence.

- ✔ Buy a programmable thermostat. It will reduce your heating bills by lowering the temperature in your home when no one is there or while you sleep. It can be set to signal the furnace to raise the temperature just before you return from work or when you wake up in the morning.

- ✔ If you seldom use certain rooms during winter months, or if you stay in one part of the house all day, why heat unused space? Close or turn down heating-duct dampers or registers so less heat will flow to those rooms. If you have zoned heat, set back thermostats located in unused areas. To keep a water pipe in the outside wall of an unused room from freezing, turn the thermostat down to fifty degrees, no lower. (If your home only has one zone, it might be worthwhile to create several zones to increase heating efficiency.) Before closing off a number of rooms, talk with a heating technician to see if the reduced air circulation could adversely affect your heating system.

Use a radiant heater instead of the furnace. A radiant heater can direct heat in your direction at a reasonable cost while allowing you to reduce the temperature in unoccupied rooms. However, be cautious about the possible dangers associated with improper use of the heater, such as young children being shocked or burned or the heater being placed too close to a flammable object. Use only a laboratory-tested room heater and be sure to follow all instructions.

Investigate the advantages of a heat pump. Consider installing a ground-source, water-source, or air-source heat pump in your home, particularly if you use electric furnace heating. A heat pump uses thermal energy from an outside source to heat and cool, and could cut your electricity usage for heating by 30 to 40 percent.[23] Depending on how cold your winters are, a heat pump can reduce your heating (as well as cooling) bills dramatically. To learn more about this option, talk with local reputable heating/cooling contractors.

MORE WAYS TO KEEP WARM FOR LESS

Deal with any open windows at night. If a family member opens a bedroom window at night to allow cool (or cold) breezes to waft in, close the door to his or her room. If there is a thermostat in the room, turn it down. Otherwise the furnace will continue to heat that room and any others on that particular zone.

Buy propane or fuel oil at off-peak times. Buy propane or fuel oil during the summer when demand is down. One year we bought nearly 450 gallons of propane for $.67 a gallon. Several months later, a gallon cost $1.40. The propane and heating oil companies love to "top off your tank" during the winter and get premium prices, so set up your arrangement on a "we'll call you" basis.

Let the sunshine in. Instead of keeping solar heat out of your windows, attract as much as you can during winter months.

• If you are serious about receiving solar gain and are willing to keep your windows clean, remove the screens on the southern side of your home to allow the maximum amount of sunlight to enter.

• Wash your windows more frequently during winter months. Clean windows allow more solar gain.

• Install heat-absorbing flooring in an area that receives lots of sunlight. For instance, dark-colored tile or brick laid on concrete will absorb solar heat during the day and release it at night.

• Open curtains, windows, or blinds on windows that receive a great deal of sun during the day. Make sure you close them at night to reduce heat loss.

Reduce window heat loss.

- Install insulating glass windows. Installing a low-emissivity coated double-glass unit with gas fill will improve the insulating value of the glass area by 40 to 50 percent.[24]
- Install insulating shutters that fit tightly inside the windows and reduce heat loss.
- Make your own insulating window shades.[25]
- Make your own storm windows using simple board frames and upholstery plastic. We have used this technique to reduce heat loss on low-quality windows.

Consider doors and entryways, too. Every time you open an outside door during cold winter months, you let warm air out and cold air in. That's the "Law of the Doorway." But you can do a few things to reduce this heat loss.

- Don't talk with someone while standing in an open, exterior doorway. Say good-bye before you open the door.
- Install a storm door that will keep a dead-air space between the cold air outside and the heated air inside.
- If your doors are colder on the inside than the inside walls, the doors are losing heat. If the doors have hollow cores, replace them with storm door/solid wood door combinations or insulated, metal-clad doors. We added a storm door to our back door two winters ago and noticed a difference right away. (Exterior doors with single-glass panes have a much lower insulating value than do solid wood doors with accompanying storm doors.)
- Pay close attention to uninsulated sliding-glass doors. We had a sliding glass door that allowed so much heat to escape that it would literally freeze shut on especially cold days. Since we didn't have the money to replace the door, and it was the only way to enter the backyard so it couldn't be sealed up with plastic, we did the next best thing: we covered it with an insulating drapery at night to reduce heat loss. (When the door still froze on really cold days, we thawed it with a hair dryer.) Solutions for that problem? Install a different door or design an insulating blanket or drapery that will reduce heat loss.

Use exhaust vents sparingly. Run exhaust fans just long enough to carry out excess humidity or odors. They carry out lots of heated air—

perhaps a houseful of heated air in just an hour—just as they'll carry out cooled air during summer months.[26]

Use an electric blanket. Using an electric blanket to keep warm at night is much cheaper than heating your entire home while you sleep. If you really want to stay warm, try putting a wool blanket underneath the sheet or mattress pad. Follow the electric blanket manufacturer's instructions carefully. Common sense tips include: Do not allow small children to use it, do not crimp internal wires, do not poke sharp objects into it, and clean it correctly.

Decorate with Your Climate in Mind

Your choice of exterior colors, as mentioned earlier, can make a big difference. (It's too bad houses don't have interchangeable exteriors: light-colored paint and shingles during the summer and dark-colored exterior paint and shingles during the winter.) We've chosen to use dark shingles and medium-colored paint.

Plant windbreaks if you live in an area where winters are harsh. If space and climate allow, plant evergreen trees and/or shrubs on the northern and northwestern sides of your home. They will break the cold winter winds. However, don't plant them so close to the house that they allow moisture to be trapped near the walls.

Wear warm clothing. Years ago, some college friends rented a poorly insulated home in a Colorado mountain ski town. It was too expensive to heat the place properly, so in the evenings they gathered sleeping bags and blankets and lay side by side on the floor to watch television. Granted, few people would go to that extreme, but the principle of wearing warmer clothing during the winter does make sense. A light, long-sleeved sweater equals almost two degrees in added warmth; a heavy, long-sleeved sweater adds about four degrees.[27]

126

Check the garage door for air leaks. If you have a garage, check the seal at the bottom of the door. If the seal isn't tight when the door is closed, take steps to keep out the cold air. That is especially important if the garage shares a wall with your living quarters.

Garage door technology has improved greatly in recent years. Consider replacing an old garage door with an energy-efficient one. When we built our addition, we purchased an R-14 garage door. No matter how cold the temperature is outside (and we've seen it dip to -30F), that unheated but well-insulated garage usually maintains a temperature of forty degrees or higher (although it may drop to thirty degrees for a day or so when it's bitterly cold outside).

Use a small heater, not the kitchen oven, when you need extra heat. Dollar for dollar, a small heater placed strategically will provide better heat more cheaply than will the kitchen oven. (Because of the risk of electrocution, do not use a portable electric heater in the bathroom or other areas that are often wet.)

Laboratory-tested kerosene heaters can be a big help in heating a specific area. Be sure to follow all guidelines concerning their use, since improper use can be dangerous. (Kerosene heaters are even outlawed in some areas.) Make sure, for instance, that your unit will shut off if someone knocks it over. It should be placed far away from flammable materials or liquids, far from where children may bump against it, and should not be placed in a small room with limited ventilation. We use kerosene heaters during emergency situations and winter camping trips. But the heaters do give off an odor and some black smoke when they first ignite, so we don't use them often.

Maintain appropriate humidity levels. Humidity is important during the winter months. A home with adequate humidity seems warmer than one that has insufficient moisture. Plus, moist air helps to keep lungs healthy, furniture from cracking, and people from shocking one another with static electricity. Instead of running a humidifier all the time, consider alternative ways to gain humidity: put a kettle on the wood stove or on radiators, and leave warm water in the bathtub for an hour or two after you bathe.

FIREPLACE TIPS

Flames licking the logs in a conventional fireplace provide a certain ambiance and atmosphere of coziness. But a conventional fireplace can actually rob your home of heat. As much as 90 percent of the heat generated by the fire goes right up the chimney, and the draft it creates also removes heat generated by your furnace. A fireplace flue can remove about 20 percent of the heated air in your home every hour.[28] If you're determined to use your fireplace occasionally, here are some ways to minimize the heat loss.

Close the dampers when the fireplace isn't being used. Be sure the damper closes tightly. If it doesn't, heated air may be going up the chimney even when the fireplace isn't being used. An open damper in a forty-eight-inch fireplace can let up to 8 percent of your heat out the chimney.[29]

Turn the furnace off when you burn, or turn the thermostat down in the room where the fireplace is located. If you use the fireplace as supplementary heat when the furnace is on, the furnace heat will go up the chimney and other rooms will get cooler. If there is a thermostat in the room where the fireplace is located, turn it down so the furnace won't produce warm air as the fire uses it up.

Close the doors and any warm-air ducts going into the room where the fireplace is burning. That will minimize heat loss.

Install a combustion air duct. Consider installing a duct that will bring in cooler outdoor air so the fire won't use as much heated indoor air for combustion. If you can't do that, open a window an inch or so while the fire is burning.

Use the heat more efficiently. Why not install a convective or radiant grate in the fireplace opening?[30] Better yet, install an efficient fireplace stove insert.

Install tight-fitting, tempered-glass doors on the front of the fireplace. That will allow radiant heat to enter the room but will help prevent a draft from carrying the house's heat up the chimney.

6

Hail! Wind! Fire! And Other Household Hazards

We heard it coming for fifteen minutes. A loud, rainlike sound without any rain. Suddenly it hit. Ice cube-sized hailstones pounded the roof, punching holes, denting a skylight. The lights of our camping trailer shattered. Newly stained siding on the house became scarred with pockmarks and scratches. The tomatoes in the garden flattened. And the hailstones dammed up a roof valley, causing water to pour in through the ceiling. It was an event for which one buys homeowner's insurance. Fortunately we had a good policy and a good company that stands behind it.

The right homeowner's insurance policy can save you money by protecting your home and its contents, providing liability coverage while other people are on your property, and paying additional living expenses you may incur if your home is severely damaged. For most people, homeowner's insurance is mandatory because they don't actually own their homes and their mortgage companies require adequate insurance coverage to protect their investment. With careful shopping, you can save hundreds of dollars or more on your homeowner's insurance.

Homeowner's and Tenant's Policies: Get the Best You Can Afford but No More Than You Need

The right coverage will protect your home, your possessions, and your financial security from loss due to various perils and liability. Without it, you may risk losing years of hard work, so it is important that you determine how much and what kind of coverage you need.

TYPES OF COVERAGE

Policies differ from company to company. The most basic HO-1 policy covers only your house and its contents against eleven different perils. The broad policy (HO-3) covers many more kinds of losses than the basic policy, including the weight of ice and the freezing of a plumbing system. A special policy (HO-5) covers the house and its contents for all perils, except those your policy specifically excludes. A tenant's policy (HO-4) covers a number of risks to personal property and provides limited liability coverage, not including liability resulting from the use of an automobile. Other homeowner policies are tailored for older homes (HO-8) and condominiums (HO-6).

CHOOSE THE PERSONAL PROPERTY COVERAGE THAT FITS YOUR SITUATION

Standard coverage will repair a damaged item or pay you its current value, whichever is less. *Replacement-cost coverage* will pay the full cost of replacing or repairing damaged property with like kind and quality at current prices, but you must maintain coverage for at least 80 percent of your home's replacement value. Actual cash value coverage usually pays for the cost of replacing the damaged property minus depreciation. *Scheduled coverage* is used to insure items of special value at an additional premium. Each item must be appraised and listed separately.

Typically, your personal effects are insured up to half the face value of your policy. If you want more coverage, you'll have to pay a higher premium. Some policies spell out the specific limits on various categories of valuables. Any and all guns, for instance, may be insured up to a thousand dollars total under basic property coverage. Rare coins may only be insured for a few hundred dollars. So if your valuables are worth quite a bit of money, if your grandmother gave you her set of sterling silver flatware, if you own expensive jewelry, or if you collect rare antiques, it would be wise to insure such items separately. The money you save doing many small tasks may disappear in an instant if a valuable but uninsured item disappears or is damaged.

MAKE SURE THE COVERAGE YOU BUY MEETS YOUR UNIQUE NEEDS

Become familiar with which types of losses various policies cover. Ask your agent questions about your specific needs. Find out how much liability coverage you should carry for your level of income and assets. Make sure your policy covers any detached structures you may have on your property and that your agent knows you have a swimming pool or other unique features that may add to your liability. Do you need special coverage if you rent out a portion of your home? What special coverage do you need if you operate a business out of your home (such as coverage for business equipment or additional liability)? If you have animals other than typical household pets, make sure your liability coverage includes any damage they might do to others. If you have a home with a mortgage, be certain that you are familiar with the insurance requirements of the mortgage company. You don't want to be caught without proper coverage.

LOCATE A GOOD INSURANCE COMPANY

An insurance company only meets your needs when it meets its obligations to you. Research the reputation and financial health of a few insurance companies at the library, using the publications of A. M. Best Company, Moody's Investors Service, Inc., and Standard & Poor's Corporation. Talk with friends and neighbors, too, and find out which companies have paid on losses promptly. Some companies are reluctant to meet their obligations.

COMPARE COVERAGES AND RATES CAREFULLY

Will your policy automatically adjust for inflation? Can you get replacement-cost coverage that repairs whatever is damaged or stolen with items of similar quality and kind? Compare replacement-cost insurance rates with nonreplacement-cost rates. In many instances, the annual cost differences may be small. If your insured property is damaged, it's easier to have it replaced than it is to try to figure out how much money the insurance company owes you. Also, if your home is only insured for part of the replacement cost, you may have to pay the rest yourself if a loss occurs.

EVALUATE YOUR LIABILITY COVERAGE

If someone gets hurt on your property, wind causes your pine tree to fall on the neighbor's porch, or your dog bites a visitor, liability insurance goes into effect as long as the injury or damage was not intentional or committed by a child under age thirteen. The key is to pay for the coverage you may need and no less. Your agent should be able to help you determine your personal liability needs.

Don't sign anything you don't understand. If a particular clause in your policy isn't clear to you, ask the insurance agent to explain it.

EVALUATE POLICY EXCLUSIONS AND LIMITATIONS CAREFULLY

If you live in a flood-prone region, are you covered for flood damage? What about snow and ice damage? Sewer backups? Plumbing leaks? Earthquakes? Will smoke damage or theft be covered? If your home is damaged, will the company pay for you to live elsewhere until the house is fixed? What about vandalism if you're gone for a few weeks on vacation? What if your freezer quits working and your food spoils?

FIND OUT WHETHER YOU
ARE ELIGIBLE FOR A DISCOUNT

Talk with the agent about discounts. Sometimes you can obtain cheaper rates if:

- Your car and your home are insured by the same company.
- You install smoke, sprinkler, and/or burglar alarms in your home.
- You have excellent fire protection.
- You seem to be "low risk" because of few claims and/or the neighborhood in which you live.
- You have marked your valuables with engraved identification numbers.
- You work at home.
- You are a senior citizen or are retired.
- Your home is brand new or nearly new.
- You don't smoke.
- You have installed fire extinguishers and/or deadbolt locks.

Maintaining a Good Policy

Many people who are pleased with their homeowner's policies find it easy to think about other details from year to year. But like other insurance policies, a homeowner's policy needs to be evaluated periodically.

KEEP YOUR COVERAGE CURRENT

If you've made improvements to your home or construction costs have gone up, you may be underinsured. If you're not sure how much coverage to add, ask your agent to come out and assess the replacement value of your home. Remember, you need to insure for the replacement value, which may be different from the market or resale value. Just because the market value of your home declines doesn't mean the replacement cost has declined.

If your home is not insured for all of its replacement value, the insurance company won't give you full replacement payment. And if it's not insured for at least 80 percent of replacement cost, the company won't even pay the full amount on a claim, up to the limits of your policy.

For instance, let's assume that your home is worth $100,000 and you're insured for $85,000 of replacement-cost coverage (not counting the foundation and basement walls). If your home burns down, the company will pay $85,000, minus your deductible, to replace it. If a hail storm tears up the roof to the tune of $4,500, the company will pay you $4,500, less your deductible. But if your home is only insured for $79,000 (79 percent of the $100,000), the company won't pay all of the $4,500.

An insurance administrator provided us with this simple formula: The (amount of insurance you carry) divided by the (amount of insurance required) multiplied by the (loss) equals the (amount you will recover). It pays to obtain good coverage and keep it current.

> Change to a higher deductible when it is cost effective to do so. Maybe you are earning more money than you were a few years ago. If you can pay $500 out of pocket instead of $250, get a deductible of $500 if the difference in premium cost is significant.

INVENTORY YOUR BELONGINGS

It's always wise to know what you own in the event you suffer a loss. Close your eyes for a moment. Can you remember everything you own and what kind of shape it is in? If not, take photographs or videotapes of key items. Photograph or videotape antiques and special collections, furniture and kitchen cabinets, tools in the garage, and pictures on the wall. Photograph or videotape open drawers, open cabinets and open closets. Write descriptions of your goods, including serial and model numbers, prices paid, and where and when you purchased them. Locate appraisals and receipts for expensive items. Inventory everything in the attic, basement, and garage. Go outside and photograph the boat, the shed, the trees, the landscaping.

Does that sound like a lot of work? It is. But if you ever need that list, you'll be glad to have it. When you're finished, put the photographs or videotape and item descriptions in a place *other than your home.* If there is a major theft or fire, this inventory will make it easier for you to recall exactly what you have lost and prove to the insurance company that you indeed owned the merchandise.

For More Information

To learn more about homeowner's insurance, contact the Better Business Bureau for your area, the state insurance commissioner's office, or the Insurance Information Institute, 110 William Street, New York, NY 10038, (212) 669-9200.

SAVING MONEY
ON WHAT YOU WEAR AND EAT

7

Buying and Caring for Clothing

E ver since Adam and Eve ate the forbidden fruit in the Garden of Eden, clothing has been an unavoidable need in human life. We need it to protect us from weather and to make us feel comfortable in the presence of others. But clothing has come to mean much more than personal protection. We use it as a symbol of our identity, as a way of revealing our financial or social status, and as a way of influencing the opinions others have of us.

With such hidden motivators influencing our clothing choices, it's no wonder that the amount of money we spend on clothing gets out of hand. Yet there are many ways to reduce that expense. Many of the following suggestions can be easily put into practice with little noticeable change in lifestyle, whereas others may challenge the fundamental way you think about yourself and your clothing. Whether you choose to make small or large changes, you can reduce the amount of money you spend on clothing.

---

*Broaden your horizons regarding
where you shop for your clothes.
Doing so can enable you to save money.*

Buying clothing is a personal activity. Some people like to go into a store, walk directly to the rack that has countless options in their size, and walk out with a selection. Others prefer to go from store to store, comparing outfits, costs, and styles. Still others stop in second-hand stores every so often, patiently waiting for great bargains. Some people shop primarily via catalogs and telephone. So please don't view the following suggestions as an attempt to tell you what to wear or where to shop. Instead, use them as a resource to help you save money as you make clothing choices that fit your personality and lifestyle.

Save Big Bucks on Clothing by Making Wise Choices

How and where you shop for clothing makes a big difference in how much you spend. If you are serious about saving money on clothing, you may want to start by thinking about what motivates you to buy clothing the way you do.

WHAT KIND OF SHOPPER ARE YOU?

☐ Do you buy according to habit—shopping the way you always have without giving thought to other options?

☐ Does the time you have available to shop direct your actions?

☐ Are you limited in your shopping choices because you are unaware of better ways to buy clothing at reasonable prices?

☐ Does your attitude toward shopping limit your choices? (Some people, for example, are too image conscious or fearful to enter second-hand stores or stores that don't have just the right atmosphere.)

☐ Do you have the patience to wait until items go on sale instead of buying on impulse?

☐ Are you willing to comparison shop in person or by phone?

☐ Does the amount of money you have available to spend on clothing dictate where you shop?

☐ Are you an open-minded shopper who will consider new possibilities to find the clothes you want at lower prices?

☐ Do you have to project a certain professional image that you believe excludes some lower-price possibilities?

You know what kind of shopper you are. We encourage you to broaden your horizons regarding where you shop for your clothes. Doing so can enable you to save money. Even if you require the highest quality (and generally more expensive) clothing for work, you can shop for bargains on leisure clothing. And if you think that discount store and thrift shop clothing is all you can afford, think again. Sale prices of high-quality merchandise can rival the everyday prices offered by low-end merchandisers.

We have found that a combination of shopping habits saves us the most money. We can't stand paying high prices for most types of clothing, so we have learned to "cherry pick" thrift stores while on our way to do other errands. We buy comfortable, long-lasting clothing from catalog companies such as L. L. Bean when we need to, and we window-shop and compare prices once in a while in malls. Usually we find that carefully selected "consignment shop" clothing is even better than new clothing because we enjoy saving money and meeting our needs (and sometimes our wants) at the same time. But we also enjoy finding "just the right thing" for a special occasion at a nice department store or specialty shop—especially when it's half price!

Let's look at ways you can save lots of money on clothing and still look as good as you want to look—or even better.

BUY ONLY THE CLOTHING YOU NEED

If you are serious about saving money on clothing, it's important for you to determine exactly what you need and generally to buy only those items. For example, not long ago while Stephen was browsing in a used clothing store, he noticed several nearly new jackets that would fit our daughter. He nearly bought one, until he realized that she already had two similar jackets—one given to us and the other purchased at the same thrift store months earlier. Even at bargain prices, clothing can be expensive if you impulsively buy items you don't need.

The fact is, most people have items in their closets or in boxes that were purchased impulsively. So one of the best ways to cut down on clothing expenses is to avoid impulse buying. Often this clothing is rarely worn anyway because it doesn't fit, isn't the right color, doesn't go with other clothing, is flawed, or is simply unnecessary. We have fallen victim to impulse clothing purchases and have learned that the best way to avoid the problem is to have a list of what we need and to buy for the long term.

You can help protect yourself against impulse buying. The following suggestions can help you limit your clothing purchases to the items you really need.

- When was the last time you really looked at your clothes to see what you have? If it has been a while, take a hard look at what's tucked away in your closet.

- If you enjoy wearing what you have and have few items that are worn out, don't fit well, or don't suit your present needs, clean out the excess items and give them to a friend, to your church, or to an organization that collects and redistributes used clothing. If your money is tight or you have a number of good quality, expensive clothes, you may want to try to sell them through a consignment shop before you give them away.

- If you aren't satisfied with what your wardrobe has to offer, make a list of the items you need. Keep the list with you (or at least clearly in mind) whenever you shop. If you happen to find a great price on one of the items on the list, buy it with the confidence that you have made a good purchase.

- If your wardrobe is basically sound but needs a little pizazz, you may be able to update it by purchasing selected accessories. A new scarf, tie, belt, handbag, or piece of jewelry may be what you need to make an old standby seem new again. It's cheaper to buy accessories than to buy new basics, so add appropriate accessories to your list of clothing needs.

- Of course that isn't the only way to expand a deficient wardrobe. You can buy new outfits, or you can build on the garments you already have. It may not be difficult to make better use of clothing you already own. Perhaps you could buy a skirt, pair of pants, shirt, blouse, or jacket to coordinate with some of your existing favorites. You may be able to create an entirely new look by mixing old favorites with carefully selected new items.

When you need to buy something new, think carefully about your need before you buy. Ask yourself these questions:

✔ What is the purpose for the particular garment I need (casual use, a specific sporting activity, a dressy occasion, or everyday professional clothing)?

✔ Will the garment I am considering serve me well for the purpose I have in mind?

✔ Must the garment stand up to hard, everyday use (which demands quality fabric and construction)? Or do I plan to wear it just a few times (which may enable me to buy a less expensive garment)?

BUY FOR THE LONG TERM

Clothing manufacturers want you to think that new is necessary. They want you to toss out last season's look in favor of this season's hottest fashion. They also want your pursuit of a fashionable style to be a greater priority than practicality and long-term wearability. A key to saving money is to see through the multilayered game of fashion and to buy basic, well-made items that will stand the test of time, to buy those items at a reasonable price, and to care for them properly.

In a way all of us, by purchasing what makes sense to us, creates our own fashion. The designers make money when they create fashion; when we do it, we pocket the savings. Here are some ways you can set yourself free from the short-term clothing trap and save money by thinking long term.

Be only as fashion conscious as you can truly afford to be. Fashions come and go, but basic, classic styles can be worn for years. So don't get stuck with clothing that looks ridiculous six months after you buy it. If most of the clothing you buy is a basic style that will "stand the test of time," you will save a bundle. Unless you're a teenager, buying a "label" or "look" is less important than buying quality clothing that will meet your needs over the long haul.

Of course, in some situations you may have to be extremely well dressed. Bankers, women who sell cosmetics, salespeople, business executives, and consultants, for instance, have to maintain a professional image. But even if this is your situation, you can choose quality clothing that you can wear for several seasons. An executive business consultant we know buys what he calls "timeless" suits with moderate lapels and traditional styles. "When styles change," he explains, "I just have to buy a new tie instead of a new suit."

Shop for multiseason clothing. We've learned that if we buy clothing that can be worn for three seasons of the year, we don't have to pack up and store as many items in boxes, protect them from damage, and unpack them again when the weather changes. For example, we may buy a medium-weight coat that can be worn by itself in the fall and spring and with a liner or sweater in the winter. Some new, combination fibers make it easy to wear multiseason clothing.

Outerwear isn't the only kind of multiseason clothing you can buy. Consider thick and comfortable cotton sweaters (one of Amanda's favorites). In warm parts of the country, they can be worn from fall through spring, and in chillier areas they can be worn from spring through fall. Selected women's dresses, if the colors and patterns aren't too seasonal, can be worn for several seasons, too. (But be careful. Your favorite pastel floral dress with the lace collar may look out of place in October, as would an autumn plaid on Easter Sunday.) In many parts of the country, men can wear lightweight wool suits through several seasons, too.

---

*If clothing isn't comfortable
in the store, the odds are you
won't wear it when you get home.*

Evaluate material and workmanship before you buy. That seems logical, right? Unfortunately, much clothing today is not made well and won't last long even under normal use. Although some budget-priced clothing will last, other items will fall apart the second time you wear them. Stephen once purchased a number of shirts at a "seconds" store in Chicago and gave the nicest looking one to his father for his birthday. You guessed it, the shirt he gave his father fell apart after the second washing. It ended up being stuffed into a heating duct when his father was painting. The shirts that Stephen kept lasted for years.

When you buy clothing, check hems to make sure they are evenly stitched and pressed. Cuffs and collars should be neatly and evenly stitched without puckers. Patterns should match at the seams. Buttons should be stitched on well and be functional; buttonholes should be reinforced and the right size for the buttons. All seams should be evenly sewn and should not ripple. Sleeves should reach your wrists when you extend your arms, and zippers should lie flat. Lapels should spring back to their original shape quickly after you squeeze them, and linings should be well fitted (not hang below the hem of the garment). Pockets should be double stitched. Clothing that will receive heavy wear should be reinforced with double stitching at key stress points.

Check the "comfort factor." How does the article of clothing feel on you? Do you feel really comfortable, or does the neck pinch a little? Can you move freely without restriction? When you bend down, can you only go down halfway because the pants pull in the seat or the knees are cut too narrow? If clothing isn't comfortable in the store, the odds are you won't wear it when you get home. Save your money for something you will enjoy wearing.

GET MORE MILEAGE OUT OF YOUR CLOTHING

Buy outfits you'll wear more than once. Buying for a special occasion may be fun, but why not give yourself the option of wearing the outfit again? Think about the kinds of special occasions you normally attend and try to find something that will be dressy enough for the most formal, but not too dressy for less formal occasions.

Also consider alternative uses for special-occasion clothing. If a short-sleeved print dress is appropriate for a summer wedding, perhaps a solid-color jacket will make it suitable for the office, too.

If you must buy an outfit that you will only wear once, look first in a nice consignment shop. There's no point in spending more money than you must for a one-occasion garment.

Concentrate on a basic color group. Stephen's father once told him, "I've chosen to go with blues and grays instead of using browns, too. That way, I can mix and match." That was good advice. Stephen has saved lots of money through the years and has quite a few combinations of blue and gray clothing.

The same principle applies when you buy items that will match with other items in your wardrobe, such as buying a skirt that will go with a number of blouses you already own. Amanda, for example, focuses her wardrobe around navy blue and white. She has several navy blue skirts: one straight long skirt, one short full skirt, one long full skirt. She also has a variety of fabrics and weights: one lightweight wool skirt, one wool and polyester blend skirt, and one cotton skirt. She has a more limited selection of white skirts. She also has several blazers and jackets in navy and white. No matter what current style or length of skirt is popular, or what style of jacket is in vogue, she can mix and match these basics in a number of different ways. Mixing and matching is an easy way to create variety, especially if you pick up such accessories as ties, belts, or scarves.

Combine outfits. If a suit coat no longer fits or has become dated, you may still be able to wear the suit pants with a different suit coat. If a skirt can no longer be worn, wear the blouse with other coordinating skirts and jackets. That is a good way to save money creatively by getting more mileage out of your clothing.

Take time to survey possible combinations, using clothing you already have. Lay out several outfits on the bed and see how many new combinations you can come up with. Make a list of items you could purchase to make several more combinations.

Read clothing care labels. Have you ever pulled your clothing out of a washing machine and encountered green underwear or dress shirts that were once white? As more and more clothing is made in developing countries, that may occur more often because the quality of dyes isn't consistent. Some colors will hold up well, whereas others bleed and quickly fade.

Check the permanent care labels on clothing if you are not sure which items will need to be dry-cleaned, washed in cold water, or ironed. Permanent press, wash-and-wear clothing requires little or no ironing, so you'll save time, money, and keep dry cleaning expenses to a minimum.

If you wash an item in hot water and it shrinks, you're out the money you paid, plus the time and money it takes to replace the item. However, be aware that some manufacturers recommend dry cleaning primarily to protect themselves, not because the clothes necessarily require it. If you take the time to learn about fabrics and what happens when they get wet, you may find that you can successfully wash several garments for which dry cleaning is recommended.

Consider how "adjustable" the item of clothing is. Some people's weight fluctuates frequently. If you are one of them, you know how difficult buying clothing can be. If your weight varies by more than a few pounds, buy clothing that will fit you when you are heavier and still look OK when you weigh less. And be cautious about buying an item that may shrink. Above all, don't buy clothing that doesn't fit well just to entice yourself to lose weight. When you do lose weight, buy and enjoy clothing that fits your new look.

You also may want to see if hems can be taken out if styles change or if the seams can be adjusted easily if you gain or lose weight.

When clothing wears out in one area, repair it or alter it for a different use. If you get a hole in the elbow of a long-sleeved shirt, make short sleeves. If the elbows on your favorite turtleneck wear out, cut out the sleeves and wear the shirt under your favorite long-sleeved sweaters. If you get a hole in a pair of pants, make shorts.

Use appliqués or press-on tape in simple designs to cover a tear in children's jeans, jackets, or shirts. Children usually love the new look.

Dress down for dirty tasks. Wear older clothing when you do dirty tasks. It beats staining or otherwise damaging a good outfit. In fact, we usually change into our kick-around-the-house clothes as soon as we walk in the door. That keeps our better clothes looking their best and keeps us relaxed and comfortable.

Recycle old clothing. If you can no longer use clothing that is still in fine shape, you have several options. You can donate it to a church clothing pantry, put it in a consignment shop, sell or donate it to a thrift shop, have a garage sale, or swap with friends. Allow the clothing you no longer need to help others. Charitable organizations give IRS donation verifications.

If the clothing you no longer need isn't even good enough to give away, consider these options: Use old clothing that has little giveaway value as rags. For many years, we have used cotton tee shirts and underwear for dust rags, to wash the car, and to clean up after painting projects. There's no need to buy rags. Also, quilters may be interested in acquiring all-cotton or all-wool fabrics.

Care for your clothing. Like most things, clothing that is cared for will last longer and look nicer than neglected clothing. Here are some clothing-care tips that are sometimes overlooked.

- Take care of small tears promptly so they don't get worse.
- Repair buttons before they come loose.
- Watch for unraveling hems before an edge of the fabric tears.
- Wear old clothing to do work around the house and garage. It's not a disaster if you get oil, tar, or paint on an old shirt or pair of pants.
- When elastic no longer stretches, put in new elastic.
- Carry a water-resistant jacket with you so that you can quickly cover up a nice outfit if rain hits.
- Don't leave clothes hanging where the sun can fade them.
- Wash delicate clothing by hand in a sink. We have done this for years, and our delicate items have lasted much longer than if we had put them into a washing machine. As an alternative, buy a mesh bag and wash delicate items in the gentle cycle (if your washing machine has such a cycle) with less fuss.
- Try to keep the clothes in your closet from getting too dusty. Sometimes the dust won't easily brush off, which may require dry cleaning.
- Watch what you sit on or lean against. "Tar on the rear" or bubble gum on the sweater is not a fun experience.
- Hang clothing on wooden or plastic hangers rather than just on bare, dry-cleaner-variety wire hangers. The clothing will keep its shape better, be less wrinkled, and not stretch as much.
- Use "suit hangers" for coats, jackets, and suits. Because of their contour, these hangers keep items looking neat.
- If clothes you plan to wear are wrinkled, hang them in the bathroom when you take a shower or a bath. The steam may remove the wrinkles. (So will the fluff cycle on a dryer.)
- Use fingernail polish at the top and bottom of a "run" in a stocking to stop it in its tracks.
- Be careful not to leave nails or other sharp objects in your pockets. They will tear holes and could hurt you if you happen to fall on them.

- Although it's convenient, a dryer can be hard on clothing. Use the dryer sparingly. When you use it, use a cool setting rather than a hot one. Your clothes will be less likely to be excessively wrinkled or damaged by too much heat.

- Save buttons from old shirts. They come in handy when you need to match one on a favorite shirt. (We have a whole can of them.)

- Be careful you don't damage your clothing: getting ink marks in your shirt pocket, ripping a skirt or pants when you are too close to an open car door, getting ink on your dress from a copy machine, or poking holes in your pockets with a sharp object can be expensive mistakes.

- Find effective cleaning products for stains. Keep them on hand and use them immediately. Take action before the stain "sets." If necessary, call a dry cleaners and ask the "stain expert" what to do.

How You Shop Makes a Difference

CHOOSE CLOTHING THAT LOOKS GOOD ON YOU

We've known people who love to shop for clothing but come home with clothes that don't fit, don't match anything else they own, or are the wrong color. If you're prone to make these mistakes, relax!

- Ask a clothes-conscious friend or spouse to go with you. Second opinions can help you avoid costly mistakes. (It took a while, but Stephen finally admitted that he needs help matching his clothes.)

- Choose colors that make you look good. If you're not sure which colors are best for you, pay a good color consultant to advise you, or evaluate your clothing purchases with a knowledgeable friend.

- Choose colors that blend well, whenever possible, so you can mix separates to create a greater number of ensembles.

- Try on clothing before the purchase, whenever possible. Any given garment may run a bit smaller than usual or have a pattern that accentuates physical characteristics that you want to minimize.

- Most clothing stores have changing rooms, but many thrift shops don't. If you know a place doesn't have a changing room and the climate allows, wear lightweight clothing so you can still try on other garments. If you're buying ties or light jackets, a typical shirt will work well.

COMPARISON SHOP

Comparison shopping can be a great way to reduce clothing costs. You see, retailers do not have the upper hand. They have to choose clothing well in advance of the season, price it on arrival, and wait for consumers to come in and buy it. You, on the other hand, have your pick of clothing and can go from store to store if you care to do so.

---

*Window-shopping, especially at malls,
can be like walking the carnival fairway
and being beckoned by the hawkers.*

✔ Take advantage of clearance, going-out-of-business, or end-of-season sales. Look at sales racks every time you shop. "This is a great way to do early Christmas and birthday shopping," a woman from church told us, "especially for children."

✔ Window-shop all you want to, but beware! Window-shopping, especially at malls, can be like walking the carnival fairway and being beckoned by the hawkers. As a friend says, "For the faint of wallet, it's usually too hard to resist."

✔ When you find a product you need (or want), make several phone calls to determine if the same or a similar item is available in a local discount store. Or browse in other stores in the mall or the same part of town. If the item isn't on sale, evaluate how much you really need it and when it might go on sale.

✔ Call stores to compare prices on basic items, such as jeans, 100-percent wool socks, and so on. You can get a basic idea of price, especially if you are looking for a particular brand.

SHOP AT STORES THAT HAVE GOOD REFUND/RETURN POLICIES

If you goof and end up with clothing that doesn't fit right or isn't suitable, it is important to be able to return the clothing for credit or a refund. Otherwise, you may end up with a hanger-on in your closet, or something that just hangs on you.

✔ Keep receipts until after you have worn and washed an item. Otherwise you may not be able to return it. (If you keep all your clothing receipts in a sealable plastic bag, you'll get an idea of how well you are stretching your clothing dollars.)

✔ Learn the return policies of each store where you buy clothing. Look near the cash register for a statement of the return policy. Beware of "credit refund only" and "no cash refund" retailers.

✔ If an item of clothing doesn't satisfy you, complain politely to the salesperson and, if you need to, the store manager. Usually the store will refund your money or exchange the item for a comparable one.

Shop Seasonally

Stock up on summer items when stores shift to fall merchandise. Buy sweaters and wool hats in the spring. Frequently the best deals surface at the end of each season and are found on bargain racks. About six years ago, Stephen bought a beautiful down coat for twelve dollars in April. It was marked down from more than one hundred dollars.

"If you have children," says one woman with four children, "learn to anticipate their sizes one season ahead of time."

WHERE TO GET SPECIAL DEALS

In recent years, many discount clothing stores have opened.

Factory outlets. These stores sell a variety of items. Some outlets sell goods at reduced prices—up to 80 percent off. Others sell goods at about the same price as specialty stores. Some items sold through factory outlets may be slightly defective; others may be perfect.

During a recent visit to a factory outlet in Connecticut, Stephen purchased a fine leather belt for four dollars instead of twenty-two dollars. Curious, he asked the saleswoman why it was so cheap. The answer: "It was a salesman's sample that he carried around in his car for a little while."

Entire books are devoted to tips on shopping in factory outlets. If you are serious about finding the best deals in factory outlets, you may want to check your local library for books such as *Factory Outlet Guide to New England*. It devotes nearly two hundred pages to specific factory outlet stores in New England—what they sell, how to get there, store hours, whether they take personal checks, and even if they can accommodate handicapped shoppers. It also has a product index and other helpful information.

Warehouse outlets. You can find excellent bargains at warehouse sales. But compare quality and price carefully. Not all warehouse outlets are worth visiting.

Specialty outlets. Generally specializing in one type of merchandise such as shoes, fabric, men's suits, kitchenware, and so on, specialty outlets buy surplus inventory from manufacturers or merchandise at manufacturers' "distress" sales. The outlets may have nice showrooms or be quite basic.

There are no guarantees about the quality of merchandise you'll find in an outlet.

People travel many miles to go to a particular shoe outlet in Illinois. The selection is great, the salespeople are helpful, and the prices are incredibly low on name-brand merchandise. But when Stephen looked at a selection of shoes in a local outlet, he found nothing but damaged shoes or items made of inferior materials.

A word of caution is in order here. The word *outlet* has become a marketing buzzword. Many "outlets" are nowhere near a factory and are only 10 to 15 percent cheaper than specialty shops. But some outlets are worth the trip, so check them out.

Remember, there are no guarantees about the quality of merchandise you'll find in an outlet. So make sure you know what you are buying. Find out if the merchandise is "irregular," "overstock," "marked for flaws," or "seconds" before you buy. There can be a significant difference in the quality of these items.

Catalog shopping. Depending on what you need, you can find good deals in direct mail catalogs. That is particularly true if you are shopping for unusual or especially high quality items that you might otherwise have to find in a specialty shop. Some mail-order companies offer good products and terms, unbeatable guarantees, and reasonable prices. Others don't. Here are a few tips to ensure a satisfactory purchase.

✔ If you are not sure about a company's reputation, contact the Chamber of Commerce or Better Business Bureau, and ask if there are any outstanding complaints about the company.

✔ Beware of "contests" or "giveaways" that entice you to spend more than you need to.

✔ Be sure you understand the terms of your purchase, delivery dates, return policy, and whether or not a substitution will be made if the product you want is out of stock.

✔ If you place an order and don't receive it within thirty days, request a refund. In most instances, the company is required to provide one.

✔ Order by mail whenever you can, since postal regulations apply to companies that receive and deliver orders via mail.

✔ Keep a record of what you order, the price, description, when you placed the order, and how you paid for it.

✔ If you purchase by credit card, give your credit card number only to reputable companies. You don't want your number to fall into unscrupulous hands.

Membership discount stores. You may save a lot of money by joining a store such as Sam's, Pace, or Price Club. Although not all items in those stores are inexpensive, many are priced well below similar products in other retail stores. Before you buy, know how much items cost elsewhere and make sure it is worthwhile for you to buy in the bulk quantities generally required.

Nonmembership discount stores. We have found good buys on children's clothing, swimsuits, underwear, socks, and some accessories at these stores. But be careful. Some low-end merchandise is good quality, and some of it is junk.

Salvage stores. Have you ever wondered what happens to clothing that is slightly damaged in an accident, fire, or flood? What about items not picked up from warehouses? Quite often that merchandise ends up in salvage stores.

Sometimes the items are top quality and after a trip to the dry cleaners will be as good as new—at a cost of just pennies on the dollar. Unfortunately, some so-called "salvage" stores are only outlets for inferior goods. So be careful about what you buy.

Garage sales and flea markets. If you have the time, garage sales can be great places to find clothing "treasures." Sometimes you'll find exactly what you need. Other times, nothing turns up for weeks. We've purchased great items for literally pennies, but we've also seen clothing priced way too high. Again, know what you are buying and what it's worth to you. Sometimes you can bargain with the seller. Make an offer that is lower than the asking price but not so low that he or she will become disgusted with you.

Don't race to see how many garage sales you can get to in a half an hour. Have fun. Resist the impulse to make this activity a schedule contest.

It also helps to become familiar with your clothing requirements—and those of your family members. If you need a certain length of pants or a certain color skirt, don't settle for anything else. Carry a tape measure so you can measure garments to see if they will fit.

Second-hand/thrift stores. These stores can be found almost anywhere. They include consignment shops, charity thrift stores, and privately owned thrift stores. They generally offer used clothing, although they sometimes carry brand-new clothing, too. You can save lots of money if you shop in them regularly and know your merchandise. Look in your local telephone directory to find the second-hand/thrift stores near you, and plan a trip to visit several of them to see which ones appeal to you.

Second-hand/thrift stores are worth covering in more depth. Why? We and others we've known have saved hundreds of dollars on clothing by shopping at thrift and consignment stores. It can be a fun way to buy items for yourself or your family at a low cost. We have purchased numerous pairs of jeans ($2 each), several down jackets ($3-$5 each), a girl's swimsuit ($3), shoes ($2), winter overpants ($5), and snowsuits ($4).

Some tips to keep in mind:

✔ Dress appropriately but not in expensive clothing. If there's room to bargain, you'll lose if you look like a million dollars.

⤸ Don't put up with hard sell. If a salesperson consistently bothers you, shop elsewhere. (Usually there are too few salespersons, so this isn't a common problem.)

⤸ Bargain. Mention the weakness(es) of the article of clothing and why you think it should be priced lower. Say what you think the clothing is worth to you and expect a counter-offer. In some stores, though, price is not negotiable.

⤸ Become familiar with each store's strengths and weaknesses. Perhaps at one store nothing you like ever turns up except in the shoes or winter coats.

⤸ Go to garage sales and consignment clothing shops in exclusive neighborhoods. Get there as soon as they open. Not long ago Stephen found a great pair of shoes for Caitlin, our daughter, for two dollars. Only buy clothing that looks nearly brand new, fits well, and has parts that operate well.

⤸ Learn when special sales are held. Some stores have discounts on particular items on certain days of the week.

⤸ During the summer, wear shorts so you can try on pants. Many thrift stores do not have changing rooms.

⤸ Again, bring your own tape measure to double-check sizes.

⤸ Become familiar with which brands of clothing tend to fit you. Certain jeans have more room in the legs, and so on.

⤸ Be patient. If an item is nearly right but isn't, don't buy it. Come back the next day or the next week when new items are in stock.

⤸ Learn which alterations you can do yourself and which ones you can afford to have others do. Don't buy anything that needs alteration or repair unless you are sure you can fix the problem and enjoy wearing the garment.

⤸ Learn to scan the racks quickly.

⤸ Check wear areas carefully. Pay particular attention to the knees and seats of pants, the elbows of shirts and sweaters, (and zippers and buttons on children's clothing).

⤸ Test all buttons and zippers to make sure they work. If you don't have time to fix the problem, don't buy clothing that needs repair.

⤸ Check for stains and holes.

OTHER TIPS FOR SUCCESSFUL BARGAIN SHOPPING

- Shop when the weather is bad and the stores aren't moving merchandise. Owners may be more willing to bargain.
- Try buying several pairs of same-color socks so that if one gets a hole in it or is lost in the laundry vortex, you can substitute another one in its place.
- Generally avoid designer labels unless they're on sale or in a thrift store. They typically cost more than clothing of comparable quality, and the style may become dated quickly (although some designer wear will stand the test of style and time).
- Stock up on everyday clothing items such as socks, underwear, or nylon stockings when they're on sale.

Don't Forget Your Feet

BUYING SHOES

- Buy comfortable shoes that will complement the colors you most often wear. Make sure the shoes you buy give your feet, ankles, and legs proper support. The only thing worse than having shoes sit in your closet is having to wear shoes that don't fit properly.
- Watch for shoes sales. If you have an unusual size, you may find shoes in your size discounted frequently. Or you may not find them at all.
- Choose medium- or dark-colored shoes when you can. They don't show dirt as much as lighter colors do.
- Buy practical, conservative shoes that will stand the test of time. Trends come and go, but traditional styles last.
- Try to buy shoes that can be resoled and reheeled.
- Always try on shoes before you buy them, and walk a few steps. The way a shoe fits depends a lot on workmanship and style, not just size.
- If a pair of almost-new shoes in a thrift shop fits, buy it! Stephen purchased a nearly new pair of name-brand leather shoes for twelve dollars that normally sell for nearly ninety dollars. In case the previous owner had a communicable foot disease, spray each shoe with a fungicide before wearing it.

- Try to avoid shoes that don't allow perspiration to evaporate. Stephen bought a pair of shoes for two dollars once, but they were made of a plastic-type material. So he took the new heels off and threw away the shoes. A good lesson learned—and fortunately the lesson was cheap.
- If you're a woman who likes to match your shoes and handbag, you might consider spending more money on the shoes where quality and comfort make a big difference and spending less on your handbag purchase.

CARING FOR SHOES

- Keep leather shoes clean. If they get wet, don't put them directly next to a source of heat to dry. The leather will stiffen and may crack. Fill damp shoes or boots with newspaper and let them dry out slowly.
- Oil leather boots enough to keep them pliable but not enough to soften the leather. We use a product that lubricates and waterproofs the boots without making the leather too soft.
- Baking soda placed inside shoes will absorb moisture and odors.
- Evaluate the cost of having shoes fixed instead of buying new ones. Stephen has had one expensive pair of shoes resoled and reheeled several times for much less than he would have paid for new shoes. If you choose to go this route, don't let your shoes become too worn out before having them repaired.
- Wear boots or overboots when it's wet outside in order to protect your shoes.
- Change your shoes as requirements change. It's better to wear old shoes when cleaning or working in the garage, for instance, than to wear nice shoes from the office that will become scuffed or muddy.

Sew If You Can Afford to and Will Enjoy It

Men and women who know how to sew well can make beautiful clothing and often save money. But sewing our own clothing isn't the right option for many of us. How do you know if you should be sewing more and shopping less?

- First, are you good at sewing? How do your clothes look when you put them on? Are your seams straight and even? Do your finished garments hang right? Do you have the knowledge and dedication to do the pressing, facings, and other extras that make a garment look perfect?

✔ Do you enjoy sewing, or is it a chore?

✔ Can you make clothing for less than similar clothing will cost you on sale? (Be sure to add up what the pattern, material, zipper, buttons, elastic, hooks, thread, trim, and so on will cost.)

✔ Do you know anyone who can help you with the fitting?

✔ Do you find it difficult to find quality clothing that's right for you at fair prices? If the answer is yes, sewing may be an alternative.

✔ Do you have time to sew? For many, time is precious, and in some areas of the country quality clothing is available at prices less than what you would pay for the materials to make it.

Should you sew your own clothes? It depends. If you can buy the clothes you need for less than you can make them, then making your own clothes won't help you save money. But if you love to sew, don't stop doing it just because you might be able to buy some of your clothes for less.

Money-Saving Tips for Children's Clothing

Trees grow, weeds grow, and kids grow even faster than weeds. For that reason, buying clothes for children is an ongoing challenge.

- Be adventurous. Buy children's clothing that's a little too large because young children outgrow clothing so quickly. We've done that for Caitlin (except for shoes), and she has received much more wear out of her clothing. Just make sure clothing isn't so large that it creates a hazard, such as pants that are too long and could cause a child to trip.

- Choose basic styles of children's clothing whenever possible and you'll get by for less without sacrificing quality and style. Plus, nobody will point to your kid and say, "Ugh, that was 'in' four years ago."

- Shop discount and thrift stores regularly. One woman we know cruises such stores during her lunch hour.

- Buy next winter's coat in the spring when stores gets rid of this year's version.

- Network with your friends, relatives, and folks at church. You'll be amazed how often you'll end up giving and receiving bags of fine, used clothing.

- Be wary of tight necks and sleeves. Children do lots of bending, reaching, and sitting. Their clothing should be loose enough to allow mobility. (They often refuse to wear shirts that are difficult to slip over their heads.)

- Select clothing that can be altered when your child grows.

- Try on coats and snowsuits when the child is wearing clothing similar to what he or she will wear under those garments.

- Again, be sure all the zippers slide easily.

Remember, part of living smart is enjoying life more. Don't deny yourself a true pleasure just to save a few dollars. There are many other ways to spend less and have fun doing it.

8

Saving Money on Food

It seems that no matter what the condition of the economy is, food prices always escalate. Prices on certain items may drop temporarily, whereas prices on other items may rise quickly. At times when most food prices are following a slow but steady gain, other prices skyrocket for no apparent reason. No matter what food prices are doing at any given time, there are ways to get the best for your dollar in a supermarket. As in all shopping, advance planning is the key to spending less.

Know What You Are Buying

Buying, preparing, and eating the right foods—those that provide good nourishment with a satisfying flavor—are far more important than simply knowing how to buy food inexpensively. So if you are not familiar with basic nutrition needs and which combinations of foods make up a balanced meal, it's time to learn. Without that essential knowledge, you may work hard to get the best prices on the foods you buy without receiving the highest nutritional value for your dollar.

By learning more about nutrition, you can eat better and save money at the same time.

There are many possible sources of help for learning nutrition essentials: your family doctor, county or city health department, county extension service, local state community college or university, community adult education department, community education programs offered by a local hospital, local public library, or the U.S. Government Printing Office. By learning more about nutrition, you can eat better and save money at the same time.

READ LABELS

When you buy any kind of processed or prepared foods, know what you are buying. Prepared foods include cereals, canned goods, frozen food, ready-to-eat foods—anything you don't buy in its natural, raw state. The labels on most prepared foods reveal the ingredients and nutritional information. They list such ingredients as salt, sugar, calories per serving, additives and preservatives (but perhaps not under the names that you are used to hearing), net weight, percentage of fat, and so on. Usually ingredients are listed in descending order—the first ingredient is the predominant one, the last ingredient makes up the smallest portion of the product.[1]

Read labels carefully. Manufacturers are masters at making you think you're getting one type of product when in fact you're getting another. Sugar, for instance, can be identified by any of the following names: dextrose, glucose, maltose, lactose, syrup, corn syrup solids, brown sugar, molasses, fructose, honey, and sucrose. Upon examining the fine print, you may discover that a brand of cereal that is touted as "healthy" contains just as much sugar as the advertised sweetened cereals.

Don't be fooled. If water and sugar are the first two ingredients of your favorite fruit juice, you are really buying water and sugar. You may want to find another brand that gives you more real fruit juice.

Don't pay for ingredients you don't need or want. A friend who was staying with us bought some "sugar-frosted" cereal that cost more because of the sugar, which we didn't want anyway.

Learn all the names of any food additives that you want to avoid so you can make informed decisions about the prepared foods you buy. This is particularly important if members of your household have health conditions that require abstinence from certain substances. Your family doctor, local health department, or county extension service should be able to provide you with the various names.

BUY EARLY IN THE FOOD-PROCESSING CHAIN

You can avoid the uncertainty of prepared food labeling if you buy minimally processed foods. What kinds of products classify as "minimally processed"? Fresh fruit and vegetables, fresh meat and fish (but not smoked products), eggs, minimally processed dairy products (excluding ice cream, some cheeses, and yogurts), dried beans, dried and ground grains, and some dried fruit. Generally speaking, not enough has been done or added to those foods to warrant special labeling. When you prepare them at home, you have complete control of what goes into them, so you know exactly what you're eating.

Buying minimally processed foods often, although not always, enables you to eat better and spend less. But it also takes more time to prepare such foods, and given today's lifestyles that simply may not be practical for you. Convenience, appealing taste and texture, and quick preparation time regulate most people's food purchases. That's why supermarket shelves are filled with all kinds of convenient, prepared foods—from fruit juices to potato chips to microwavable french fries to canned peas.

We are not making a judgment against prepared and convenience foods, but we are encouraging you to know what you're buying. Why? Because the main reason for buying food is to provide nourishment. Although that fact should be obvious, it is easy to overlook when you're faced with the overwhelming, tough-sell marketing that confronts you the minute you step inside a supermarket. The sheer volume of the visual presentation of food is designed to convince you that potato chips and popcorn are more of a necessity than milk and eggs. Most supermarkets devote more space to junk food than to dairy products. More space is devoted to frozen sweets—everything from ice cream to Dove® bars to individual diet cheesecakes—than to fruit. And soda pop probably takes up twenty times as much space as dried beans.

We can't emphasize enough that nourishing foods should make up the bulk of your food shopping. Appealing, prepared foods should be the exception rather than the rule. If saving money is your goal, you must know what you're buying and determine ahead of time to buy according to nutrition first, and convenience second.

Comparison Shop for the Best Buys

We can purchase foods in many different types of stores: supermarkets, fresh "open" markets, warehouse stores, buying clubs, outlet thrift stores, and specialty stores. Each one offers unique benefits to the thrifty shopper. To make the most of your food-buying dollars, you must visit them to compare prices, selection, and quality.

DO A COMPARISON SURVEY

Comparison shopping is something you must do yourself. You must visit each store personally so that you make your comparisons according to your own needs and draw conclusions according to your own criteria. Your neighbor, your best friend—even your mother—cannot do this job for you. Why? Because no two people eat or buy food in exactly the same way.

For instance, we have three major supermarket chains in our area. Most people think that chain "A" has the best prices. A few would say that chain "C" has the best prices. Through research, however, we discovered that chain "B" has the best prices and quality for the foods we buy. How can there be such a discrepancy? Because not everyone buys the same things. Our research has shown that store "A" has the best prices on baked goods and frozen foods. Store "C" has the least expensive loss leaders and the best prices on fresh fish. Store "B" has the best prices on produce, meats, and quality frozen vegetables and dairy products—the kinds of foods we buy in greatest quantity from supermarkets.

If you have more than one option for the bulk of your food purchases, you would be wise to comparison shop. It isn't uncommon to find as much as a 10 to 15 percent difference in price on the same merchandise in different stores. Here's how you can make your own supermarket comparison. It will take time, particularly the first time, but it can help you save a significant amount of money.

1. Make a list of the food items you normally buy. Your list should include dairy products, cereals, baking needs, paper products, meats, produce, frozen foods, juices, crackers and snacks, beverages, soups, canned goods, condiments, cleaning and laundry products—almost everything you buy regularly.

2. Add columns to the right side of your list and write the name of a food store at the top of each column. Make a separate column for each store so you can record the prices of each item on your list in each store.

3. Take your list, a clipboard, and a pencil and visit each store, recording the prices for the items you've listed. If you can take someone with you to help, the job will go faster.

4. As you record prices, make sure you compare the same-size products in each store. You don't want to compare the price of a twenty-ounce jar to a twenty-eight-ounce jar. Also make sure you compare the same brands.

5. If certain items on your list are on sale, write down the sale prices as well as the regular prices of each item. It's helpful to have an idea of what each store considers a "sale" price to be.

6. When you get home, compare the prices you've recorded. Calculate the total price and the savings available in each store overall, as well as the savings for individual categories of products. The difference between your overall savings may be very low, but the differences between certain categories of products may be significant.

7. Determine which store will give you the best savings on the products you buy, and shop there. If you live in an area where several grocery stores are close together, you may choose to shop in all of them, purchasing the lowest-cost products in each.

8. Update your list periodically. The first few times you do it, you may want to update it every six months. If competition between area stores tightens, you may want to compare prices again. After you have done the comparison a few times, you may notice that the changes are so insignificant that you don't need frequent updates.

CONSIDER OTHER SHOPPING OPTIONS

Once you complete your comparison survey, you'll know which supermarket has the best prices for you—no matter what others may claim. The survey also provides basic information from which you can make price comparisons at discount supermarkets, warehouse and buying clubs, and other sources. These additional options can provide excellent savings *if* the products and quantities they offer fit your needs.

Discount supermarkets. We have found that the discount supermarket in our area generally provides a 15 percent savings on most canned goods, and when frozen juices go on sale (which is often) the savings are frequently 30 percent or more. Seasonal loss leaders—ketchup, mustard, and relish in the summer, and baking chocolate, sugar, and canned milk in the fall—can provide even greater savings. Discount supermarkets offer lower-than-supermarket prices and a wide selection but do not require you to purchase large quantities.

Buying and warehouse clubs. Buying and warehouse clubs may offer tremendous savings, too, but there are some drawbacks.

- Most require an annual membership fee. If you won't shop at the store enough to more than pay for the fee, don't join. Before you join, ask for a free pass so you can see what items the store carries and compare prices. We have joined a buying club and have saved many times our twenty-five-dollar fee.

- Compare prices. Some items may be cheaper in a supermarket than in a warehouse store. Take your calculator so you can compare the cost of products ounce for ounce and pound for pound.

- Compare the benefit of price versus quantity. The quantities usually required for a purchase in a buying or warehouse club may be far more than you can use. If food goes bad before you eat it, it's no bargain.

- Compare quality and price as well. We buy some quality products from our buying club that we don't buy at a supermarket because the supermarket price is too high. For example, a pound of Danish ham at our local supermarkets generally runs $4.98; the same ham at our buying club costs $5.16 for two pounds (two one-pound packages). We won't pay the supermarket price, but the buying club price is reasonable enough for us to buy it.

This is not a direct savings because it is possible to find a cheaper substitute for sandwich filling. However, the buying club enables us to buy a higher quality or more desirable product than we could otherwise afford. That's smart shopping, too. (Just be careful that you don't overspend by purchasing too many high quality "goodies.")

Restaurant supply houses. Savings on some food items can be found at restaurant supply houses. Again, compare quality, price, and quantity before you buy. Sometimes you come out ahead when you buy in quantity; sometimes you don't. For example, we buy tomato sauce in number ten cans. (When Amanda makes spaghetti sauce, she makes ten quarts at a time and freezes it for future "fast" food.)

Restaurant supply houses may offer time- and money-saving products you can't find anywhere else. One of our favorites is a cheddar cheese sauce mix (dry) that we can use as needed as a base for scalloped or au gratin potatoes, a sauce for vegetables, or an addition to cream soups.

Home shopping plans. These are frequently sold as freezer plans. Someone calls you on the phone or comes to your home and offers to sell you a list of food for a set price. The list may include meats, prepared foods, frozen juice, and frozen vegetables. In order to know if these are a money-saving option, total the prices of like quantities of comparable items from your price comparison survey. That will tell you what the "normal" price is for each item. If the plan costs less, then consider it but be aware of these drawbacks:

- You don't know what the quality of the products will be. Find out what satisfaction guarantees the company offers and ask your local Better Business Bureau if anyone has lodged a complaint against the company.

- If the products offered through the plan frequently go on sale and you generally buy them for less than the "normal" price listed on your comparison survey, you may not save much money even if the plan prices are a bit lower than "normal."

- When you buy a freezer plan, you no longer control your choices; someone else makes them for you. If the plan includes items you normally don't buy, your savings may be far less than you think.

Co-ops. The idea behind co-ops is to pool resources, buy in bulk, and provide food to members for less. Sometimes a cooperative buying effort saves you money; other times it doesn't.

For example, the money you save is dependent on the wisdom of the shopper. You'll benefit from the choices made by shoppers who make good buying decisions, but you will pay the price of choices made by unwise shoppers.

In some cooperative buying efforts, everyone buys what the group buys. Unless you control what you can buy from the co-op, you lose control of your shopping choices.

We have participated in the SHARE program in which you donate several hours of community service, pay a specified amount of money, and receive a box of groceries. Although the savings on the box of food was substantially less than the "normal" prices of those items, 30 to 40 percent of it was high-priced food we normally would not buy. After a few tries, Amanda concluded that she could save more money by making her own choices.

Save Money Every Time You Shop

Once you find out where you can generally buy the foods you eat at the best prices, you can do more to stretch your dollar each time you shop.

LEARN MORE ABOUT THE FOODS YOU BUY

Talk with the people who work in your supermarket. When people spend their workdays preparing and stocking food items, they learn about them. Their knowledge can save you money, and they are usually more than happy to share their best tips. For instance, talk with the butcher. Find out which cuts of meat are more tender, flavorful, or nutritious than others.

Learn how to choose the best quality fruit and vegetables. Ask the produce manager which varieties of available foods will best meet your needs. Do you know which tomatoes are best for slicing, which will be tastier in salads, and which will make the richest sauce? Do you know which varieties of apples are best for fruit salads, which ones make the best applesauce, and which don't overcook in pies? A good produce manager will know such facts and more that may help you get more value from your food dollar.

CONTINUE TO COMPARISON SHOP

Compare generic brands, house brands, and name brands. Different brands of food vary in appearance, taste, and, to a lesser extent, nutritional value. Depending on your particular needs, a low-cost generic brand may serve your purposes well. Or, you may want to stick with a name brand if consistent quality over time is important to you or if the appearance of a particular food is significant.

If generic or house brands are available, try them. If they work for you as well as the name brands, enjoy the savings. You won't know what works until you experiment a bit. Then if you find that the quality of the generic products you try isn't satisfactory and that the savings is insignificant, stick with brands you prefer. You may be better off buying generic paper or cleaning products than foods.

We buy house brand cold cereals instead of popular name brand cereals. The variety of options is limited, but the taste is only slightly different and the nutritional value is the same. We save between 40 and 52 percent on a product that has become quite expensive. Savings like that more than make up for the difference in quality.

There is a lot of talk about how you can save money by using coupons. It's true that coupons can save you money. However, most coupons are for prepared or highly processed convenience foods, which are among the most expensive foods you can buy. Our philosophy is that you will save more money if you shop for the best buys on good food than if you focus your money-saving efforts on extensive coupon shopping.

Compare convenience against cost. Usually convenience foods that have already received some degree of preparation that you could have done at home are more expensive than minimally processed foods. So compare the price of convenience to the cost of foods you could prepare yourself. Consider the following:

✔ You can often buy ten pounds of fresh potatoes for the price of one and one-half pounds of frozen fried potatoes.

✔ Frozen dinners cost much more than comparable ones you could prepare, and you seldom get as much food.

✔ Ready-to-cook oatmeal costs much less than premeasured and preseasoned packets of instant oatmeal.

✔ Frozen vegetables cost much less in bulk bags than those packaged in individual boiling pouches.

✔ Individually wrapped items such as cheese slices cost much more than a block of the same cheese that you cut or grate yourself.

✔ Although kids love them, single-serving containers of yogurt, pudding, and fruit are very expensive—sometimes five times as much as the normal packaged variety. If these sizes are convenient for you or help your kids eat good foods they wouldn't normally eat, purchase similar-sized plastic containers and fill them from the larger containers.

✔ Microwave popcorn is another budget buster. It is much cheaper to buy bulk popcorn and pop it according to the method you prefer.

✔ Be aware of the exceptions to the general rule, however. Concentrated juices and certain canned or frozen vegetables are often cheaper in their prepared states than in their raw, unprocessed states.

Compare packaging and pricing. Many stores have unit pricing. That is, they list the total cost of each item and the cost according to a common measurement—per ounce, per pound, square feet (for paper towels), and per item (for vitamins, tablets). To find the best buys, compare the unit price of each item.

Meat is expensive. If you can make a dent in your meat costs, you can make a dent in your food bill.

Beware, however, of inconsistencies in unit pricing. Different sizes of the same product may not be unit priced in the same manner. The small size may list a per-ounce unit price, whereas the large size lists a per-pound unit price. The solution? Take your calculator along and recalculate the unit prices according to the same unit.

In addition, remember these points regarding packaging:

- Not all large sizes are more economical than smaller sizes. In fact, some "economy" sizes are more expensive than standard sizes. Check the unit prices to determine which sizes are the better buys.

- The size of a package is less important than how much is inside. Compare the weights and volume of similar products. Sometimes there is a significant difference.

- Weight can be misleading for liquid-packed foods. It's difficult to tell just how much food is actually in a can. Generally speaking, smaller fruits and vegetables (beans corn, peas) fill a can more densely than larger fruits and vegetables (peaches, pears, asparagus spears). Some manufacturers now list total weight as well as the food weight on their labels.

- Consider carefully how many portions a given package will provide. Stephen used to buy cheap hamburger that had lots of fat in it. When he cooked it, however, he ended up with what seemed like half of what he started with.

- Don't buy according to the number of portions suggested, although that may be helpful in making comparisons between similar products (if the portions are the same size). Remember, a portion size is a relative term. An average teenager may eat two or more "portions" in one sitting.

Save money on the meat you buy. In general, meat is expensive. If you can make a dent in your meat costs, you can make a dent in your food bill. Here are some ways to do it.

- Don't assume that the least expensive form of ground beef is the best buy. Compare the price of lean beef versus regular beef. Also, look for alternative sources. For example, premium ground beef (20 percent fat) in our area costs $1.58 to $1.87 a pound. However, even leaner round steak often goes on sale for $1.49 a pound. So we buy round steak on sale and have it ground up (a free service at most stores). The end result is high quality ground beef for a reasonable price. We don't buy regular ground round because that is $2.29 to $2.59 a pound.

- Buy whole chickens instead of cut-up ones.

- Buy meat that has a lower percentage of bone.

- Buy a whole ham, and ask the butcher to cut it up for you.

- Buy whole turkeys when they are on sale and freeze them. The larger ones give you more meat for the dollar.
- If you live near the ocean, go to an open market where you can buy fish, crabs, and lobsters as they come off the boats. Be sure to know the deals, though, since some open-market items can cost more than supermarket items.
- Compare the costs of processed meats (bacon, bologna, and so on) with other meats. Processed meats are relatively expensive and contain preservatives and additives.

BUY AT A LOWER PRICE WHENEVER POSSIBLE

One great thing about food prices is that they are always subject to change, and sometimes that change is in your favor. If you learn how to take advantage of price changes, you can make big cuts in your food bill.

Stock up during sales.

- Read the weekly supermarket advertisements in local newspapers, and make your choices accordingly. (When chicken goes on sale, quess what we eat that week.)
- Remember that not every item in a sales flyer is sale priced; some prices may be "everyday low prices."
- Especially watch for "loss leaders" that you'd normally buy anyway, which are often featured in newspaper ads. Stores sell those items to you at or below their cost to attract you into the stores. We often go "cherry picking" during these sales.
- Be willing to plan your menus according to the foods that are on sale. If bananas are on sale and apples are high, pack a banana in your lunch instead of the usual apple.
- Know which staples you use regularly, and stock up when they are on sale. (An extra freezer can really help here, but you don't have to have one to save plenty of money.) When our favorite breakfast cereal was on sale for 30 percent off the usual price, we bought ten boxes. When frozen juice is half price, we buy as much as we will use in a reasonable amount of time.
- Know when a bargain isn't a bargain. No matter how well priced a sale item may be, evaluate how much money and time you'll spend

getting to the store to buy it. If you'll only save a dollar, think twice about your trip.

✔ No matter how good the sale price is, don't buy it if you or your family won't eat it.

✔ Don't be so "brand loyal" that you won't switch to something else that goes on sale and will provide comparable quality.

✔ If the sale item(s) is sold out, ask the store manager or manager of that department to give you a "rain check" that will enable you to buy the item(s) at the sale price when it is restocked.

Watch weather patterns in key growing areas. When frost hits major growing areas, such as California and Florida, crops may be damaged and prices will go up. Keep an eye on the media. If you can stock up on a food you use before the damage pushes prices way up, you'll save. (But hoarding is not the objective here.)

Watch for discounted foods. Watch for dated foods that are about to expire and carefully consider the reduced-price foods. Meats, dairy foods, and produce are commonly marked down that way. Sometimes we end up getting items for about half price. Look for markdowns in all the stores in which you shop. Some stores have significantly better markdowns than others.

Look for packages that have coupon and refund offers. Even in the same bin or area, not all the packages may be the same. Some of the packages may have coupons attached that you can use to purchase that item.

SHOP WITH SAVINGS IN MIND

No matter how much research you do, you may still make mistakes once you're inside a grocery store. So be on your guard and don't fall prey to marketing gimmicks. Merchandisers use sophisticated techniques to entice you to buy impulsively. For instance, they put related items together, such as ice cream and ice cream topping. They use banners and displays at the end of aisles and put high-priced items at eye or hand level. The following tips will help you minimize the most common shopping mistakes that cost you money.

• Once you have purchased everything on your list, leave.

- Resist the temptation to buy nonfood and nongrocery items at the supermarket. These items often have higher markups and probably can be purchased for less in a discount store. (Supermarkets use these items to improve their profit margins.)

- When you "taste test" an item in the store, don't feel obligated to buy what the salesperson is selling.

- Keep an eye on the lower and higher shelves. Often supermarkets put higher-priced merchandise at eye level.

- When you go in to buy a sale-priced item that is located near expensive foods, come home with nothing more than the item you went in to buy.

- Don't buy impulse items you first see when you enter the store or items at the ends of aisles that look as if they are on sale but often aren't.

- Notice pricing strategies. Are you tempted to buy "four for a dollar" instead of just one item for twenty-five cents?

- Plan your meals ahead of time. That way you'll know what you need to buy and save time and money by not having to return to the store to buy items you forgot.

- Don't shop under pressure. If your stomach is growling or you only have a few minutes to buy a week's worth of groceries, go shopping another time. You'll be able to buy more efficiently, plan better, and avoid mistakes. You shouldn't shop when you're exhausted or when the store is packed (as it is at 5:00 p.m. the day before Thanksgiving).

- Shop alone when you can. It's amazing how much a child, teenager, or spouse can add to a grocery cart!

  Guard against impulse and convenience traps.

- If you're willing to cut a ham thinly or carve the cheese to make your sandwiches, you can save a lot of money. Convenience usually costs! When you can, ask the butcher to slice up the meat you buy for sandwiches. In our area, they do it for free.

- Control how many soft drinks you buy. Soft drinks are expensive and aren't nutritious, so drink "sun tea" or other fluids when you can. If soft drinks are a requirement, however, try generic brands and buy them in the sizes that are cheapest per ounce as long as you'll use them before they lose their fizz.

- Control the number of cakes, cookies, and other goodies that you buy. They are not healthy or inexpensive, and can add many dollars to a food bill.

- Shrimp, lean steak, exotic fruits, and other expensive foods can be almost habit forming. Watch how often you eat them, or your budget will suffer. Eight dollars a week adds up to $416 a year.

Buy "family" quantities. Sometimes the price per pound is reduced if you purchase a set size of food. For instance, meat is often cheaper when purchased in a larger size. We sometimes buy larger sizes, use what we need, and repackage, freeze, or put the remaining food into a canister. If you do that, make sure the food doesn't go to waste or that you don't eat more than you normally would just because you have more.

Don't let down your guard until you're out of the store.

- As you stand in the checkout lane, keep children (and yourself) from picking up the many small items, such as candy, batteries, and magazines, that are waiting for the unwary.
- Watch for pricing mistakes. Sometimes the price the computer reads on an item doesn't reflect the sale price. If you notice this, you may get the item free or at least will get a credit on your bill.
- When a product isn't what it should be, take it back. If the milk sours two days after you get it home or the ham smells bad when you open the package, take it back for a refund or substitution.

Preserve Your Savings

If you do a great job shopping but don't store the food properly, you will lose some of the money you've worked hard to save. First, the food won't last as long or remain as nutritious. Second, you and other members of your family may get sick and have to receive medical treatment.

- Buy frozen and refrigerated foods last, and make sure you choose items that are still frozen or cold. They will stay cold during your trip home and maintain their quality.

- If you live in a warm climate, consider packing a cooler in your trunk to keep foods in good shape during the ride home.

- Frozen foods should remain frozen until use. Thawed foods should be refrigerated around forty degrees Fahrenheit. If you aren't familiar with how long various foods should be stored, contact the U.S. Food and Drug Administration, U.S. Department of Agriculture, your county extension service, or look up books on the subject in your local library.

- Store dry staples such as sugar, rice, flour, and cereals in glass jars or sealed plastic containers to keep bugs out. Grain-based foods, such as flour, may have bugs in them, so freeze them for a week or so before storing them.

- Store canned goods in a cool, dry place, not near heating pipes or furnaces.

- Watch for bulges on cans or rust on seams, and return or throw away cans that look bad. We once brought home several large cans of sauerkraut that apparently weren't perfect. Two months later, one of the cans blew up. Boy, did that apartment stink!

- Use frozen foods that have been partially thawed and then refrozen as soon as possible. If the color or smell is bad when you thaw it again, throw it out.

- Keep fresh vegetables in the refrigerator, and eat them quickly. If you can't eat them fast enough, freeze, can, or dry them while they're still in good condition. Contact the U.S. Department of Agriculture or a local county extension agent for information on preserving fruits and vegetables.

- Keep thawed meats, seafood, and poultry cold. Seafood, especially, should be eaten right away or frozen.

- Keep meats, seafood, and poultry frozen until you need them and then thaw them only as long as necessary so they're ready for cooking.

- Use leftovers wisely. Combine leftovers in microwavable plates at the end of the meal, or store leftover vegetables in the freezer until you have enough for soup. By using bits of leftovers, you can make the food you buy stretch for more meals than you had planned.

By becoming a thrifty food buyer and making the best use of the food you buy, you can make a bigger difference in your food expenses than you may think!

SAVING MONEY
ON HOW YOU TRAVEL

9

Caring for a Car (Including Pickup Trucks, Vans, and So On)

There's no doubt about it: cars are expensive. They require gas, oil, tires, and regular maintenance. They also break down and may require expensive repairs. Drivers have to pay for insurance, taxes, license fees, and sometimes parking fees. And many people purchase cars on credit and pay finance charges every month to pay for their cars.

So it is important to buy the best (not necessarily newest) car you can afford and to care for it properly so it will last. When we use the term "best," we mean one that runs well. The advertising slogan that says a car "is your freedom" isn't true. A car is just a car. It has nothing to do with your freedom—unless it doesn't run.

In this chapter, we'll show you how to reduce the expense of owning and operating a car. Maintaining your car the best you can—whether it's one week or ten years old—will help keep it from wearing out and may prevent an accident that could cost you thousands. Maintenance is especially important these days because the average age of an automobile (7.8 years) is higher now than it has been since World War II.[1]

Reduce the Cost of Maintaining Your Car

Obviously the best way to cut automobile-related expenses is to avoid owning a car. If you are fortunate enough to live near efficient public transportation, perhaps you don't even need a car. Perhaps you can ride a bicycle to work; we know an architect in Boston who does that. But if you can't get along without a car, maintaining it properly can save you lots of money.

Although most of us use automobiles quite often, we easily overlook their basic maintenance. We may keep the rugs in our homes clean, wash the dishes, and dust the furniture, but we forget to check the air pressure in our tires, change the oil and air filters, or do other basic auto maintenance. Yet the benefits of regular auto maintenance can save far more money than many other things we do. The financial benefits of regular maintenance include: savings on fuel economy, increased safety, higher resale value, lower repair bills, fewer expenses and headaches caused by mechanical breakdowns, and a vehicle that will last longer and pollute the air less.

YOUR BASIC MAINTENANCE OPTIONS

We all have a few basic options in caring for our cars. We can: (1) learn when and how to do basic auto maintenance; (2) learn which maintenance is required when and either pay someone or ask a friend to do it; (3) choose to know little or nothing about auto maintenance and trust a repair shop or friend to do the work.

"Many people would avoid car problems if they'd only become familiar with the owner's manual."

Today our 1983 Honda Accord has 162,000 miles on it, and our four-wheel-drive Scout (a necessity in our area during the winter) has

186,000 miles. They still run well, but through the years we have learned much about maintenance through ownership of not-so-new vehicles such as these.

The following proven tips will help you save money on the maintenance of your gasoline-driven vehicle. Some maintenance tasks are quite simple and require no tools. Others require basic tools and, if you are not inclined toward mechanical things, assistance from a reputable auto mechanic. Regardless of which ones you choose to do yourself, become familiar with them all so you can get the most efficient and safe use from your vehicle while spending the least amount of money on it.

If you have a diesel or air-cooled vehicle, not all of the following tips will apply. Check with your mechanic to see which maintenance tips you should follow. And no matter what kind of vehicle you drive, don't do any mechanical work unless you know the requirements of your vehicle and can do the work properly and safely.

EASY, DO-IT-YOURSELF MAINTENANCE

Before you start, it is vital that you practice safety procedures when working on your car. These include: not smoking when you work on your car, being careful of hot engine parts, tying back long hair so it won't get caught in moving parts, jacking up the car properly, and using the appropriate tools carefully so you don't injure yourself.

Be very careful when you jack up the car. If the car will be kept up for a while, use rated jack stands instead of a jack to hold the car up. *Never go under a car that is only supported by a jack.* The jack could fail and let the car down suddenly, seriously injuring or even killing you. Be sure the car's emergency brake is on, that the car is level, and that you have blocked the wheels so the car can't roll.

The second most important maintenance procedure is to read the owner's manual for your car. (If you don't have one, try to order one.)

As one mechanic told me, "Many people would avoid car problems if they'd only become familiar with the owner's manual."

Now let's look at the specific ways in which you can care for your car.

Care for your tires. To achieve maximum longevity from your tires, buy a pressure gauge and check the air pressure regularly. It's best to check the tires before you start driving because if you check them after you've driven more than a mile, the pressure will be up a few pounds.

Heat and cold influence tire pressure, too. For every ten-degree (Fahrenheit) drop in temperature, tire pressure will drop one pound per square inch. Hot weather can cause a tire to lose several pounds per square inch per month.[2]

✔ Keep the tires inflated to the proper level. Tires with low pressure create more friction, which lowers gas mileage, increases outer tread wear, and increases the chance of dangerous tire failure. Tires that are too highly inflated, on the other hand, wear out more quickly on the middle of the treads. Plus, the wrong tire pressure may cause your car to handle unsafely and possibly lead to serious injury or death. Check with your tire supplier or read your owner's manual to learn the right pressure for your tires under your driving conditions.

✔ Drive in a controlled way. Driving around corners too fast, accelerating quickly, and stopping quickly will cause your tires to wear out faster.

✔ Replace a worn tire. If a tire's tread gets down to one-sixteenth of an inch, replace it. Insufficient tire tread is unsafe and will reduce your car's gas mileage.

✔ Monitor tire alignment. If your front tires start wearing more on one side than another, if they develop bald spots in the tread, or if the car doesn't steer well, have the alignment checked and adjusted if needed. Call several shops first to obtain estimates. (Caution: Some old cars with older front-end parts won't quite align properly. If things aren't perfect but the car handles well and the tires aren't wearing badly, don't worry. Don't let a repair shop sell you parts you don't need.)

✔ Rotate tires periodically to gain the best tread life. If you do this yourself, check with a tire dealer first to determine the best tire rotation system for your tires.

Also, learn how much you should tighten the lug nuts. If they are not tightened enough, damage could occur—your wheel could even fall off! If you tighten a lug nut too much, it could snap off or distort the brake rotors or drums.

Some tire stores include free, periodic tire rotation and inspections as part of the sale price of their tires. That can be a great deal, but be cautious. Some stores use "free" tire rotation as a way to drum up business. Get a second opinion before having a tire shop do any repair work they discover while rotating your tires.

Keep an eye on the shock absorbers or struts. Test the shock absorbers or struts on your car by pushing down hard on each front and back fender. The car should stop bouncing immediately when you stop pushing down on it. If the car bounces up and down several more times, you probably need new shocks or struts. Also look at each shock or strut to see if it is leaking oil. That's another sign that it's worn-out. Driving with bad struts or shocks is unsafe and will cause your car to handle poorly, decrease your car's stability, and increase tire wear.

Check the oil regularly and add it as needed. Oil, the lifeblood of an engine, keeps parts lubricated so they don't wear out as quickly.

To check the oil level if the engine is cold, park the car on level ground. Then pull out the dipstick, wipe it off with a cloth or paper towel, and reinsert and recheck it to get a good oil level reading. If you don't know where the dipstick is, ask someone to show you or look in the owner's manual. If you just turned off the engine, wait a few minutes before checking the dipstick so the oil can flow back to its normal level in the crankcase.

Put the appropriate quality oil into the engine. Use the right weight and brand of oil. Oil is rated by how it responds at different temperatures—its viscosity—and it isn't all the same. When it's minus twenty degrees Fahrenheit, an oil that's too thick may prevent your car from starting. If the weather is one hundred degrees Fahrenheit, a different level of protection is needed. Check the owner's manual or ask a trustworthy mechanic which oil is best for your particular engine. Don't mix viscosities.

The first numbers on the oil container (10W40, for instance) show the oil's performance characteristics. The number before the "W" shows the oil's low-temperature (winter) performance characteristics; the number after the "W" shows it high-temperature characteristics. If the oil only has one number, it is a single grade; if the oil has two or more numbers, it is a multigrade. So, a 10W40 oil has the performance characteristics of a 10W oil when the engine is cold and that of a 40W oil when the engine is warm. We use 10W40 oil in our cars because it is good for all kinds of weather. But if you have a turbo engine, you may need a 20W50 oil when it's hot and a 10W30 when it's cold. And if you live in a very cold area, your engine may need a 5W30 oil.

The oil label should also read, "Exceeds car manufacturers warranty requirements." That means that it will protect your engine. On the oil container, you will see letters such as SC, SD, CC, CB, CA, and/or SE. If the "S" is first, that indicates that the oil meets or exceeds established standards for use in gasoline engines ("SE" is the highest rating); if a "C" is first, the oil will work in diesel and commercial engines.

Shop around for the best price on oil. We buy our oil by the case at discount stores, sometimes in five-quart containers. It's much cheaper than buying it by the quart at a service station, convenience store, or supermarket.

Don't overfill the engine with oil, but don't let it get too low, either. (An easy way to put oil into the engine without making a mess is to make a funnel by cutting the bottom off a clean, tall, plastic bottle such as a one- or two-liter pop bottle.) Unless you know exactly how much oil to add, pour it in gradually and keep checking the dipstick until you reach the desired level.

Change the oil and oil filter regularly. Oil lubricates moving parts, reduces noise, fights rust and corrosion, acts as a seal for the pistons and rings, and carries bad substances to the oil filter for removal. But oil gets dirty and breaks down after a while. Engine combustion creates dirty residue. Friction in the engine causes small particles of metal to come loose, and the air entering the engine contains dirt.

Keep the battery terminals clean. . . .
You'll be less likely to be stranded somewhere
—an event that almost always costs money.

By putting clean oil into the engine regularly, you can remove dirt particles before they damage the delicate insides of the engine. We change the oil and filter about every 2,500 miles. (Conventional wisdom says to do it every 3,00 to 5,000 miles.)

After someone shows you how to change the oil and filter the first time, you can probably do it yourself. It costs about ten dollars for a filter and enough oil to refill the crankcase and takes about forty-five minutes until you get faster at doing it.

Pour the dirty oil into a leak-proof container and take it to a gas station that will add it to a used-oil tank. You may have to pay for that service, since oil is now considered "hazardous waste" and the stations may have to pay to dispose of the oil properly. (Although many people commonly put used oil into the trash, that is not advisable because just one gallon of oil that leaks into the earth at a landfill can taint the water supply of nearby residents.)

If you are not mechanically inclined, don't have any tools, or have no place to dispose of the dirty oil, go to a quick-lube place or maintenance shop and let them do it. The key is to change your oil regularly.

Care for your car battery. Keep the battery terminals clean. Your battery will last longer, and you'll be less likely to be stranded somewhere—an event that almost always costs money.

That yellowish/whitish powder—acidic corrosion—reduces the battery's effectiveness, but you can neutralize the corrosion with a mixture of baking soda and water. Be careful! The film and deposits on the outside of the battery are corrosive, so don't get them on your hands, in your eyes, on the garage floor, or on your clothes. Battery gases are explosive, too, so don't smoke or create sparks by allowing a metal object to touch both battery terminals at the same time.

If the corrosion is bad, wipe off the terminals first with a rag that has a solution of baking soda and water on it and throw the rag away. Use a wrench to take the negative (–) terminal off the battery first and then take the (+) terminal off the battery. Use medium sandpaper to lightly sand the battery posts and inside the ends of both terminals until they are shiny again. If you need to use more baking soda and water, do so in small quantities. It will bubble and sizzle a bit as it neutralizes the acid. Carefully wipe everything dry, put petroleum jelly on each terminal (or anticorrosion rings that you buy at an auto supply store), and put the terminals back on the battery (the positive one first, the negative one last).

Caution: Be sure to put the correct terminal back on the correct post, and tighten the terminals so they make good contact with the battery. If you become confused, ask a knowledgeable friend or professional before rehooking everything.

If your battery isn't sealed up (maintenance free), gently remove the battery lid and make sure all the holes are filled with distilled water or cared for according to the battery instructions. If in doubt, call the store where you bought the battery or a reputable mechanic.

Maintain brakes properly. Check the brakes regularly. Some pads and brake shoes squeal when they are worn out; others don't. (One time ours didn't squeal, which cost us nearly $300 when they finally wore down to the metal.) Some brake shops will check your brakes for free. If you set up an appointment, you may not have to wait as long to have them checked.

Pay attention to unusual braking. If your car pulls to one side or the other, you hear metal noises, or the brake pedal feels "mushy" or pushes way down to the floor, have the brake system checked. Those are classic symptoms of a master cylinder going bad, a leak in the brake line, worn brake parts, or other potentially major problems. By catching the problem(s) early, you can prevent or minimize expensive damage.

Check the brake fluid level in the master cylinder periodically. The master cylinder uses the pressure you put on the brake to multiply the force so that the brakes work. It looks like a little box and is on the driver's side near the firewall. If you don't know where it is, ask a friend to show you.

When you remove the caps on the master cylinder to check the fluid level, be sure no dirt enters the master cylinder. If the level isn't up to the top, add the brake fluid rated DOT (Department Of Transportation) that your brakes require. If the fluid level is more than half an inch from the top, you have a leak somewhere. Track down and repair the leak immediately.

Care for the transmission.

✔ Check the level of transmission fluid and add more if necessary. Do this when the engine is warm and running, the parking brake is on, and the car is either in neutral or park (according to your owner's manual). The transmission fluid dipstick is generally located between the engine and the passenger compartment.

✔ Remove the dipstick, wipe it off with a clean rag, put it back in, and then check the fluid level again. If it's low, add more of the type of fluid your engine requires. You may need a funnel to do this.

✔ Use the proper transmission fluid. If you're not sure which kind of fluid to use, check your owner's manual or ask the dealer or your mechanic.

✔ Don't overfill the transmission; you can damage it. Again, if you have doubts about your ability here, have a mechanic or a friend help you the first time you do this.

✔ Have the transmission serviced periodically. If your car has an automatic transmission, it's a good idea to have a mechanic change the transmission fluid and filter according the service schedule in the owner's manual. If you have a manual transmission, the fluid needs to be replaced periodically.

✔ Watch for danger signals. If there's a leak from the transmission or you hear funny noises as the engine shifts, have a professional inspect the transmission.

Keep fittings and other parts lubricated

Learn which parts need lubrication. If you drive an older vehicle, some fittings probably need to be greased. (The fittings on many newer cars can't be greased; the parts just wear out and have to be replaced.) When we bought the Scout, we asked a mechanic to show us which fittings needed regular lubrication.

Use the appropriate kind of lubricating grease or oil. The Scout needs special gear oil in the transfer case and the differential, for instance, but not all manual transmissions use gear oil. Check your owner's manual or talk with a mechanic if you're not sure about which kind of grease/gear oil to use in which places. There are many different lubricants suited for specific purposes (wheel bearings, transfer case, transmission, and so on), and using the wrong one can be costly.

If you don't feel up to doing your own lubrication, that's OK. It may be more convenient for you to take the car to a quick-lube shop. Also, you may not have confidence in your mechanical ability and indeed could make a costly goof.

Buy the gasoline your car is designed to use. Start with the basic octane needed. If you're not sure which octane rating your engine needs, check the owner's manual or call a dealer who sells cars like yours. Many people think that buying a higher octane gasoline makes a huge difference. It seldom does. Our Honda is rated for eighty-seven octane and runs well on that. So we don't buy a more expensive, higher octane. Nor do we buy a lower octane, which causes the engine to make a rapping sound, or "knock," resulting from uncontrolled combustion in the cylinders.

Go to a higher octane when necessary. Sometimes the engine needs a higher octane. If your engine "knocks," it is being damaged. Sudden acceleration, high altitude, spark timing, and the age of the car can also cause knocking. If knocking occurs, purchase the next higher octane and see how the engine responds.

Try different brands of fuel. If your car is fuel injected or has other special features, you may discover that certain brands of gasoline cause your engine to run better and that others clog up the fuel injectors. Experiment with discount gas (which may come from the same refinery as the name brands) to find out which ones work best in your vehicle. A lower-price brand may work just fine.

Replace the air filter regularly. The air filter catches dust and dirt in the air that's going into the engine. Without the filter, vital engine parts would become clogged with dirt, dust, and residue, which reduces your gas mileage, causing the engine to stall, and possibly leading to expensive repairs.

The air filter is located in the air cleaner housing on top of the engine. Usually you can simply undo a wing nut or a few snap clips to get to the filter. To learn whether the filter needs to be replaced, take it out, tap it lightly on a flat surface, and hold it up to a source of light. If you can't see much light through the filter, replace it with a new one designed for your car.

Buy a filter that has double filters—an "extended life" filter—if you can. It costs a bit more than a standard filter but catches more dirt. (When you put things back together, don't overtighten the wing nut and damage the body of the carburetor.)

Care for the cooling system. Check the coolant level every two months or so when the engine is cool. If your car has a coolant reservoir—a plastic jug-like container with radiator coolant in it—you can check the level without removing the radiator cap.

Use the proper mixture of antifreeze and water. If the radiator needs fluid, add a fifty/fifty mixture of antifreeze and tap water so you don't accidentally reduce the antifreeze protection.

To test the cold protection strength of the antifreeze in the radiator, use an inexpensive tester. Follow the directions on your particular tester. When you test, be careful that you do not drop the tester into the radiator. That happened to us once. Fortunately we were able to fish it out with a pair of meat tongs.

Antifreeze is a poison and is tasty to many pets. If you spill any on the ground, dilute it with water immediately, and dispose of used coolant properly. Pets that lick up coolant can die.

If your engine loses a lot of water from a broken hose or leaky radiator while you're driving and you can only add water to get on the road again, remember to put the right mixture of antifreeze and water back into the radiator as soon as possible. Straight water, mechanics tell us, can destroy aluminum engine parts as well as cause freeze-ups.

Follow safety guidelines. Never put cold water or antifreeze into a hot engine. You can damage the engine because the cold coolant flowing suddenly into the hot passages can crack the engine block. Translation? Lots of money down the tubes. Also, be careful when removing the radiator cap of a hot engine. There is a lot of pressure in there, and if you don't allow the engine to cool down first you could be sprayed with boiling water.

Drain the cooling system periodically. Every year, or according to your car manufacturer's guidelines, drain the cooling system, flush it out, and add new antifreeze. This helps to get rid of any rust and scale that could clog the engine's fluid passages or radiator, and it also lubricates the water pump that circulates the water.

Be careful if you do the flushing yourself. A friend who was "learning" ended up with a fountain of water spouting out of the carburetor! Some cars require certain flushing procedures, so always read the owner's manual or talk with a knowledgeable mechanic before getting in over your head. Mistakes can be very expensive.

Air conditioning: too cold to touch! If your car has air conditioning, a mechanic should maintain it seasonally by charging the system, adjusting the compressor drive belt, and so on. Do not do this yourself. Freon®

can freeze your fingers instantly or blind you. Many people have been seriously injured when they instinctively put a rag over a Freon® leak.

A few minutes of easy maintenance beats standing by the side of the road.

Replace the fuel filter periodically. In most cases, a fuel filter between the fuel pump and the carburetor keeps dirt and dust in the gas tank from entering the engine. (Some cars have fuel filters in other locations, too.) It's best to change this filter every year, or sooner if your car's maintenance requires it. This is especially important during a gas crisis, when gas stations may pump gas right down to the bottoms of their tanks where sediment, rust, and water accumulate. Tip: if you pull into a gas station when a tanker truck is unloading fuel, go to another station. The filling process stirs up the sediment in the tank.

When a fuel filter goes bad (becomes clogged with dirt), your engine will typically have less power and will sputter and "miss" when it starts to work hard. If the filter becomes too plugged, the engine won't run at all. Some unwary consumers have paid for expensive engine work, only to find out later that a clogged fuel filter (which is relatively inexpensive to replace) was the source of their engine problems.

Routinely check the fan belt(s), power-steering belt, and water-heater hoses. Broken belts and leaky hoses are among the most common causes of roadside breakdowns. A few minutes of easy maintenance sure beats standing by the side of the road watching steam come out from under the hood or having your alternator light go on because the battery isn't being recharged.

Monitor the condition of the belts. Replace a belt that is frayed, has large cracks in its underside, or is especially worn. Tighten a belt that has more than half an inch of "give" in it when you push on it. If you're not sure about the condition of your belt(s) from a visual check, ask a trusted mechanic to show you what to look for.

Pay attention to water hoses. Immediately replace a hose that has a leak or is swollen, cracked, or soft in any spots.

Keep the engine tuned up. Keeping your car tuned up, which means installing new spark plugs (maybe a condenser, distributor points, distributor cap, and rotor if the engine doesn't have electronic ignition), and adjusting engine timing and the carburetor can reduce gas consumption by as much as 10 percent and make your engine start easier. (New cars that have electronic ignition don't have points, distributors, or condensers. When the electronic ignition unit goes bad, it must be replaced.)

Although almost any backyard mechanic used to be able to do a tune-up, new cars today can seldom be tuned up properly without expensive tools and equipment. However, if you know your car's maintenance schedule, you can have your car tuned up at the right time, which will save you money on gasoline and help avoid costly repairs.

Wash and wax the car regularly to keep the finish in good shape. A well-maintained finish can add dollars to the resale value of your car. Fix scratches in the finish quickly so exposed metal won't rust. Sun, salt, tar, and dirt all work together to wear down your finish. If area road crews use salt to melt ice during the winters, wash and wax your car more often. Be sure to spray underneath the car, too.

Be cautious about using automatic car washes that use rotating brushes. The brushes can wear down a wax job, scratch the finish, and even knock side molding loose.

Park a little farther away from other cars whenever possible. Your car will be dented less often by car doors, which may result in a higher resale value when you decide to sell the car.

Whenever possible, keep your car in a garage or under a carport. Sun can bake the upholstery and fade the paint, hail can dent the metal, and tree sap can ruin the paint.

Keep the interior in good shape. Buy floor mats or thick plastic to protect the carpets. We cut plastic to fit and then use regular mats on top of it. Your carpet will last longer and look nicer, which may add to the resale value of your car.

Check the condition of the wiper blades. Ineffective wiper blades can be dangerous in heavy rain or snow or even a light drizzle. New wiper blades aren't expensive, but they can be tricky to take on and off. Ask someone in an auto parts store to show you how to do it.

When you replace wiper blades, replace only what you need. Some cars require a whole new wiper-arm assembly every time you need a new blade. On other cars, you have the option of replacing just the rubber blade.

Check the exhaust system. Are pipes loose or hanging down? Do you see any holes in the muffler(s) or pipe(s)? Is the vehicle louder than usual? Can you smell fumes when you drive down the road? If so, have the system checked at a repair or muffler shop immediately. Carbon monoxide fumes, which have no color or odor, can be deadly.

It's often best to have a specialty shop do exhaust system repairs rather than attempting to do them yourself. But before you have work done, shop around. Costs can vary by nearly 100 percent. If you don't plan to keep your car long, don't pay extra for a "lifetime" guarantee.

Monitor the power steering unit. Check the fluid level periodically. You can check power steering fluid levels by removing the cap on the power steering pump. If the level is low, put in the right fluid type for your car. (Honda, for example, requires its own type of power steering fluid.) Be careful not to drop any dirt into the power steering pump, and don't add too much fluid.

Don't forget about the PCV valve. This little valve, usually mounted in the valve cover, controls the flow of partially and completely burnt gases going back into the combustion chambers. In some vehicles, it's possible to take it out and shake it up and down to test it. Other vehicles require a special tester to measure the air circulation through the crankcase during an idle. Signs of a bad PCV valve are poor gas mileage and rough idling.

Keep an eye on the power steering fluid lines. Have your mechanic replace one that is going bad. Stephen once decided to "wait a while" after a mechanic pointed out a worn line. It blew apart as he was driving down the road. He lost the ability to steer the car, and the fluid that sprayed out caught on fire. Fortunately he was able to put out the fire and damage was minimal, but he had to pay to have the car towed to a repair shop. Maintenance really can save you money.

Keep the windshield wiper fluid reservoir full. If a big truck goes by and throws dirty water or slush on your windshield, you need to be able to get that dirt off quickly without the fluid freezing. Add windshield fluid that won't streak to the reservoir. (Do not confuse the windshield reservoir with the coolant reservoir.)

In the summer, you may dilute the wiper fluid one to one, but before the onset of winter make sure the fluid in the reservoir is at full strength.

Check the ignition (spark plug) wires for cracks or bare spots. If you hear a popping noise when the engine is running, electricity may be jumping from a bad wire to another part of the car. (A cracked distributor can also do this.) You may be able to see the sparks at night. If so, get it fixed right away.

Don't touch or pull on a bad wire while the engine is running. Some electrical systems carry more than 35,000 volts, which is enough to induce a heart attack.

Reduce the Cost of Operating Your Car

TIPS FOR GAS SAVINGS

In addition to maintaining your car properly, you can do a number of things to reduce the cost of your car's daily operation.

Treat the engine right.

- Don't idle the engine for more than a minute. Turn it off instead. It requires less gasoline to restart an engine than to let it idle.
- On a cold day when your car is parked outside, start the car and let it run for a very brief time before you start to drive. Long warm-ups waste fuel. Today's modern oils are designed to protect the engine when it's not warmed up, and you can add specialty products to your oil to dramatically reduce engine wear that occurs when you first start the engine. Ask a mechanic or the auto parts store about such products.
- On bitterly cold days, you may want to put a piece of cardboard in front of the radiator so the engine will warm up faster. If you do that, be sure to take the cardboard off when the weather warms up or your engine may overheat and be damaged.

- Don't "race" the engine when you first start it. Let the oil circulate well before you increase friction unnecessarily.

- Accelerate smoothly to reduce tire wear, increase gas mileage, and reduce overall engine wear.

- Use the car's gearing correctly. If you have a manual transmission in your car, shift as soon as you have the speed to do so rather than waiting for higher revolutions per minute. You'll keep the engine running at a slower speed, which will save gas and reduce engine wear. But a mechanic also advises not to lug the engine by shifting too soon (at too low a speed) because that is hard on engine bearings.

  Streamline your car.

- Whenever possible, keep the car windows closed when you drive and use the vents. The air resistance of open windows reduces your mileage.

- If you must open a window, consider opening a number of them so that the air can come in and out freely, creating less drag.

- Particularly at high speeds, running your car's air conditioning is preferable to opening windows. However, air conditioning can cut your fuel mileage by 10 percent or even more. Use the air vents instead whenever possible.

- If you don't need a roof rack or other items on top of your car, remove them. They resist the air flow.

The average car uses 17 percent less gasoline at fifty-five than at sixty-five.

Plan your shopping to minimize unnecessary driving. Doing several errands in one trip saves time, reduces operating costs, and allows your engine to warm up fully, which means it will run more efficiently and use less fuel.

- Before we started working at home, we often ran errands on the way home from work. Now, we list the places we need to go in logical order so we minimize the distance we have to drive and don't forget any stops.

- Do initial shopping by phone. Once you know which store has what you need at the price you want to pay, drive to purchase it.

194

- Shop at businesses that offer free or cheap delivery, if their quality and prices are comparable to others. For instance, we paid a little more for lumber when we built our home addition because the lumber yard provided free delivery. This is an easy way to reduce your car's operating costs.

Other ideas for saving gas.

- Clean out the car. Don't carry more weight in your car than you need. It will reduce your gas mileage, put strain on suspension parts, and wear out the brakes faster.
- Anticipate when you'll need to stop for a light or a stop sign. Try to keep the car rolling instead of having to stop for every light. We are sometimes successful at this. Much depends on how the lights are timed and the traffic volume.
- Avoid stopping and starting constantly. Tailgating, for instance, wreaks havoc on brakes, engine parts, and drivers' psyches—your own and those of the people in front of you.
- Don't race up hills. If your car's speed drops a bit, live with it—and save gas. Downshift instead of lugging the engine.
- Don't change lanes constantly. Doing so decreases gas mileage and increases your chances of an accident.
- Go fifty-five miles an hour instead of sixty-five. The average car uses 17 percent less gasoline at fifty-five than at sixty-five.
- Carpool to work. Talk with co-workers who live near you or on the way to work, and ask if any of them would like to carpool. This arrangement works best if everyone leaves work about the same time.
- Use public transportation. Bus, subway, and train facilities in many cities are well run and much cheaper to use than driving your car.
- Don't fill the gasoline tank all the way to the top in hot weather. As the tank warms up, the expanded volume will cause the gasoline to overflow, wasting your money and possibly taking the wax off your car. Plus, the extra gas can saturate a part called a purge canister and damage it. When the pump clicks off, stop pumping.
- Use the transmission to gear the car down on steep grades. You'll reduce wear on your brakes.
- Take advantage of cash discounts. Some gas stations give cash discounts, and they can add up.

- If your car's gas cap doesn't lock, buy one that will. When times get hard, some people siphon gas from other people's cars.

- If you have to siphon gas out of your car, use a pump rather than your mouth to get the suction going. Gasoline is toxic, and going to the emergency room is expensive. As a teenager, Stephen once got a mouthful of gasoline, and he burped gasoline for two days.

- Drive defensively. Scan the traffic ahead constantly so you are prepared for difficult driving situations. Failing to do that can cost you plenty in repair bills and insurance rates. Once Stephen was slowing for a traffic light and noticed a car coming up behind him in his lane at a high rate of speed. Stephen switched lanes quickly, and when the other car screeched to a halt he and the other driver were eye to eye.

- Record your car's mileage on a regular basis. If it suddenly drops, find out why.

TROUBLESHOOTING

It is important to learn your vehicle's idiosyncrasies. If it starts operating differently, take note and investigate. When Stephen drove our old pickup truck recently, he noticed that the brakes were pulling a bit. Since he was working hard on this book, he asked our mechanic to check things out. The truck's axle seal had started leaking, and the brake shoes on one wheel were coated with fluid, making them ineffective.

On another occasion, while hauling heavy loads of wood in the same truck, Stephen had a "gut feeling" that something in the brakes wasn't right. So he stopped hauling, removed the brake drums, and found a small leak in a wheel cylinder. That small leak could have become a serious problem while transporting more than a ton of wood over a mountain pass.

Each vehicle has its own peculiarities. By paying attention to your car's sights and sounds, you'll be able to reduce repair costs and avoid inconvenient breakdowns.

Learn to listen to what your vehicle tells you.

✔ Learn what your car's warning lights mean. If one comes on while you're driving, pull over and figure out what happened. (A friend of Stephen's once destroyed his engine by continuing to drive after the oil warning light went on.)

✔ Do you feel unusual vibrations all of a sudden?

✔ Do you see anything strange? Red leaks (transmission fluid)? Water leaks (engine seal, radiator, hoses)? Dark oil leaks under the engine or the differential? Try to figure out where the leaks are coming from.

✔ Do you hear strange noises from the engine? Rear end? Brakes?

✔ Do you smell something odd? Oil or grease? Steam? Oil coming from the tailpipe? A strange film on the inside of the windshield?

Troubleshooting tips.

✔ Wiggle the cooling fan blade from front to back. Is it very loose? Do you hear "growling" noises? The water pump that circulates water throughout the cooling system may be going bad.

✔ Listen for a funny clunk when you put the car into gear. If you hear one, a U-joint may be going bad. This joint, in the rear (and sometimes both ends) of the drive shaft, allows the drive shaft to change angles. (If you've ever seen a car on the side of the road with a long, wrist-sized metal tube hanging down on the road, the odds are the U-joint snapped and the drive shaft dropped down.) Detecting this problem early can save you plenty of time and money.

✔ If your engine starts missing, have the spark plugs, choke, and fuel mixture checked. When one of these goes bad, your gas usage may increase significantly.

✔ Is the heat coming out of the heater warm enough? If not, the heat sensor or the thermostat that helps your car engine warm up isn't working correctly, which increases fuel consumption.

✔ Is the engine idling at too high a rate? The fuel system needs to be adjusted.

✔ Do you hear squealing or growling noises when you turn the steering wheel? The power steering pump may be low on fluid or going bad.

✔ Is the fan belt singing? Tighten or replace it.

✔ Is the engine suddenly making metallic clicking noises? Stop immediately and find out why. Perhaps the engine oil is low or is badly overheated and has lost its ability to lubricate moving parts. Maybe engine coolant has leaked out and the warning light didn't go on.

✔ Do you smell burned rubber? Maybe a brake shoe is stuck or your brakes are overheated. Or a rubber hose may be touching a hot engine part. Have it fixed before a major problem develops.

✔ Do you smell gasoline? Perhaps a fuel pump is leaking, there's a leak in the gas line, or the carburetor is leaking. Be careful; if there is gasoline or fumes on or near the engine, a spark could set it off. Track down and repair the problem immediately to prevent the loss of gasoline or a fire.

✔ Do you hear a hissing noise? A vacuum line may have come detached, which may reduce your gas mileage.

Emergency tips. Pack emergency items in the trunk. These should include whatever tools you need to perform on-the-road repairs you know how to do. Consider these: a set of jumper cables to start your car if the battery dies, a spare fan belt, a gallon of antifreeze, a flashlight, two quarts of oil, extra fuses, a funnel, a cross-shaft lug wrench to aid in tire changing, several kinds of screwdrivers, an adjustable wrench, a role of electrician's tape, and two extra radiator clamps. Also consider a warm blanket or sleeping bag, some change for the phone, and a coffee can full of food such as candy bars, granola bars, and so on. Such items can save you money on towing charges, telephone calls, and could even save your life in a blizzard.

If your engine starts to overheat in heavy traffic but still sounds OK, try these tips.

✔ Turn off the air conditioner (if it's operating).

✔ Turn on the heater, which will pull some heat out of the engine and cooling system.

✔ Put the car into neutral and give the engine a bit more gas so the water will circulate more quickly.

✔ Pull off to the side of the road if the temperature keeps rising. Keep the engine running with the hood up until the engine cools down. (Never remove a hot radiator cap.) Then find out why the problem occurred, unless it's obvious.

Carry a small fire extinguisher or bag of baking soda in your car in the event of a fire. Keep it in an easy-to-reach place.

Keep the gas tank at least half full at all times during the winter. This will reduce the chance of condensation (water) accumulating in your gas tank, which can cause the gas line to freeze. If the line freezes, add some "dry gas" to the tank and wait a while until the water is gone. If you travel in extremely cold weather, you may wish to add "dry gas" to every third tank of gasoline.

If your lock freezes, warm up the key with a match or a lighter before inserting it into the lock. (If the lock doesn't have a spring-loaded dust cover that closes when you take out the key, put masking tape over the door lock to help prevent freezing.)

If your battery dies, you may be able to get your car started with "jumper cables" instead of having it towed. Put both cars in "neutral" or "park," put on the parking brake, and turn off the car with the good battery. If the batteries have removable caps, remove them from both batteries to release potentially explosive hydrogen gas. (NOTE: Never try to jump start a car that has a frozen battery. The battery could explode. If you see ice in the battery, don't jump start it until the fluid thaws.)

Connect the red, positive (+) end of the jumper cable to the positive terminal of the good battery and then the other red, positive cable end to the weak or dead battery's positive terminal. Then connect the black, negative (–) end of the jumper cable to the negative terminal of the strong battery and the other black, negative end of the jumper cable to the unpainted frame of the car that has the weak or dead battery. (Attach it far away from the battery or carburetor.) That will keep any sparks that may fly from being too close to the weak or dead battery, which is potentially explosive. Never allow the jumper cable ends to touch each other.

Now try to start the car with the weak battery. If the engine won't start, don't crank the starter too long. You can damage it or drain the other battery.

If the engine starts, remove the cables carefully, one at a time. Be careful to keep the ends from touching one another as you remove them.

A mechanic also offers this tip: "Be sure to turn off the car with the good battery before jump starting. Otherwise, the alternator of the good car will be working to meet the needs of both cars and may be damaged."

MORE MONEY-SAVING TIPS

Get traction when you need it.

- If it snows quite a bit where you live, carry a few covered coffee cans of sand, kitty litter, or gravel in your car. They can help give your tires traction if your car gets stuck.

- If you drive a rear-wheel-drive vehicle, you might carry several burlap bags or pillowcases of sand above the rear wheels. The additional weight can help your wheels gain traction. Taking these preventive measures will help you avoid missing work, having to call someone to pick you up, or having to call a tow truck.

- If studded snow tires are legal in your state, consider using them. They are great for snow-packed and icy roads and may help you reach your destination or avoid an accident.

- If you use tire chains, always put two chains on the front (front-wheel-drive car) or two on the back (rear-wheel car). One chain alone is dangerous because the other tire will spin. Make sure the chains are installed snugly and fit correctly. If they are too loose, they may damage your tires.

- If you use snow tires every winter, buy an extra pair of tire rims (low-cost used rims are a good option) and have snow tires mounted on them. That way you can take the snow tires on and off when you need them and store them during the summer months without having to pay for remounting and balancing each time.

Keep the engine warm during bitterly cold weather. If your car doesn't start when it's really cold, try these tips before calling a repair service or selling your car.

- Consider installing an engine heater to help your engine start.

- Put a heavy blanket over the engine when you turn it off at night to help it retain heat. But be sure to remove it before you try to start the car.

- Consider a plug-in heater. We've known people who used them, but a reliable mechanic says that the dipstick-type heaters can burn the oil. So proceed cautiously.

Save money on routine auto parts.

- Buy auto parts you use routinely when they go on sale in reputable discount stores. For instance, we stock up on oil filters and oil so we always have a supply on hand. You can easily save up to 50 percent by watching for good sales.

- When you shop for tires, compare warranties and prices carefully. Check the ratings and how much difference there is in price between whitewalls and blackwalls and whether any low-cost, cosmetically blemished tires are available. Also find out if the tire mounting and balancing is free or not.

- Join a warehouse club, if one is available, so you can save money on tires and batteries. We just bought a highly rated battery that had more cranking amps than most batteries in the parts stores and cost at least twenty-five dollars less than comparable batteries.

Hold onto those keys. Are you tired of "losing" your car keys? Stephen made a key board on which he can hang keys as soon as he enters the house. Having to pay a locksmith to replace lost keys is an avoidable expense.

If you're going on a family trip, make sure that someone other than the driver has a spare set of keys. It's maddening to try to break into your own car, and it's expensive to call a locksmith.

If you don't know how to change a tire, ask someone to show you how . . . so you don't have to pay for emergency service.

Watch your foot. Don't "ride" the clutch or brake out of habit. You'll wear them out prematurely. Even very light pressure on the pedal activates the brake system.

Watch out for holes. Deep holes and curbs are hard on tires and front-end alignments. (So are railroad track crossings when taken too fast.)

Reduce parking fees. If you commute to a location where parking is a problem, take time to find out which lots are the cheapest, including monthly rates. Better yet, find an area a mile or so from work where you can park for free and then walk to work.

Learn how to change a tire. If you don't know how to change a tire, ask someone to show you how (on a nice day) so you don't have to pay for emergency service. Most vehicles are fairly easy to jack up, as long as the jack is still in the car, the lug wrench is the right size, and the ground is level and firm. (Stephen once stopped in a snowstorm to help a guy whose new four-wheel-drive had a flat tire. Together, the two of them couldn't figure out how to remove the spare tire, so the guy had to leave his vehicle on the side of the road. It pays to learn ahead of time how things work.) Be sure to use safety procedures, such as changing a tire on a level surface, blocking the wheels so the car won't roll, and making sure the jack is secure before you pull off a wheel.

The Bottom Line

Use what you've learned in this chapter to make better choices about your car's maintenance. If you can apply some of these tips yourself, you'll save money, learn new things, and have fun. And if you choose to have someone else do the maintenance for you, you'll still save money because you will make better decisions.

10

Saving a Bundle on Car Insurance

Buying insurance is a bit like wondering if you need to carry an umbrella. Some days you'll do fine without one; other days you'll get soaked. Insurance coverage is a vital part of preserving your assets, and selecting the wrong company or policy could result in costly expenses. So choosing an insurance company, and the coverage you need, is very important.

For the average consumer, insurance is a major expense. Yet many people spend little time evaluating their insurance needs and don't comparison shop. If you neglect to shop for insurance, you may pay more than you should, get coverage you don't need, lack coverage you do need, or put yourself and others at risk if your company refuses to pay your claim.

Recently, for example, a teenager rear-ended our car, injuring Amanda. But our insurance company is handling the medical bills, the teenager's insurance company paid us for the damage to our car, and we're going onward.

Understanding Types of Coverage

Car insurance is necessary and, in some states, mandatory. Without insurance, an accident subjects you to liability that could wipe out your assets. Auto insurance is divided into several types of coverage.

PROPERTY DAMAGE AND BODILY INJURY LIABILITY COVERAGE

This coverage protects your assets because it pays for damage your vehicle does to others and their property for which you are liable. If you should hit another car and hurt someone and are found to be at fault, you are liable to pay for the damage and medical care. Liability coverage insures you for that cost.

Given the high cost of medical care, it pays to have adequate liability coverage, and possibly more, given the money that juries sometimes award victims. Often this coverage is described by three numbers. The company insuring a person who has 100/250/100 coverage will pay up to $100,000 to any one person injured in a single automobile accident, a maximum of $250,000 for total bodily injuries when more than one person is injured in an accident, and up to $100,000 per accident for property damage.

COLLISION COVERAGE

If your car collides with another object or turns over, collision coverage pays for the repairs. It makes sense to carry collision coverage if your car is worth quite a bit, but if it's not worth more than $2,200 or so, don't carry it. The insurance company will only pay you the value of the car anyway, and the money you save on premiums could be used toward a future car purchase.

COMPREHENSIVE COVERAGE

Comprehensive coverage pays for theft and damage done to your car by something other than a collision, such as fire, vandalism, hail, flying rocks, windstorms, fire, lightning, or riots. If your car is fairly new or contains expensive stereo equipment, you should carry comprehensive coverage. The car's fair-market value is the standard by which payment is given. Even if your car is older, this coverage can easily pay for itself in repaired windshields, repaired damage committed by vandals, and hail dent removal.

UNINSURED/UNDERINSURED MOTORIST COVERAGE

Uninsured/underinsured motorist coverage pays for the medical bills related to your injuries if another driver who injures you or a family member has no insurance, doesn't have enough insurance, or flees the accident scene and can't be located. In some states this coverage is required. Even if you have good disability, life, or health insurance coverage, you may want to purchase extra coverage of this type.

MEDICAL PAYMENTS COVERAGE

This pays the medical bills for you and your passengers if injury occurs while in, entering, or leaving your car—no matter who is at fault. It can cover such costs as funeral expenses and lost wages, too. Your insurance company pays these costs without your having to prove that the other party involved was at fault.

"NO-FAULT" COVERAGE

Designed to eliminate expensive, ongoing lawsuits to find out who was at fault in an accident, "no fault" insurance means that your own coverage pays for your injuries, regardless of who is at fault in an accident. Your insurance company will pay for the injuries you and perhaps your passengers sustain from an auto accident up to the no-fault policy limits. It will pay for such losses as medical and hospital expenses and loss of income. It also covers any person driving your car with your permission but does not cover damage to vehicles. If your state has no-fault insurance, your insurance company will pay your medical expenses. If statutes permit, your company will then collect any money that is due from the other party's insurance company. Not every state has a no-fault law, so check with an insurance agent or state insurance official to determine what your insurance needs may be.

Choosing a Policy

Auto insurance costs are on the rise. Cars cost more to build and repair. People cost more to repair. Car theft is rising in some cities. Plus, injury cases often lead to litigation and high settlements. People are driving smaller, more vulnerable cars. And complex insurance laws and regulations ensure that skilled attorneys often are necessary to wade through claim-related paperwork. The end result means higher claims losses and higher premiums. So it pays to save what you can on auto insurance. Do that by determining what coverage you need—no more, no less—and comparing the prices that various companies charge for that coverage. The difference may be amazing.

Being underinsured is not
a smart way to save money.

SELECT HIGH DEDUCTIBLES

The deductible is the amount you must pay for a loss before the insurance company starts paying. If you have a deductible of $250, you must pay the first $250 and the insurance company then pays the rest. The general rule of thumb is to choose the highest deductible you can afford in order to reduce your premiums. If you can afford to pay the first $500 of a claim, evaluate the premium cost of a $500 deductible versus that of a $250 deductible. For the extra premium you would probably pay every year for a $250 deductible, the $500 deductible may save you much more money.

Also consider the benefits of having higher collision and comprehensive deductibles on a newer vehicle and dropping all comprehensive or collision insurance on an older vehicle (unless it is a valuable antique).

BE SURE TO CARRY ENOUGH
INSURANCE FOR YOUR SITUATION

Being underinsured is not a smart way to save money. If you have quite a few assets, you'll want more protection because a plaintiff may sue you. If you have adequate coverage, it may pick up where another driver's insurance stops paying your medical bills. Raising liability amounts may not cost much more in light of the added protection you'll receive.

SELECT THE RIGHT INSURANCE COMPANY

Ask state insurance officials or workers, friends, and associates about any company in which you're interested. Some companies have a good reputation for servicing and paying claims, whereas others fight their obligations every step of the way. Contact your state's insurance commissioner's office, and ask for materials that will help you compare insurance coverage and rates.

Using an insurance company rating guide at the library, compare companies to see which ones are financially strong and pay their claims. A. M. Best Company, Moody's Investors Service, Inc., and Standard & Poor's Corporation all rate insurance companies. Try to choose a company that has an A-plus or higher rating, and remember that a financially strong company may not necessarily be large.

> When you choose a company, remember that the lowest-priced premium may not always save you the most money. If an agent is knowledgeable and reliable, and the company he or she represents has a good reputation, consider paying a slightly higher premium than you would if you bought insurance offered by a less reliable, less cooperative company. When you suffer a covered loss, the few dollars difference in premium won't matter anyway.

Be sure to note the different ways in which the rating organizations conduct their ratings, and keep in mind that even a company with a strong rating can become insolvent quickly. We've noticed more articles about the weakness of insurance companies lately; many companies overextended during the real estate boom and made risky investments. So it is wise to monitor the financial stability of the company you choose.

COMPARE PRICES OF VARIOUS COVERAGES

Once you've selected several companies that seem to have excellent overall records, call local agents and compare coverages and prices over the phone. (We usually call three or four.) Also talk about your insurance needs with one or two agents who represent several companies. Make sure you use the same deductibles and coverage limits so the quotes you receive will be truly comparable. Sometimes agents give wrong figures, so ask them to send you written quotes, too.

Listen to the proposals, and consider policies carefully. If you don't understand something, ask questions. What you don't understand could cause you to pay more for your insurance. So don't be in a hurry. After all, it's your money at stake. A few calls may save you as much as 50 percent on your insurance premiums.

If you are turned down by a few companies, for whatever reason, keep looking. Don't be sucked in by a "we can insure anyone" company that charges too much, pays out too little in claims, and may not even be around when you need it.

WHEN YOU DECIDE TO MAKE A CHANGE

Keep the old policy in force until the new one kicks in. If you are switching from one company to another, be sure the old policy won't lapse until the new one is in force. You could lose a lot of money (and could face prosecution) if you have a lapse of coverage.

Read the new policy carefully. Accidents can happen, and so can clerical errors. Therefore you must read everything in the policy carefully before signing it. Check coverages, discounts, and so on. If you don't understand something, don't sign it. Ask your agent to explain all coverages and answer all of your questions. What perils will the policy cover? What won't it cover? What conditions are you agreeing to follow?

Evaluate premium payment options. Paying your premium annually may save you money. Companies have to do more paperwork if you pay monthly, and many of them charge extra for that service. On the other hand, don't forget the time value of money. Your lost income on money spent for an annual payment may more than offset the extra service charge.

Other Ways to Cut Car Insurance Costs

PURCHASE CARS WITH GOOD SAFETY AND REPAIR RECORDS

Certain makes and models of cars are cheaper to repair or safer than others. Check with your insurance company to find out the coverage rates of the particular kind of car you plan to buy. Some cars have a higher rate of theft, some have poor injury records, and others are inordinately expensive to repair. In short, there are statistical factors that affect insurance rates that differ from what we might conclude based on common sense.

DRIVE CAREFULLY

Accidents and tickets jack up insurance rates. Insurance companies know that someone who is ticketed is more likely to be involved in an accident and that someone who has been involved in one accident is more likely to be involved in another one.

When your driving habits change, your rates may go down.

If you haven't done particularly well in the past, start now. Keep your record clean, inform your insurance company of your improved driving habits, and compare coverages and prices regularly.

MOVE TO A DIFFERENT AREA

In some cases, you may be able to move to an area with lower insurance rates. That may be accomplished simply by moving out of a city and into a suburb.

TAKE ADVANTAGE OF DISCOUNTS

Find out if you are eligible for one or more insurance discounts commonly offered to the following categories of drivers:

• Those with a good driving record.
• Young drivers who earn good grades and/or complete driver education classes.

- Drivers who complete defensive driving/accident prevention courses.
- Women over thirty who haven't had an accident.
- Families with two or more cars insured with the same company.
- Nonsmokers and/or nondrinkers.
- Those who install antitheft devices in their cars.
- Those who have etched window glass on their cars.
- Senior citizens.
- Carpoolers.
- Those whose cars have automatic seat belts and air bags.
- Those whose cars have antilock brakes.

KEEP YOUR AGENT POSTED

When your driving habits change, your rates may go down. For example, we have lower rates now that we work in our home and don't commute. Have you changed jobs and shortened your daily driving distance? Are you taking public transportation to work instead of driving your car? Do you only use a car for pleasure driving? Are you carpooling? Is your reckless spouse no longer driving the car? Have you moved to the country or to a smaller city?

STAND UP FOR YOUR RIGHTS

Occasionally even a good company may not treat you the way you think you deserve. For instance, years ago a hit-and-run driver rear-ended Stephen's car, and our insurance company wanted to raise Stephen's rates. A short letter to the state insurance commissioner's office straightened out that problem.

If you have problems, first talk with your agent. Then contact the state insurance commissioner's office by letter and send a copy to the head of the insurance company and also to a local consumer group. If all else fails, contact a lawyer, whose influence will probably carry more clout than yours.

To receive further insurance-related information, contact the Better Business Bureau for your area and the state insurance commissioner's office.

11

Reducing the Expense of Flying

Every week, nearly eight million people in the United States board a regularly scheduled airplane.[1] You may be one of them. You may travel for business purposes, to visit grandchildren or grandparents, to take a long-awaited vacation, to see friends, or for any number of other reasons. Air travel is one of the most widely used methods of transportation, can be quite expensive, and has a complex rate structure. That's why we've concentrated on money-saving tips for air travel.

Experienced airline travelers often become experts at saving money on air travel. However, even those travelers who are planning their first flight can easily save a lot of money on air fare. The following tips aren't all-inclusive—such a list would take up a whole book. But these proven suggestions will help you better understand how the airlines work and will enable you to save money on your next trip.

A Travel Agent Can Save You Time and Money

WHY USE A TRAVEL AGENT?

Obviously you can walk up to an airline counter and buy airline tickets. You can also call an airline's 800 number to make your reservations and payment arrangements, and pick up your tickets at the ticket ·counter. You can call several different airlines that serve the cities you travel to in order to find the lowest air fares. By doing so, you may pay the lowest available air fares to your destination—or you may not. But you don't have to do all the work of finding the lowest fares yourself. You can have a travel agent do the work for you.

---

*The trick is to find out which airline,
fare, and schedule will give you the
greatest value for the dollars you spend.*

Using a travel agent costs you nothing. Travel agents are paid on a commission basis by the airlines and other providers of the services they sell. So the ticket will cost the same amount whether you buy it directly from the airline or through a travel agent.

The airlines offer the same fares to everyone, but the trick is to find out which airline, fare, and schedule will give you the greatest value for the dollars you spend. By using a reputable travel agent, you can increase the odds that you'll obtain the best prices and most convenient schedules. Why? Because a good travel agent has access to the fares and travel restrictions of all the scheduled airlines. He or she can ferret out the best fares for your needs and has the resources on hand to do this quickly, which saves time.

In addition, a good agent will be able to help you with related travel details such as arrangements for a rental car, hotel reservations, cruises, or tour packages. Often a travel agent will enable you to save money on these services too.

SELECT AN AGENT CAREFULLY

Some travel agents are better than others, so it's important to find a skilled and reputable one. Here are some ideas.

↙ Before selecting an agent, talk with friends and family members to see whom they recommend. You can also ask local businesses that use airlines frequently to give you a recommendation.

↙ Call several different travel agents—those recommended to you and others—and give each one *exactly* the same information regarding an upcoming trip. Describe when you'd like to travel and where you plan to go. Tell them you'd like to go the cheapest way possible and find out which options (such as staying over a Saturday night, going a few weeks earlier or later, or flying on off-peak days) could save you money. Sounds easy, right? It is, but chances are good that the prices you are quoted will vary greatly due to the agents' expertise and knowledge of changing fares and restrictions.

↙ Look for an agent and agency that has a good rapport with the airlines you like to use. Your agent's relationship with the airlines can make a difference at those times when you need special waivers or refunds for unexpected changes or travel problems.

↙ Find an agency that has twenty-four-hour emergency service. That enables you to have an agent's help even when the office is closed.

↙ Although many people work through a local travel agency, agencies with 800 numbers can serve clients all across the country. You may find that the best agency for you is in a distant city.

↙ Select an agent who will return your telephone calls. A few days after fares plummeted in the spring of 1992, our agent told us, "We got so many calls we couldn't return them all. So we had to pick which ones we'd return. I picked my loyal customers first, both corporate and individual. People I didn't know, or those who just left a first name, had to wait." Some of the people in that latter group weren't able to make the travel arrangements they wanted to make.

↙ Find an experienced travel agent who not only knows prices but can compare them effectively. Let him or her know that cost is a factor. Why pay more for a ticket when a slight change in plans may save you hundreds of dollars?

↙ Be courteous and thankful. A good agent who finds you the lowest fare works hard and receives less money for doing so. Express your appreciation.

✔ After you select and begin using an agent, contact a different one every so often just to make sure the one you prefer to use is doing the best job for you. Repeat the procedure as often as necessary in order to maintain confidence in your agent.

Once you find a well-trained travel agent who knows the fares, is friendly, and will work for and with you, be loyal. You'll save hours of time and get in on travel bargains. Talking with Janet, our travel agent, is always enjoyable. She's friendly, courteous, and knows the ins and outs of the travel business. Best of all, she treats us as if we're her most important clients even though we normally fly less than a dozen times a year.

"I just thought you'd want to know," she said one morning, "that fares just dropped dramatically. If you're planning any trips, get your tickets soon. These prices may not last long."

"We'll call you back soon," Amanda said. Within two hours, we finalized plans for our family vacation to the East Coast and business trips to California and Texas. We ordered our tickets that day and saved about seven hundred dollars. Once again, Janet had saved us money through her knowledge of air fares and prices.

Avoid Paying Full Fare

YOU MAY BE ELIGIBLE FOR A DISCOUNT OR REDUCED FARE PROGRAM

Sometimes airlines offer discount fares to certain individuals or groups. If you are a student, a child or teenager, a senior citizen, a member of a family flying together, in the military or the dependent of someone who is, look into discounts carefully. You may have to comply with certain restrictions, but you can save quite a bit of money.

Don't feel guilty if the person next to you paid hundreds of dollars more than you did to fly to the same city. You did your homework and took action so you wouldn't have to pay full fare!

PLAN AHEAD

Make your reservations well in advance so you can meet purchase restrictions on the best fares. Otherwise, you will have to pay a higher fare, since the airlines design restrictions to keep travelers who can't make reservations weeks ahead from receiving promotional fares. If the fare drops after you have paid for your advance ticket and you still meet the restrictions of the new fare, ask for your ticket to be reissued at the lower fare. Most airlines will do that, although some airlines and agents levy a service charge (now approximately twenty-five dollars) for reissued tickets.

Use a Home Computer to Link Up with a Travel Data Base

You can research your own fares using your computer. However, you sometimes have to pay telephone fees, enrollment fees, and computer database charges to find the appropriate information. A price search of fares between two cities is the easiest type of search, thereby the cheapest. Before you make a commitment to use such services, talk with people who do this to make sure you understand how the system works and to see how well it has worked for them.

When you purchase tickets from a travel agent, pick them up at his or her office rather than at the airport. Or ask the agent to deliver or send the tickets to you. As of this writing, the airlines charge twenty-five dollars for a prepaid ticket to be picked up at the airport. If you're away from home and have to make changes that require the purchase of new tickets, it is usually less expensive for your agent to send the tickets to you overnight express than to pay the airport pickup fee.

ASK FOR A WAIVER

If you have to make last-minute travel plans and it looks as if you will have to pay full fare, ask your travel agent to request a waiver from advance-purchase restrictions so you can fly more cheaply. Sometimes the airlines will agree to a waiver if it looks as if they will have unsold seats at departure time. The airlines generally prefer to sell seats at a reduced price rather than not selling them at all.

OBTAIN SPECIAL MEETING FARES

If you and a number of others (ten or more) will fly to a meeting or convention, check with the organizing group to see if any airlines are offering a discounted meeting fare or special promotion. If the airlines will do that, you will need to provide a special code when you make your airline reservation.

ASK TO GET ON THE WAITING LIST FOR A PROMOTIONAL FARE

As soon as you hear that an airline is offering a promotional fare that will benefit you, try to make your reservations quickly since there is usually a limit on the number of promotional fares that will be sold. Get on the waiting list if the promotional tickets are already sold out. If you plan to travel with others, ask your travel agent to list each person separately because the computers will pick people based on when they got on the list and how many there are. If your group must travel together and some of you clear the waiting list and others don't, you can always turn down the promotional offer.

EXPLORE AIR PASSES THAT LET YOU FLY TO VARIOUS CITIES

A pass can be a great way to travel internationally. But rules and restrictions vary, so know exactly what you're getting and how the benefits you receive compare to individual ticket prices. Find out which passes are available and plan a trip around them. Senior citizens can purchase passes for domestic air travel that enable them to fly (with certain restrictions) anywhere in the United States a specified number of times.

COMPARE ONE-WAY FARES TO ROUND-TRIP FARES

If you're flying one way, compare the price of that ticket to the price of a round-trip ticket at a promotional fare. If the round trip is cheaper, buy it. You don't have to use the return ticket. (Some people have an ethical problem with this practice. Use your own judgment.)

Keep an Eye on Rates

WATCH FOR LOWER PRICES AFTER YOU BUY A TICKET

If you have purchased a ticket and the price goes down, you or your travel agent may be able to negotiate the lower price or get a refund for the difference between the two fares. (Factors that determine whether or not you can successfully make a fare change may include: flying in the same fare class and meeting all restrictions.) It has taken several months, but we recently received 25 percent of a fare back. (If you used a travel agency, ask the travel agent to use the computerized fare-check system to make sure the price you paid remains the cheapest.)

READ A BIG-CITY NEWSPAPER TO FIND BARGAINS

Watch for ads in the Sunday newspaper (high readership) and on television or radio. Airlines tend to advertise in media that will give them the most exposure and fastest results for their advertising dollars.

INVESTIGATE THE BENEFITS OF A TRAVEL CLUB

A travel club can offer you big discounts on tours, cruises, travel packages, and so on. Compare travel clubs closely, determining which ones use cities you can travel to cheaply, how much the membership fee is, how the membership renewal system works, and so on. But be careful! Some travel "clubs" have proved to be nothing more than scams. If a club seems too good to be true, it probably is. Check with the Better Business Bureau in the city in which the club is located to see if any complaints have been filed against the club.

WATCH FOR SPECIAL PROMOTIONS

Maybe you should visit that friend you haven't seen in ten years. Maybe you can buy one ticket and get another one free. Promotional tickets sell quickly, so move quickly. But if the price seems too cheap, watch for hidden fees, gimmicks, or hidden package costs. Is the airline, for example, charging you for one full-fare ticket when perhaps you could obtain two round-trip excursion tickets for the same price by meeting certain restrictions? Also, the promotion for a new route may include cheap introductory fares.

LOOK INTO TRAVEL PACKAGES THAT COMBINE YOUR AIR TRAVEL WITH OTHER ARRANGEMENTS

Airlines, travel agencies, and tour operators put packages together. Some are great deals; others are more expensive than buying the items separately. Do careful research and you may come out way ahead, perhaps even getting the package for less than you would have paid for the airline tickets alone. Ask your travel agent to price your proposed plans both ways.

If you're flexible, you can get in on great deals.

Caution: Ask about all restrictions and hidden fees. Note occupancy requirements at hotels, how long you can stay in any one location, and so on.

TAKE ADVANTAGE OF SPECIAL COUPONS

Special coupons may be found in the newspaper, discount coupon books, and so on. Make sure you read the fine print! Restrictions usually apply.

Be Flexible

To save money, we have flown on different airlines, changed our flight times at the last minute, flown to alternate cities close to our destination, and returned home earlier or later than we'd first planned. We've even taken flights that required a stop or plane change when those flights cost significantly less than nonstop flights. If you're flexible, you can get in on great deals.

CHECK IN EARLY

Whenever possible, arrive for check-in at least one hour before your scheduled departure. Since the airlines release reserved seats that are not checked in thirty minutes prior to flight time, an early check-in minimizes the chances that you'll be bumped. Plus, an early arrival gives you plenty of time to get a boarding pass if you don't already have one. If you are traveling during a peak time, you may want to arrive even earlier. Don't worry about check-in for your connecting flights, because when you check in for your first flight you are automatically checked in through to your destination.

WHENEVER POSSIBLE, STAY OVER SATURDAY NIGHT

The money you save on airfare—often four hundred dollars or more—will more than cover the cost of an overnight hotel stay.

BE WILLING TO LEAVE EARLY OR ARRIVE LATE

You may save lots of money in airfare by taking "red-eye" specials. Late-night or early morning flights work well as long as you aren't on a tight schedule and can handle an odd-hours arrival without showing it too much the next day.

TRAVEL TO FAVORITE VACATION SPOTS DURING THE OFF SEASON

Air fares may be lower, planes and airports may be less crowded, and related travel costs may be lower if you don't travel at peak times. As an added bonus, you generally will have more spur-of-the-moment lodging options, although advance reservations are always a good idea. Also, when you visit a prime vacation area during the off season, you gain more of a feel for the natural beauty or native charm of the area as it really is rather than the bustling tourist area it becomes when the main tourist season is in full swing.

LEAVE OR RETURN ON KEY HOLIDAYS

Amanda once made last-minute plans and flew from Chicago to surprise her parents on Christmas Day. She walked in just as her dad was cutting the turkey. It isn't impossible to make travel arrangements just before a major holiday. About one week before the holiday, airlines may offer reduced fares for the days of travel that aren't yet filled. For instance, they may offer reduced fares for travel on Christmas Day and waive certain restrictions.

By traveling on what are generally low-travel days, such as Thanksgiving Day, Christmas Day, or New Year's Day, you may get a low-priced ticket and avoid some airport delays and hassles. Also, the normal high-travel days (such as the Sunday after Thanksgiving and the Sunday after New Year's) are usually blacked out for discount fares.

If you are traveling to several cities, check the lowest air fare to each one. Just because you live closer to one city doesn't mean you'll pay less to fly there. Be flexible about the order in which you visit the cities on your itinerary. You may save money by flying to the most distant city first.

Travel during the middle of the week. Flights may be cheaper if an airline wants to fill up empty seats.

Make your reservations at an off time. The travel agent may have more time to assist you in tracking fares.

Be willing to fly on a small carrier if the fare is cheaper. We've flown on smaller carriers and saved lots of money.

Instead of flying nonstop, be willing to fly through an airline's hub. You may have to change planes in that hub city on the way to your final destination, but you can save quite a bit of money. Allow plenty of time to switch planes and plan to adjust for weather-related delays, especially during winter months.

AGREE TO BE "BUMPED" IF YOU HAVE TIME TO WAIT

During a recent trip to Connecticut, the airline offered passengers on three of our flights free round-trip tickets if they'd get off and take another flight. (We didn't take the option. Our seven-year-old daughter was waiting for Mom and Dad to join her for our vacation.) The key here is to have carry-on luggage and not to be in a hurry. Learn what restrictions may exist on the use of the free tickets or coupons. Find out if the airline guarantees you a seat on the next available flight. Many times the next flight will be equally overbooked, and if you are given standby status you may have to wait through several flights before you receive a seat.

If you think your scheduled flight may be full, check in advance with the airline on which you are flying and find out what its policies are for "bump" tickets. If the terms are suitable, let the agent at the departure gate know that you'd be willing to be bumped.

FLY INTO ALTERNATE AIRPORTS

Sometimes you will pay a significantly lower fare by flying into an alternate airport. We have family in Massachusetts, Connecticut, New Jersey, and Maryland and have saved as much as one hundred dollars a ticket by flying into Baltimore, Newark, or Providence, depending on which city had the best fare at the time.

ASK ABOUT JOINT FARES

Let's say, for example, you can obtain a good fare to a city that is close to your final destination. A joint fare will allow you to fly into a city on a major airline and then transfer to a different (usually smaller) airline for the final leg of your trip—all for one fare. If you ask, you may be able to pay that fare, arrive in the first city, and then catch a flight to your final destination on a different airline without paying more money. If you learn how the system works, you can benefit greatly.

BE OPEN TO FLYING COMPETITIVE ROUTES

Flying different routes can save you money even if you need to drive to an airport farther away or take a bus or train once you reach your destination. Competition between certain cities keeps air fares low.

FLYING OVERSEAS?

Consider buying a low-priced ticket to a city on a competitive route that's not your ultimate destination and then arranging alternate transportation (train, bus, rental car) to the city of destination. For example, perhaps you can get a great rate to London and then travel via ferry and train to Paris. The disadvantages include the additional arrangements you must make and the time delay you will experience. But if you're not in a great hurry and have a helpful travel agent, why not do this?

Special Needs

BUY A NONREFUNDABLE TICKET ONLY WHEN YOU'RE SURE OF YOUR TRAVEL ARRANGEMENTS

If you become sick or injured and can't travel, ask your doctor to document that in a letter. In most instance you'll receive a refund. If sickness, injury, or death occurs in your immediate family and your travel is restricted as a result, you'll also need a doctor's letter or other documentation.

When approached in a polite manner, an agent will often give a refund.

If something other than the above reasons happens to prevent your travel, contact your travel agent or the customer service office of the airline and try to reschedule your flight. Airlines generally are more willing to reschedule than to refund your money.

IF YOU NEED TO ATTEND A FUNERAL FOR A FAMILY MEMBER

Some airlines give lower fares or waive advance-purchase restrictions for family members who need to attend a funeral or be with someone during an emergency. You may need documentation to prove the emergency is real (a fax, letter, telephone numbers, and so on). You may, however, not always be able to negotiate a special fare. Stephen once had to pay six hundred dollars to attend a family member's funeral (when the discounted fare at the time was less than half that amount). If you can, let a travel agent handle this for you.

WHAT TO DO WITH NONREFUNDABLE TICKETS

Although it is a fairly common practice for individuals to sell airline tickets they can't use, you should know that it is against federal law to travel under someone else's name.

You can, however, try to get a refund for a ticket you can't use. Take it to the ticket counter and explain to the agent that you can't use the ticket and ask if you can receive a refund. When approached in a polite manner, an agent will often give a refund. If the first agent refuses, don't give up. Ask several agents at different times—you only need one to say "yes."

If a refund appears impossible and you want to fly to your destination at a later date, ask the agent to reissue the ticket to accommodate your new plans. If your new schedule involves travel on the same days of the week and the same length of stay, the airline will rarely refuse your request, although you may be charged a reissue fee (usually twenty-five dollars).

Other Tips That Can
Save You Money on Plane Fare

ENROLL IN FREQUENT FLYER PROGRAMS

Frequent flyer programs have many changing rules and conditions, but they provide members with such benefits as special fares, discount coupons, bonus miles, mileage credits for staying at certain hotels, and using certain rental-car companies. In time, those miles add up! If you fly even three or four times a year, you'll be surprised by how many bonus miles you can earn.

Join the programs of every airline you fly. Use them as often as you can. To gain the greatest benefit for your travel dollar, compare restrictions, bonus-mile setups, relationships with hotels and car-rental companies, awards, and the mileage you need to take advantage of them.

PAY BY CREDIT CARD

If an airline has filed for protection from creditors (and we've flown on ones that have), it will often use low fares as an enticement to generate more business and cash. Take advantage of these low fares, but pay for your ticket with a credit card so you have recourse to a refund, subject to certain limitations, if the airline stops flying.

REDUCE COSTLY LUGGAGE-RELATED PROBLEMS

Don't check valuable items. If you must, arrange extra coverage from the airline. Otherwise, what the airline pays you for your lost bag won't come close to covering the replacement cost of what is missing. Never pack valuable items such as medicines, eyeglasses, or ongoing tickets in your luggage.

Know each airline's baggage requirements. In the United States, usually you can check one or two bags and carry on one or two others if they fit under the seat and in the overhead compartment. If you have more baggage than that, it will cost you. In other countries, you will face a weight requirement. In some cases, you may fly out of the United States or Canada with heavy luggage and then be told in another country that you have too much, or that you must pay an airline an extra charge to transport it. (That charge can be very steep.)

Reduce your risks of having luggage lost or damaged. Lost or damaged luggage can cost you money in several ways. You may have to buy new luggage because you have to travel on business before the damaged luggage is repaired or replaced. You may have to replace items that are lost and pay higher prices than those you originally paid.

The following tips can help you reduce the risks:

- Try to travel lightly, with only on-board luggage that can be stowed under your seat and in the overhead compartments.
- Check your luggage at the ticket counter rather than at curbside. The fewer people who handle your bags, the better.
- Try to get to the airport early. A rushed ticket agent could put the wrong destination tag on your suitcase.
- Remove old destination tags from your luggage.
- Always verify that the destination tag the agent puts on your bag is your destination. If you don't understand the tag code, ask the agent to tell you what it is.
- Put your name, address, and telephone number on the outside and the inside of your luggage. (Use a business address whenever possible so that no one has access to your home address while you are gone.)
- Don't pack your bags too full. They might break open or tear in transit, spilling items.
- Don't pack fragile items in your bags. The airlines' insurance policies won't cover breakage.
- Don't pack items that are of great value to you, such as that special manuscript or drawing. You may never see them again and may have to invest time and money regathering information or redoing a project. Worse yet, you may lose business or an account because you

missed the delivery deadline. Never carry anything in your checked luggage that's essential to your trip. Keep your minicomputer, business plan, and file folders with you.

- If a bag is lost or damaged, report it immediately. Don't wait around, hoping. Maybe your bag is on the plane but wasn't unloaded. Fill out the official claim form at the airline counter and keep a copy of it. Don't just tell an agent verbally about the damage, or *you* may have to pay for a new suitcase. Nearly every time we travel, an airline damages one of our suitcases. We're getting good at filling out those forms quickly.

- When you file for lost or damaged baggage, some airlines will tell you that you must come to the airport to retrieve lost or repaired baggage. Politely remind them that they are obligated to deliver it to you.

- Hold onto your baggage claim form. It's the proof that you checked in your luggage. Not having it could cost you the value of your luggage and its contents.

WHEN PROBLEMS COME UP

Sometimes problems come up when you fly, and you can save money by knowing your legal rights.

1. If you have a confirmed reservation for a flight, you checked in at least thirty minutes prior to departure, and the airline "bumps" you because they overbooked, you are entitled to compensation. That may include guaranteed seating on the next flight to your destination, a seat on a competitor's next flight to your destination, vouchers for future tickets, or overnight accommodations. Since deregulation, the airlines have been able to write their own rules on compensation for overbooked flights, so procedures vary from airline to airline and are subject to change. Check with your travel agent or the airline ticket counter so you know your rights as a passenger on each particular airline.

2. If you miss your flight due to your error, apologize to the ticket agent. Hopefully he or she will put you on standby status for the next available flight to your destination. But you will have to pay for your meals and lodging until you leave.

3. An airline ticket is just like cash. If someone else uses the ticket, you're out of luck. If you lose a ticket or it is stolen, you may have to

replace it at full fare. However, always ask if the airline will waive the advance-purchase requirement for the new ticket so you may purchase it at a reduced fare. Or, you can apply for a refund, which may take quite a while and cost you a fee.

4. If your flight is delayed and you miss a connecting flight too late in the evening to catch another one, the airline must either put you up at a hotel for the night and arrange for your transportation the next morning, or the airline must charter a van and drive you to your destination or pay the cost of a rental car.

SAVING MONEY
ON THE REST OF LIFE

12

Enjoy the Benefits of a Spending Plan

One of the best ways to save money is to allocate it wisely. With a wise spending plan (or budget, as it is more commonly called) to guide you in spending your resources, you can plug money leaks and take steps to reduce debt. It's also easier to save money for wise purchases and just plain fun times with family and friends.

Why Have a Spending Plan?

A spending plan is simply a helpful tool in financial planning. Stress caused by financial worries contributes greatly to the lack of well-being felt so widely in our society. Although everyone's financial situation is different, a spending plan offers advantages to everyone:

1. It reveals how you (and your spouse) spend money so you can accurately reduce or eliminate unnecessary spending.
2. It enables you to prepare for and survive lean economic times with grace and style.[1]
3. It helps you use your current and estimated income more effectively.
4. It gives you accurate information so you can make wise choices, meet needs, satisfy wants, and attain desired goals.
5. It can help you prepare for uncertain economic times, since you will know where you stand financially and will be prepared to make adjustments when life throws curves at you.
6. It helps you measure your progress in saving money and reducing unnecessary spending.
7. It may improve your standard of living.
8. It gives you a base from which to discuss fun ideas and financial goals with your family.
9. It can lead to your having more money available for investments and charitable giving.
10. It is a key element in reducing debt—or eliminating it altogether.
11. It can give you the options to buy items you want as well as those you need.
12. It motivates others around you, including family members, to participate in the saving process.
13. It gives you the resources to take advantage of true "bargains."

A Spending Plan Doesn't Have to Be a Pain

I know all about a spending plan, you may be thinking. *It's a disguised budget. Why should I bother to take the time to do it?*

Some people view a spending plan as a whip-cracking slave driver that pushes them in ways they don't want to go. To them a spending plan is to be avoided at any cost. They wouldn't use one unless they were forced to do so by debt or a court of law.

Let's assume, however, that you realize that a properly used spending plan can lead to great rewards. It's true that developing and living by a spending plan is not as much fun initially as spending money any way you want to. However, over time a good spending plan can give you much greater financial opportunities. It can be written in a day or two (including your research into past spending), and only takes an hour or less a month after that to maintain.

Many excellent books have been written on how to develop and stick to a spending plan (or budget). In fact, even grocery stores sell booklets on the subject. But a spending plan can only work for you if you put it into practice. If you truly believe that you can save money by allocating your resources differently, the following guidelines will get you started.

LIST YOUR ASSETS AND LIABILITIES

Assets include: money in savings, checking, and money-market accounts; cash; investments that can be liquidated for cash such as government securities, stocks, bonds, mutual fund shares, CDs, and insurance policies; equity in your home; value of appraised collections; IRA and Keogh funds; pension plan; profit-sharing plan; real estate (current value); debts owed to you; value of automobiles, equipment, appliances, furniture, jewelry, business shares, and so on.

Separate your assets into two categories: liquid assets (which you can convert to cash easily), and nonliquid assets (which may take time to cash out). Also, if you are married and you each own things separately, make a column for each of your personal assets and liabilities.

One of the best ways to find out where your money is going is to look at your checkbook.

Liabilities include: unpaid bills; installment debts on such items as a car, furniture, or appliances; promissory notes; money left on your home mortgage; balances on other mortgages; taxes due; pledges you have made to Christian ministries or charities; and personal loans outstanding.

When you add up your total assets and subtract your total liabilities, the remaining figure is your net worth.

DETERMINE YOUR ANNUAL EXPENSES AND INCOME

Look at all your bills, checkbook(s), savings passbook(s), receipts, and income statements, and figure out how much you earn compared to how much you spend. Going back at least six months will help you spot trends. Going back a year is even better. We know that it takes discipline to do this, but say "aaahhh" and swallow it anyway. It will lead to great things soon enough. (See the "Spending Plan" section in Appendix A for basic columns that will help you make your own worksheets.)

Review expenses. Be dreadfully honest here. No cheating. This exercise is for your eyes only, and it may reveal trends that need to be corrected. For instance, maybe you have too much debt or your money is "disappearing" into areas of wants rather than needs.

One of the best ways to find out where your money is going is to look at your checkbook. Other places to look are at your charge-card receipts and bills you've paid with cash. It may take a while to track where your money has gone, but keep at it.

You may separate your expenses into two categories: fixed expenses (the ones you must pay regularly) and variable expenses, which come up from time to time and in varying amounts. An easy way to figure these categories is to make a list for each month of the year on which each of the following categories is listed.

Fixed expenses include: insurance payments (property, medical, life, disability, dental, automobile), taxes (federal, state, property, automobile), monthly telephone charge for basic service, mortgage or rent payments, car payments, debt payments, ongoing medical care, educational costs, business dues, tithes, and monthly savings. Be as specific as possible. If you have two cars, list them separately. Once you've listed the figures under these categories, add them up.

Variable expenses include: utility costs (water, electricity, propane, natural gas), expected bills, routine home maintenance, food, clothing, laundry, transportation (gas, auto repairs and parts, parking fees, train tickets, tolls), personal care, entertainment (movies, tickets, travel, hobbies, eating out, books), unreimbursed medical and dental expenses and prescriptions, gifts and contributions, and that catch-all: miscellaneous (for all those small purchases that add up to a lot but never seem to be worth bothering with). Again, be specific. If you contribute to a number of charitable organizations each month, list each one.

Once you've listed all of those figures, add them up and add the total to your fixed costs to find out your total expenses.

Review your income. List money coming in from your wages, investments (interest, dividends, annuity payments, and so on), pension, child support and alimony, part-time work, Social Security, trust, tips, royalties, rent from tenants, and so on. Next to each source of income, write down when it comes in: monthly, quarterly, semiannually, or once a year.

Once you know your total income, compare the number to the total amount of your fixed and variable expenses. If the amount you bring in is more than you spend, you're living within your income. If not, don't panic; the spending plan will help you get things straightened out.

Divide your income and expenses by twelve to determine how much you bring in and spend each month. You may be surprised at what you find. Maybe you will see that soon you'll be able to save money again and that things aren't as bad as they seemed. Or you may realize for the first time how much money you actually spend in certain categories.

ANTICIPATE CHANGES IN PROJECTED INCOME AND EXPENSES

Now think about how your income could change during the next months or years. Could your salary be frozen? Is a layoff possible? Do you plan to do some moonlighting for extra income? Will you be eligible for Social Security? Will you receive money from a pension, annuity, or trust? Anticipate what may happen so you're prepared. Be conservative. You may not get another raise for a while.

Do you have a special expense coming up in a month? Are you going on a trip to visit relatives? Are car repairs needed? Will you have to buy a car? A bicycle? Pay for an operation? Do you need to buy Christmas gifts? Will you need dental work? If so, take the projected cost of each item, divide it by twelve, and add that monthly figure to your expense section in a separate category for special situations. If certain expenses need to be paid four times a year, set aside a specific amount every month for three months so you'll have that money.

When possible, set up a reserve fund so you can pay unexpected emergency expenses out of your own funds and not have to borrow them from a family member or financial institution. If you are self-employed, as we are, you'll need more in this reserve than somebody else will.

233

EVALUATING YOUR FIGURES

Now you can see clearly where you stand by comparing what you spend to what you earn. If you spend more than you earn, you need to make changes. Even if you don't spend more than you earn, you may still decide to spend your money more wisely. Knowing whether your cash flow is positive or negative is a key point. You now know whether you are living within your means or not, and you are better able to determine the areas in which you are not spending wisely and the areas in which you are doing well. With this knowledge, you'll be better prepared to know how much money you'll need and when you'll need it.

Tips for Setting Up and Maintaining a Spending Plan

- ✔ At the beginning, you (and your spouse) need to spend time each week evaluating how well your spending plan is working and making necessary adjustments.

- ✔ If you need to have everything accounted for perfectly, do it. If not, and you come close, that's OK, too. But if you don't come close, pay more attention to details.

Be willing to revise the spending plan as your needs, goals, and wants change.

- ✔ Gain the cooperation of key family members. If your spouse isn't willing to following a spending plan, conflicts will arise.

- ✔ Reflect the needs of individual family members in the spending plan. One child may need more money for sports equipment, for instance; another may need money for camp.

- ✔ Be conservative. If more money comes in than you expect, great. But if it doesn't, you'll be in stronger financial shape.

- ✔ Give each responsible family member a little money to spend that doesn't have to be accounted for.

- ✔ Set money aside for taxes when your income first comes in. We deposit all income into an account, but we set aside a percentage for taxes and don't consider that money to be "usable funds." Other people put tax money into a special savings account.

- Realize that your spending plan is a flexible planning tool. It should not be set in concrete. An unexpected expense, for example, may cause one or more other areas to shift. (For example, a forty-five-dollar doctor's visit may have to come out of "entertainment" if there are no more funds in the "medical" budget.)

- Be willing to revise the spending plan as your needs, goals, and wants change.

- If you spend too much money in one category, be patient with yourself. Pull from another category temporarily and try again next month. Avoid going further into debt.

- As you cut spending, remove money from a number of categories instead of dramatically reducing one category (unless it is superfluous).

- Stick with your spending plan until you have your income and expenses well in hand and can follow the basic plan naturally. If at any time you begin to lose control of your spending, return to the basics again.

13

Building Relational Riches: Free or Low-Cost Family Activities

F amily activities don't have to cost lots of money. In fact, some of the most fun ones cost little or nothing. But there's much more at stake than saving a few dollars here or there by taking a walk instead of eating out or by going bike riding instead of to an amusement park.

We live in an entertainment-oriented culture. If the television program isn't what we prefer, we change channels. When we go to the mall, we may be able to choose from three, five, or even ten movies. Our entertainment options would boggle the minds of our great-grandparents: roller coasters, water amusement parks, high-tech gear for water skiing at high speeds, a wide variety of restaurants, mountain bikes, huge botanical gardens and museums, and so on.

Critics of culture point out that we have lost something in the process—our ability to relate to one another, especially family members, in intimate ways. We often bounce by one another without connecting. Our days are hectic, the pace frenetic, and our energy demands kinetic.

Two friends of ours, Doug and Jan, decided to downscale a few years ago in order to reverse that relational trend in their family. Doug left a corporate marketing position to do informal counseling through a nonprofit Christian organization, and Jan volunteers at church and is involved in women's ministry.

"We wanted to spend more time together, to learn how to have fun together as a family," Doug told us. "We realized that we needed to practice and learn that. It's easy for families to use activities as a substitute for deep relationships, and we were doing that, too. So we stopped long enough to ask ourselves what we felt quality of life should consist of. We ruled out materialism, because money in and of itself doesn't satisfy, and began to focus on relationships with one another.

"To no one's surprise, our children quickly felt deprived. The older ones were used to having the latest and greatest toys, and when our income dropped by more than half and Jan and I could no longer just go to a store and buy a new—and popular—item, the kids didn't like it. Jan and I, like other parents, could give up lots in order to save money or achieve other goals. But when you have children, the scenario changes. Children live in a world with other kids, and they can't help but pick up values from the culture."

"As a family, we are not materially rich; we are relationally rich. We've learned to use activities as vehicles for relationship and have learned how to share experiences together."

Realizing that their children had good reasons for feeling deprived, Doug and Jan determined to make their free and low-cost family activities fun and challenging and to develop strong relationships with their children and with God. "Since Doug left the corporate world," Jan said, "we've been helping our children replace certain values with other ones. Simply taking away valued items just creates a feeling of deprivation, which causes anger and frustration."

"For instance," Doug added, "if we take steps to save money and don't provide our children with other values besides materialistic ones, the kids understandably view themselves as 'have nots' because their friends may have better toys and more money for entertainment. But if we replace activities and things with *relationship,* which enhances activities and things, the picture changes. Our kids know that we seldom buy new things, for instance. But they also see that many of their friends hardly see their own parents, much less have fun with them as friends. As a family, we are not materially rich; we are relationally rich. We've learned to use activities as vehicles for relationship and have learned how to share experiences together. So our low-budget family activities, although they save us lots of money, have become opportunities for relationship rather than a money-saving end in themselves. In many respects, we 'have nothing, and yet we possess all things.'"[1]

Ideas to Get Things Rolling

The following family activities can be ways for you and your family to cultivate relational riches and save money at the same time. Feel free to pick and choose, blend and mix. Brainstorm as a family and create your own list!

GAMES

▶ Play "punchball." We made this game up, so you probably don't know it. Buy a cheap, lightweight plastic ball about a foot in diameter and set up a place in a room where two children can hit the ball along the floor. Both players sit on the floor opposite one another, maybe ten feet apart. The players take turns hitting the ball with their fists toward one another, trying to get it past the other player. It's great for kids ages 5 to 8, since it's active, teaches coordination, and costs virtually nothing.

▶ Play "store." Almost anything can serve as money: pine cones, buttons, pennies, or circles cut out of colored paper. "Restaurant" is a fun way to play store, especially if the child(ren) has some real or make-believe dishes and glasses.

▶ Divide into teams on a cold or rainy day. One team moves items in one room in obvious ways while the other team waits in another room. (Changes may include turning things upside down, putting books the wrong-way in, or turning chairs backward.) The other team gets points for the moved items they notice and loses points for the ones they don't see. Then the teams switch.

- Buy puzzles at garage sales or thrift stores and put them together. Stephen once bought thirty puzzles at an auction for a dollar.
- Make your own bean bags out of tightly woven material and fill them with dried pinto or navy beans that have been heated in a 200-degree oven for one hour (so they won't germinate). Don't put too many beans into each bag or it will be too hard. Then see who can toss the bean bags the greatest number of times into a circle you've made with string.
- Play croquet in your yard. We picked up a set at a thrift store for three dollars.
- Throw baseballs, footballs, or frisbees.
- Have water-balloon fights or squirt gun battles (but limit your attacks to active participants, not passersby).
- Bob for apples in a large washtub, with hands kept behind your backs.

CRAFTS

- Draw the rooms of a house on a large piece of paper. Then find pictures in magazines and furnish the house. Add people, too.
- Have a special drama night when you assume different roles and act them out. Make and wear funny costumes.
- Make cards and gifts for friends (and one another) instead of buying them. Clip photos and funny sayings out of advertisements. Draw your own pictures and caption them yourself.
- Make a neighborhood out of boxes. Cut out or draw doors and windows. Add chimneys, sidewalks, pools, and so on.
- Go sightseeing and notice unique craft ideas that you could make yourself. Then come home and do it. (We're thinking about making various kinds of wind chimes.)
- If you live in a cold, snowy climate, make snow sculptures. Start simple (maybe a turtle), then let your imagination and creativity run wild. Make a giant with an axe, a horse, a car, or a wagon. Sprinkle the snow with water to make it last longer.
- Build a birdhouse or bird feeder.
- Make simple hand puppets out of socks and put on your own puppet show.

- Carve wooden spoons out of pieces of hardwood that are ten or fifteen inches long and two or three inches wide. All you need is a pencil, a pocketknife, a way to sharpen the pocketknife, a rasp, sandpaper, and a way to determine how deep your cuts should be.[2]
- In the winter, fold squares of paper in half diagonally to make triangles, and fold them in half again. Keep folding until you decide to start making snowflakes. Using a scissors, begin to cut pieces out of each triangle. When you open up the triangles, you'll have beautiful snowflakes.
- Draw faces on balloons with magic markers.
- Have a special crafts night to make Christmas or birthday gifts.
- At Christmastime, make your own gift wrappings out of maps, fabric, decorated brown bags, butcher paper, aluminum foil, newspapers, or magazines.
- Develop hobbies you can do together: collecting seashells, driftwood, elk antlers, matchbook covers, antique toys, insects, and so on.
- Draw an African plain on cardboard and cut out pictures of animals that would live there. (Or draw a jungle, a forest, or a mountain.)
- Gather small blocks of wood left over from projects or discarded from a building site. Be sure to sand off any rough spots and to remove any sharp points. You can build houses, towers, apartments, and so on.
- Check out a craft book from the library and get new ideas.

SKATING

- Ice skate in a park or on a friend's pond. (Make sure the ice is thick enough!)
- Roller skate at a rink during off nights or weekends when special discounts apply.
- If you live in an area that gets cold enough, make your own ice skating rink. Lay boards end to end on a level area to form a rink, and pound stakes on the outside of the boards to keep them in place. Lay clear polyethylene on the ground and up the sides of the boards, lapping any joints by several inches. Seal the joints by running cold water slowly over them when the temperature is below freezing.

Finally, flood the rink with a garden hose until the ice is about two inches thick, being careful not to freeze the outside faucet in the process.

Happy skating! In the spring, before the grass starts to grow, remove the plastic.

Movies or Special Television Programs

✔ Go to matinee films at off hours. In our area they only cost about three dollars.

✔ Have a special video night. Rent a video or two during the middle of the week at a reduced rate, and cook up some popcorn.

✔ Watch a special television program.

PHYSICAL ACTIVITIES

✔ Go on family "bike hikes." If the kids are small, buy a bike trailer, child backpack, or bicycle seat. (Note: Be sure to have an approved helmet for each rider, check the tightness of bolts and nuts and the tires regularly, and obey all traffic laws.)

✔ If you live near a lake or the ocean, find out how much it would cost to rent a small sailboat for a day. Or buy one that's in poor shape and restore it.

✔ Have a camping trip in your backyard, at a friend's home, or in a national forest. If you don't own a tent, rent or borrow one. Many people have tents they don't use. Pick up sleeping bags and other gear at garage sales, thrift stores, or on sale, or make your own camping gear. (Older camp-craft books tell you how to make your own sleeping bags out of blankets.) Or, if the weather and bugs permit, sleep out under the stars.

✔ Invite friends to pay a game of "capture the flag" in the park.

✔ Play tennis or basketball on a public court. Contact the local park and recreation department for the location of free or low-cost courts and reservation information.

✔ Rent a racquetball court at the local high school for an hour.

✔ Fly kites on a windy day.

✔ Play badminton in your yard.

✔ Find special shells by the ocean.

✔ Make sand castles.

✔ Go sledding.

✔ Take up cross-country skiing. There are no lift lines or fees—just you and nature and the opportunity to enjoy good exercise with your family and friends. Sometimes you can find good used skis at ski swaps or resale shops.

Going Places

NATURE

✔ Walk along a river or in a forest preserve or park.

✔ Take a nature walk on a trail.

✔ Go bird watching.

✔ If you live near open fields, contact the owner and ask permission to pick wild flowers for a special table decoration.

✔ Get involved in a 4-H program.

✔ Buy a used canoe or rowboat and take a "cruise."

✔ Go to a rodeo or other outdoor sporting event and sit in the "cheap seats" section. The trick is to get there early so you can have a family picnic and then get the best seat in that section.

✔ Visit a working farm.

✔ Hike in the country and try to see how many birds, plants, and animals you can identify.

✔ Find out if someone in your area raises a special breed of animals and arrange to visit.

✔ Contact the National Park Service and visit a wildlife refuge or other point of interest.

✔ If you live in the Northeast where sugar maple trees abound, find out if you can watch or participate in the syrup-making process.

✔ Fish. Many cities provide stocked ponds. Or you may live in an area near the ocean or lots of private and public lakes and streams.

✔ Visit a public garden.

✔ If you live in a cold climate where there are lakes, find an experienced ice fisherman who will take you and the family ice fishing. People have been doing it for centuries, and there's nothing like a great fish dinner after a long, cold time on the thick ice. (NOTE: If you haven't done this before, be sure to learn all safety procedures and dress warmly. Ice can be treacherous and thin in some parts of the lake or river.)

CULTURAL ACTIVITIES

✔ Contact local colleges and universities regularly to find out about concerts, lectures, poetry readings, film series, plays, and so on. Ask to be put on their mailing lists.

✔ Attend an art exhibit.

✔ Learn about a certain type of music and listen to radio shows on public radio stations.

✔ Attend a family-oriented play.

✔ Visit a circus.

✔ Tour local museums.

✔ Go to a zoo.

NEW AND UNIQUE SPOTS

✔ Contact the state tourism office and travel agencies and learn about free, low-cost, unique points of interest. (Whenever possible, talk to the people in person.) Find out about hidden "ghost towns," special cultural weekends, parades, art exhibits, festivals, concerts, and so on. For example, we visited an old, out-of-the-way museum in southern Colorado that was brimming with old muskets, mounted animals, and antiques.

✔ Ask to take a tour of a fire station and talk with the firemen.

✔ Purchase a Golden Eagle Pass (for those under age sixty-two) from the National Park Service and tour national parks, historical sites, recreation areas, and monuments. If you are sixty-two or older, purchase a Golden Age Passport. There's also a Golden Access Passport for disabled people.

✔ Attend the county or state fair.

✔ Go to an auction. You can find them listed under the "auction" section of the classified ads in the newspaper. You can also call auctioneers listed in the Yellow Pages and ask to be put on their mailing lists.

✔ Visit garage sales and flea markets. You never know what you'll discover.

✔ Visit a local radio station and talk with the deejay.

✔ Go berry picking.

✔ Go to an orchard or farm and pick your own fruit or vegetables.

✔ Visit historic Spanish, English, and French sites, including Civil War battlefields, Pony Express stops, early settlements, Native American cultural sites, Oregon and Santa Fe trail sites, and immigration monuments.

VACATIONS/TRAVEL

✔ Extend a business trip. If you or someone in your family has to drive somewhere on business, try to work it out so all of you can go. Plan to stay a bit longer in that city or area.

✔ Travel with friends. If you have good friends (who will still be friends after a few days or a week of traveling together), consider taking a trip together and sharing expenses. The old adage "The family that travels together unravels together" is sometimes true. Make sure that the people with whom you travel are able to be patient, flexible, trustworthy, loyal, helpful, friendly, courteous, kind, obedient, and cheerful, especially when the hotel just filled up, the food is cold, the closest bathroom is thirty miles away, and a tire goes flat on the desert road.

✔ Vacation at home. Put the answering machine on or turn the phone off altogether. Tell close friends you are going on vacation, but don't tell them where. Then do the things you've always wanted to do in your city, at home, and so on.

✔ Rent a small trailer for a weekend.

✔ Rent a cottage for a week during the off season.

More Ideas

EXERCISE YOUR GREEN THUMB

Plant flowers—perennials, biennials, annuals—in special areas around your home. Your home will be ablaze with colors at different times. Check with local gardening shops to see which plants will be best suited to your particular climate and requirements. Children of all ages can help.

FUN WAYS TO COMMUNICATE

✔ Make your own envelopes out of magazine advertisements or funny cartoons, and send them to special friends. Just be sure they fit the standard sizes required by the Postal Service.

✔ Make a "letter on tape" (cassette or videotape) and send it to grand-parents or friends.

✔ Draw a large picture or write a special letter to someone in the hospi-tal or living in another state. Let everyone participate, and make the process a fun craft time as well as a way of remembering someone.

✔ Develop a family newsletter that you can send out at Christmas or just about anytime. Each member of the family can write an article, draw a picture, help to take photographs, and so on.

✔ Sing Christmas carols at people's homes. We've done that several times, and it has brought joy into the lives of elderly people who sel-dom leave their homes.

✔ Bake cookies or brownies and take them to a friend or a shut-in from your church.

TAKE ADVANTAGE OF SPECIAL CLASSES

✔ Find out about county extension service activities.

✔ Call the nearest YMCA and find out about their activities and classes.

✔ Investigate classes that interest you at local colleges, trade schools, and universities. Some offer discounts to seniors.

CREATE INDIVIDUAL EXHIBITS

Choose topics each person would like to study. Each family mem-ber then prepares a simple exhibit about that particular topic, i.e., how fossils are made, the history of a certain kind of dinosaur, or what Mars looks like.

Take time to talk. Sit around and catch up on what is really going on with one another. You may be pleasantly surprised by how much fun this can be.

Visit mall exhibitions. Attend special activities at shopping malls. To increase store traffic, malls often schedule special events such as historic car shows, home improvement shows, and garden shows.

Organize a swap meet. Organize a neighborhood swap meet when you and your neighbors can trade clothing, tools, and so on. It will work especially well if the neighbors have children a bit younger and older than yours.

Study people. Go "mall walking" or "airport watching." Decide which person you see is the most unique.

Buy a special book. Invite all the readers in the family to go to a used bookstore and pick out read-aloud books. Then schedule a reading evening.

Try thrift shopping as a family. Cruise discount stores, charity stores, and bargain basements for special items that people may be almost giving away. It's fun whether or not you buy anything.

WORK AND PLAY SIDE BY SIDE

For centuries, parents and children worked side by side, learning from one another and enjoying natural time together. If you don't already do that, try it. Pull weeds together. Wash windows or the car. Rake leaves.

Buy a family pass to a YMCA, and use the pool, the basketball court, and the volleyball net.

USE THE LIBRARY

Check out books, videotapes, cassettes, and records, and enjoy them as a family. The selections may astound you. Schedule a regular reading session at the library if your children are old enough. Check with the library to learn about upcoming programs. We've taken our daughter to special film series and enrolled her in a reading program.

HOLD A SAVING MONEY PARTY

Meet with friends to discuss ways in which all of you save money. Encourage the children to share their ideas, too.

JOIN IN THE CELEBRATION

Attend the grand opening of a new business. It will probably provide balloons and free food, and you'll be able to browse and see their merchandise. The key here is to hold onto your money. The business obviously wants you to buy during your visit.

A CHANGE OF PALATE

- ✔ Have lunch at an "all-you-care-to-eat" cafeteria. Call first to verify that prices are reasonable.
- ✔ Go to a restaurant that serves tasty appetizers from 5:00 to 7:00 in the evening. You'll be able to sample delicious items for just the price of milk, pop, or coffee.
- ✔ Use discount dining coupons and try a new eating spot once in a while.
- ✔ Invite elderly people, singles, or couples who don't have family in town to join you for a meal.
- ✔ Get together with two other families once a month for a meal and rotate houses. Add to the fun by planning special foods or foods from other countries.
- ✔ Invite good friends over for a potluck dinner. You'll have enough people to pay fun games, and you won't have to do all the cooking.
- ✔ Invite someone from another country to fix a special meal for you, or fix a special meal for someone from another country.
- ✔ Get take-out foods from the grocery store and have a picnic.
- ✔ Invite friends to drop in at your house between 4:00 and 7:00.
- ✔ Enjoy a "game feast." Invite neighbors and friends to bring duck, bluefish, elk, deer, antelope, rabbit, and so on.
- ✔ Instead of eating full meals at restaurants, stop in for an appetizer, soft drinks, coffee, tea, or dessert.

BEFRIEND AN INTERNATIONAL STUDENT

Contact a local college or university and befriend an international student. You and your family will learn a lot about another country and be able to give much in return.

GIVE AWAY SPECIAL GIFTS

Give someone a coupon saying, "This coupon is good for one evening's work. The _____ family will do any or all of the following tasks: gardening, washing windows, mowing the lawn, painting (and so on)." It's a great way to share yourself and your talents with others.

BECOME INVOLVED IN CHURCH ACTIVITIES

Find out about Wednesday evening potlucks, movie series, Bible study classes, drama group, or choir.

THE LAST WORD

14

Why Save Money?

It may seem strange to ask this question at the end of this book. Saving money is good, right? We think so, or we wouldn't have written this book. Most likely you agree too, or you wouldn't be reading it. But why do you want to live smart and spend less?

If we asked you and other readers to tell us why you want to save money, we'd receive thousands of different reasons. They might include:

"To cut our electric bill."

"To reduce our food and clothing costs."

"To spend less on the car."

"So our family can take a vacation."

"The old car is getting tired; we need another one."

"Our daughter needs braces."

"The dog needs an operation."

"My kid heads to college in two years, and I doubt it'll be on a scholarship."

"I want to enjoy my retirement."

"I want to live in a bigger apartment."

"Somebody stole my bicycle, and I want another one."

"I want to support a Christian outreach."

"I feel more secure when there's money in the bank."

"So I can spend less money on the essentials and more money on the things I want to enjoy."

"We'll feel better, since we'll be better stewards of our resources."

"So we can do more things as a family and go more places."

"We only go around once, so why not get the most out of it?"

What your smart living truly accomplishes is determined by the priorities of your heart.

All of those hypothetical reasons are legitimate, but most of them are superficial. They reveal the benefits people often hope to gain when they save money but don't reveal the underlying reasons that people wanwant or choose to save money.

You may be sensing that a philosophical or spiritual statement is coming. It is, but relax. It's a simple one: *Money is a resource, and the reasons you save and spend money reveal your real life priorities and your spiritual perspectives.*

Every dollar saved through living smart is a resource. When you access greater resources, you can make better choices regarding what you'll do with your dollars and cents. That's why it is important for you to discover the real reasons you choose to save money. What your smart living truly accomplishes is determined by the priorities of your heart. How much you save is actually less important than how you use the new resources available to you because of your choices.

Think About Your Reasons

Consider the following checklist. It may help you discover your real reasons for living smart. Honestly look at why you save, or would like to save, money.

☐ I want to be like other people I know.

☐ I want more security.

☐ I want to feel good about myself.

☐ I want others to feel good about me.

☐ I want to be able to help others.

☐ I'm afraid that unless I maintain a certain lifestyle, people won't think I'm successful.

☐ I tend to gauge how well I'm doing in life by what I own or what I've purchased.

☐ I'd like people to notice me.

☐ I don't want to be hassled by creditors.

☐ I feel guilty about how I've spent my money in the past and want to turn things around.

☐ I want to be in control of my life, and having money will help me do that.

☐ I want to provide a better living for my family.

☐ I want the freedom that money can bring.

☐ I realize that this life is short, and I want to use money to make a difference in the lives of people around me.

☐ I'm tired of watching my dollars disappear with little to show for my efforts.

☐ I want the way I live to count for something beyond myself.

☐ When I die, I want to be remembered for my charitable contributions.

☐ I'm not sure why I want to save money; it just sounds like a good thing to do.

☐ I want to be in financial control of my life, to be independently wealthy.

☐ Maybe money doesn't bring happiness, but I'd like to have enough money to find that out for myself.

☐ I want to honor God by the way I live.

☐ I'm afraid of what life can dish out, and having money will help to insulate me from what could happen.

☐ I enjoy reaching my goals, and having money is one of my key goals.

☐ I earn money by using my skills, so why not use skills in saving it?

☐ If I save a dollar here, I can spend a dollar there.

☐ I want to prove that I can "make it."

☐ I don't like what I see happening in the government, and if everything collapses I don't want to go down the tubes, too.

☐ I want options in life so I can explore and use my gifts and abilities more fully.

☐ I want to prove something to my family.

☐ I want to support a worthwhile cause.

☐ I really don't care about saving money (I'd rather spend it), but my spouse (or parent) is pressuring me to save.

☐ I believe that what I have is a gift to be used wisely.

☐ I want more money because it will open doors for me.

☐ If I can't make a lot of money, maybe I can move up the ladder a rung at a time.

☐ _____ (Fill in your own reason).

Now be a little bolder and respond to the following questions and statements.

If I had $____, I would _____ .

I believe money is important because _____ .

If I were to die tomorrow, people would remember me this way: _____ .

My most important possession is _____ .

This is most important to me: _____ .

The financial gift that has meant the most to me is _____ .

If I had enough money to do anything I wanted to, I'd _____ .

I have learned _____ from other people about money.

If I were to use some percentage of the money I'll save for a special purpose, that purpose would be _____.

The sharing that gives me the most satisfaction is _____.

My spiritual beliefs affect my view of money in the following ways: ____
_____.

What priorities and attitudes are revealed by your answers? Are you surprised by the motivations underlying your actions?

A Simple Illustration

Sometimes saving money for a good reason can be motivated by the wrong reasons. Permit us, once again, to share an experience from our lives that illustrates that. When we bought our present home, we stretched ourselves to the financial limit. To be honest, we would not have qualified for the loan if the owner hadn't carried part of it privately and the other part hadn't been assumable. We simply didn't earn enough money to "prove" to a loan officer that we could make the mortgage payments. But we knew we could live well on little, for a short time or for many years, and we carefully analyzed our projected income and expenses.

It was a good decision, one we've almost never regretted. However, for a while we were motivated to live smart and spend less for the wrong reasons. A few weeks after the closing on the house, Stephen learned he would no longer have a job. We'd have to pay our own health insurance. Amanda was pregnant. The roof started leaking.

Fear, rather than faith, became a key element in our lives. *What if we can't pay the mortgage?* we thought. *We'll lose the land. Let's get the land paid off so we can be secure.* We began to live as if we owned what we had, as if having more money would insulate us from difficult circumstances, as if it would guarantee future security. Then we realized that we had to reevaluate our attitude toward what we owned. For us, the key question became, *Is God who He says He is or not?* Quite a lot stood or fell on our honest answer to that question.

Fear is a great motivator, but it also exacts a high price. You see, when we live fear-based lifestyles, we begin to focus on ourselves—on our needs and desires—rather than on other people's needs and our need to know God. We make what may be good decisions for the wrong reasons. And we start living as if we could control every aspect of our lives. But a few simple laws constantly throw wrenches into our formulas.

Law One: We will all die one day. It'll happen no matter how much we have saved, how often we exercise, how properly we eat, and how careful we are. No matter how much we accumulate, we can't take it with us. So it would be wise to ask, "Do our choices have eternal consequences?"

Law Two: We cannot control life's circumstances. The amount of money we accumulate can't protect us from difficult circumstances that inevitably arise.

Law Three: Money itself cannot provide lasting inner peace and joy. Money is limited in what it can provide. Many song lyrics have communicated that money alone is not enough to win someone's heart, much less lead to a deeper sense of meaning and purpose. Likewise, the business trail is strewn with tired people who believed that if they earned so much a year and gained the trappings of wealth, they'd be able to fill the void deep inside. Personally, we've discovered that only a relationship with God through Christ can provide lasting peace and joy.

Law Four: Enough is seldom enough. Have you noticed that having money often fuels the desire to acquire even more money, which leads to more financial pressures? Have you noticed that whether you have little or much, obtaining money can be consuming? Just as spending money carelessly can ruin lives and families, being miserly can lead to misfortune and selfishness. And greed, which can be easily hidden in a culture that tends to worship "success" and individual achievement, leads to great pain.

Law Five: Money can be used to create good or evil consequences. History provides many illustrations of that.

Make Your Choices Carefully

As you save money, you will have to make even more choices concerning how to use the money you save. Will you, as one couple we know, use the benefits of living smart to help others? (They have provided food, clothing, and education to more than thirty Third World children and their families since 1975.) Will you help a family pay for necessary medical care? Will you help young people participate in short-term missions projects? Will you help to stock a local food bank? Will you give friends who have less money a gift certificate for a meal out and baby-sit their children for an evening? Will you help a financially strapped college student with tuition? What about inviting a person (or couple) to live in your home until he or she can overcome a setback? Ultimately, how you spend money is an issue of the heart: "Where your money is, there your heart will be also."[1]

Three Pieces of Bread

While waiting in line at the airport in Madras, India, about eight years ago, Stephen noticed several people going to the front of the line to board the aircraft. One of them was Mother Teresa.

She sat across the aisle from him, looking as frail as her photographs in the magazines. Stephen couldn't help but glance at her from time to time.

As the airplane reached cruising altitude, a flight attendant served juice and rolls. Stephen eagerly bolted them down, then heard a rustling noise. Mother Teresa was carefully wrapping up two rolls.

She noticed his gaze, gave him a warm smile, and said, "For the children. For the children."

How are we using the resources God has given us? To whom are we offering the bread we have to share? Perhaps, just as Jesus multiplied a few fish and pieces of bread in order to feed many people,[2] He will use some of the money you save in special ways—even if you only start with two small rolls.

It's your choice.

Appendix A:
Spending Plan Worksheets

Previous Monthly Expenses

FIXED

Food	$ _____
Shelter:	
Rent/mortgage	$ _____
Taxes	$ _____
Maintenance	$ _____
Property Insurance	$ _____
Clothing	$ _____
Transportation:	
Automobile:	
Gas/Oil	$ _____
Insurance	$ _____
Car Payments	$ _____
Maintenance	$ _____
Plane	$ _____
Bus	$ _____
Train	$ _____
Other	$ _____
Medical:	
Doctors & Dentists	$ _____
Drugs	$ _____
Other	$ _____
Debt:	
Credit cards	$ _____
Other	$ _____
Household Utilities:	
Water/Sewer	$ _____
Telephone	$ _____
Gas	$ _____
Electric	$ _____

Oil	$ _____
Propane	$ _____
Trash Collection	$ _____
Child Support/Alimony	$ _____
Insurance:	
Life	$ _____
Health	$ _____
Homeowner's	$ _____
Disability	$ _____
School	$ _____

VARIABLE

Personal Entertainment	$ _____
Gifts	$ _____
Recreation	$ _____
Miscellaneous	$ _____

Special

(Divide these by twelve so that you can budget these figures into your monthly budget.)

FIXED

Estimated Taxes	$ _____
Insurance Payments:	
Auto	$ _____
Homeowner's/Rental	$ _____
Disability	$ _____
Health	$ _____
Life	$ _____
Other	$ _____
Taxes:	
Property	$ _____
Estimated Income Taxes	$ _____
Repairs and Maintenance:	
Home	$ _____
Car	$ _____

Memberships/Dues $ _____
Gifts:
    Charitable Donations $ _____

VARIABLE

School:
    Tuition $ _____
    Books $ _____
    Other $ _____
Gifts:
    Holiday $ _____
    Vacation $ _____
Expected Purchases:
    Furniture $ _____
    Car $ _____
    Other $ _____
Investment Contributions:
    Pension Fund $ _____
    IRA $ _____
    Other $ _____

Expected Monthly Income for Next Twelve Months

Wages/Salaries:
    Person A $ _____
    Person B $ _____
Investments:
    Dividends $ _____
    Interest $ _____
    Capital Gains $ _____
    Other $ _____
Part-time Employment $ _____
Gifts $ _____
Pension $ _____
Social Security $ _____
Commissions $ _____
Unemployment Compensation $ _____
Alimony/Child Support $ _____

Profit-sharing $ _____
Sale of Assets $ _____
Tips $ _____
Bonuses $ _____
Interest $ _____
Royalties $ _____
Pension $ _____
Annuities $ _____
Life insurance $ _____
Rental Property $ _____
Other $ _____

Appendix B:
Helpful Resources

Organizations, Associations, and Government Agencies

Literally thousands of agencies, associations, businesses, and organizations are available to answer your questions and provide helpful information at no or low cost. Following are a few ideas to get you started.

BETTER BUSINESS BUREAUS

Supported by local businesspeople, these nonprofit, independent organizations are affiliated with the national organization and are very helpful consumer resources. They can provide information on various companies, including past complaints filed against them, answer many consumer questions, refer you to other resources, and so on. They can assist in settling disputes between businesses and consumers, but they don't give legal advice or credit-rating information. They also provide free pamphlets on a variety of subjects. Use them also for referrals to others who can help you.

CITY AND STATE AGENCIES

Many cities and states publish information for their residents. To learn more about them and what they offer, call government listings in the phone book, check with local city departments in your area of interest, talk with the local reference-desk librarian, and/or talk with the editor of the local newspaper.

TRADE ASSOCIATIONS

A number of trade associations will provide free or low-cost information on their subject areas. Browse through a book of associations or contact local businesses involved in your interest areas to find out which associations are on the cutting edge.

FEDERAL GOVERNMENT AGENCIES

The government offers more than twelve thousand booklets and books to consumers at bargain prices. Contact the U.S. Government Bookstore, World Savings Building, 720 N. Main Street, Pueblo, Colorado 81009 for more information and a catalog. Or contact the Superintendent of Documents, U.S. Government Printing Office, Washington, D.C. 20402.

Consumer's Resource Handbook is one such publication. It lists consumer offices nationwide; Better Business Bureaus; state utility, insurance, banking, and agricultural authorities; some federal agencies, and so on.

Books, Magazines, Newsletters

Libraries and bookstores are full of helpful magazines and books on virtually any topic. As we've researched this book, we've come across entire books on key subject areas.

If you're not sure how to track down what you need, ask a reference librarian. If he or she can't meet your needs, you'll most likely learn where you can go for help and/or more information.

The following materials may prove helpful to you.

Bakule, Paula Dreifus, ed. *Rodale's Book of Practical Formulas: Easy-to-Make, Easy-to-Use Recipes for Hundreds of Everyday Activities and Tasks.* Emmaus, Pa.: Rodale, 1991.

Burkett, Larry. *Debt-Free Living.* Chicago: Moody, 1989.

_____. *The Coming Economic Earthquake.* Chicago: Moody, 1991.

Clason, George S. *The Richest Man in Babylon.* New York: Hawthorn/ Dutton, 1926.

Derven, Robert, and Carol Nichols. *Successful How to Cut Your Energy Bills.* 2d ed. Farmington, Mich.: Structures, 1980.

Dulley, James T. *Cut Your Utility Bills: 50 Utility Bills Updates and Columns.* Cincinnati: Starcott Media, 1989.

Federal Reserve Board, Office of Thrift Supervision. *Consumer Handbook on Adjustable Rate Mortgages.* Washington, D.C. (20580): GPO, n.d.

Federal Trade Commission, Office of Consumer/Business Education. *Funerals: A Consumer Guide.* Washington, D.C. (20580): GPO, n.d.

Federal Trade Commission. *The Mortgage Money Guide.* Washington, GPO, n.d.

Foehner, Charlotte, and Carol Cozart. *The Widow's Hand Book: A Guide for Living.* Golden, Co.: Fulcrum, 1988.

Fossell, Peter V. *Keeping Cool: A Sensible Guide to Beating the Heat.* New York: Putnam, 1984.

Gill, Doris B. *My Houseful of Hints: How to Solve Problems at Home and Away.* Walnut Creek, Calif.: Crab Cove, 1989.

Gottlieb, Kathryn. *Home Free: The Complete Book on How to Furnish Your Household.* New York: Crown, 1973.

Herbert, Ralph J. *Cut Your Electric Bills in Half.* Emmaus, Pa.: Rodale, 1986.

The Homesteader's Manual. Blue Ridge Summit, Pa.: TAB Books, 1983.

Myerson, Bess. *The Complete Consumer Book: How to Buy Wisely and Well.* New York: Simon & Schuster, 1979.

Reader's Digest Back to Basics: How to Learn and Enjoy Traditional American Skills (Pleasantville, N.Y.: Reader's Digest, 1981).

The Reader's Digest Complete Do-It-Yourself Manual (Pleasantville, N.Y.: Reader's Digest, 1981).

Rees, Carol. *Household Hints for Upstairs, Downstairs, and All Around the House.* New York: Henry Holt, 1982.

Rinzler, Carol Ann. *What to Use Instead.* New York: Pharos, 1987.

Roebuck, Alan D. *509 Practical Money-saving Tips for Homebuilders.* Blue Ridge Summit, Pa.: TAB Books, 1982.

Roscoe, George B. *Today's Energy Saver's Guide for Homeowners.* Washington, D.C.: Acropolis, 1978.

Stevenson, Robert P., and Roy Doty. *The Popular Science Illustrated Almanac for Home Owners.* New York: Popular Science, 1972.

Wilson, Alex, and John Morrill. *Consumer Guide to Home Energy Savings.* 2d ed. Washington, D.C.: American Council for an Energy-Efficient Economy, 1991.

U.S. Department of Housing and Urban Development. *A Home of Your Own: Helpful Advice from HUD on Choosing, Buying, and Enjoying a Home.* Washington: GPO, 1991.

Mail-Order Catalogs/Newspapers

Christian Book Distributors (discount Christian books), Box 6000, Peabody, MA 01961-6000. Telephone: (508) 977-5050

Gander Mountain (sporting goods catalogs), Box 248, HWY W, Wilmot, WI 53192. Telephone: (800) 558-9410

J. C. Whitney & Company (vehicle parts and accessories), 1917-19 Archer Avenue, P.O. Box 8410, Chicago, Illinois 60680. Telephone: (312) 431-6102

Northern (products for do-it-yourselfers), P.O. Box 1499, Burnsville, MN 55337. Telephone: (800) 533-5545

Today's Family Times (discount Christian books), Melton Book Company, P.O. Box 140990, Nashville, TN 37214-0990

Notes

CHAPTER 1

1. For a startling look at Uncle Sam's spending and its consequences, see Larry Burkett, *The Coming Economic Earthquake* (Chicago: Moody, 1991).
2. Larry Burkett, *Debt-Free Living* (Chicago: Moody, 1989).
3. Proverbs 28:23, 26.
4. *Fair Debt Collection*, Office of Consumer/Business Education, Bureau of Consumer Protection, Washington, DC 20580

CHAPTER 2

1. Luke 19:1–7.
2. Matthew 8:1–4.
3. Mark 12:41–44.

CHAPTER 4

1. *A Home of Your Own: Helpful Advice from HUD on Choosing, Buying, and Enjoying a Home.* U.S. Department of Housing and Urban Development, Washington, DC 20410, May 1991.
2. *The Mortgage Money Guide: Creative Financing for Home Buyers.* Federal Trade Commission, Division of Credit Practices, 6th & Pennsylvania Ave., N.W., Washington, DC, 20580 (1989); *Consumer Handbook on Adjustable Rate Mortgages*, Federal Reserve Board, Office of Thrift Supervision, Washington, DC, n.d.

CHAPTER 5

1. James T. Dulley, *Cut Your Utility Bills: 50 Utility Bills Updates and Column* (Cincinnati: Starcott Media, 1989), 1–6.
2. *Tips for Energy Savers*, U.S. Department of Energy, Washington, DC, 20580, p. 13.
3. Ibid.
4. Doris B. Gill, *My Houseful of Hints: How to Solve Problems at Home and Away* (Walnut Creek, Calif.: Crab Cove Books, 1989), 78.
5. George B. Roscoe, *Today's Energy Saver's Guide for Homeowners* (Washington, D.C.: Acropolis, 1978), 8.
6. Dulley, *Cut Your Utility Bills*, contains simple instructions on how to do this in Section VIII-2.
7. Ralph J. Herbert, *Cut Your Electric Bills in Half* (Emmaus, Pa.: Rodale, 1986), 86.

8. *Tips for Energy Savers*, 12.

9. Robert Derven and Carol Nichols, *Successful How to Cut Your Energy Bills*, 2d ed. (Farmington, Mich.: Structures, 1980), 103.

10. Ibid., 102.

11. *Tips for Energy Savers*, 19.

12. Carol Rees, *Household Hints for Upstairs, Downstairs, and All Around the House* (New York: Henry Holt, 1982), 22.

13. Derven and Nichols, *Successful How to Cut Your Energy Bills*, 25.

14. Peter V. Fossel, *Keeping Cool: A Sensible Guide to Beating the Heat* (New York: Putnam, 1984), 55.

15. Herbert, *Cut Your Electric Bills in Half*, has a sample insulation contract in section XIV–2 that can help you if you decide to hire someone.

16. *Tips for Energy Savers*, 8.

17. Herbert, *Cut Your Electric Bills in Half*, 46.

18. *Tips for Energy Savers*, 10.

19. Alex Wilson and John Morrill, *Consumer Guide to Home Energy Savings*, 2d ed. (Washington, D.C.: American Council for an Energy-Efficient Economy, 1991), 113.

20. Dulley, *Cut Your Utility Bills*, V–3.

21. *Tips for Energy Savers*, 7.

22. Roscoe, *Today's Energy Saving Guide for Homeowners*, 50.

23. *Tips for Energy Savers*, 6.

24. Ibid., 22.

25. Dulley, *Cut Your Utility Bills*, has a simple plan for making insulating window shades in Section V–3.

26. *Tips for Energy Savers*, 5.

27. Ibid., 8.

28. Derven and Nichols, *Successful How to Cut Your Energy Bills*, 112.

29. *Tips for Energy Savers*, 6.

30. Ibid., 7.

CHAPTER 8

1. The Nutritional Labeling Education Act passed in November 1992 will take effect by the middle of 1994. It will provide requirements by which foods will have to be nutritionally labeled and clarify which foods will be exempted from such nutritional labeling.

CHAPTER 9

1. *Cost of Owning & Operating Automobiles, Vans and Light Trucks 1991* (Washington, DC: Federal Highway Administration, Office of Highway Information Management, U.S. Department of Transportation, 1992), 3.

2. *Consumer Tire Guide*, Tire Industry Safety Council, Box 1801, Washington, DC 20013.

CHAPTER 11

1. Based on 1991 domestic passenger-boarding statistics of 412,269,000 people, provided by the Air Transport Association, 1301 Pennsylvania Avenue, N.W., Washington, DC 20004.

CHAPTER 12

1. Read Larry Burkett, *The Coming Economic Earthquake* (Chicago: Moody, 1991) for a challenging perspective on what lies ahead for our nation and the world economy as a whole.

CHAPTER 13

1. 2 Corinthians 6:10.
2. *The Homesteader's Manual* (Blue Ridge Summit, Pa.: Tab Books, 1983) has a section on carving on pp. 220–23.

CHAPTER 14

1. Luke 12:34.
2. Matthew 14:13–21.

Index